The Photographic History
of The Civil War

The Cavalry

j

"STAND TO HORSE!"—AN AMERICAN VOLUNTEER CAVALRYMAN, OCTOBER, 1862

"He's not a regular—but he's 'smart.'" This tribute to the soldierly bearing of the trooper above was bestowed, forty-nine years after the taking of the picture, by an officer of the U. S. cavalry, himself a Civil War veteran. The recipient of such high praise is seen as he "stood to horse" a month after the battle of Antietam. The war was only in its second year, but his drill is quite according to army regulations—hand to bridle, six inches from the bit. His steady glance as he peers from beneath his hat into the sunlight tells its own story. Days and nights in the saddle without food or sleep, sometimes riding along the 60-mile picket-line in front of the Army of the Potomac, sometimes faced by sudden encounters with the Southern raiders, have all taught him the needed confidence in himself, his horse, and his equipment.

The Photographic History of The Civil War

The Cavalry

EDITOR

THEO. F. RODENBOUGH

Brigadier-General United States Army (Retired)

Contributors

THEO. F. RODENBOUGH
Brigadier-General United States Army (Retired)

CHARLES D. RHODES
Captain, General Staff, United States Army

HOLMES CONRAD
Major Cavalry Corps, Army of Northern Virginia

JOHN A. WYETH, M.D., LL.D.
Captain Quirk's Scouts, Confederate States Army

THE FAIRFAX PRESS
New York

This 1983 edition is published by The Fairfax Press,
distributed by Crown Publishers, Inc.

Manufactured in the United States of America

Library of Congress Cataloging in Publication Data
Main entry under title:

The Photographic History of the Civil War. The Cavalry.

Reprint. Originally published as v. 4 of: The photographic history of the
Civil War / Francis Trevelyan Miller, editor-in-chief; Robert S. Lanier,
managing editor. 1912, c1911.
1. United States—History—Civil War, 1861–1865—Cavalry operations.
I. Rodenbough, Theophilus F. (Theophilus Francis), 1838–1912.
E470.P45   1983b   973.7′4   83-1682

ISBN: 0-517-411474

h g f e d c b a

CONTENTS

PHOTOGRAPHIC DESCRIPTIONS THROUGHOUT THIS BOOK
    Roy Mason

FOREWORD

ON April 14, 1861, Fort Sumter underwent a thirty-four-hour bombardment by the Confederate Army. As the fighting drew to a close, Union officer Major Robert Anderson lowered the flag and turned the fort over to the Confederacy. The American Civil War had begun. It would be four long, hard-fought years before the guns would finally be silenced.

The Photographic History of the Civil War: The Cavalry captures the images of both intense drama and horror created by this internal national conflict. This unique collection of black-and-white photographs takes the reader into the campsites and onto the battlefields where victories were won and lives were lost. The superb text and photograph descriptions present an authoritative yet sensitive portrayal of the War Between the States.

The cavalry was an important fighting force for both the North and South during the Civil War. The main objectives of these mounted men included the destruction of supply centers, the cutting of railroads and lines of communication between these centers and the enemy, and engaging in battle. The cavalry also provided guides, orderlies, and grooms for staff officers. Scouting was another important role assigned to the cavalryman. *The Photographic History of the Civil War: The Cavalry* outlines the makeup of both the Federal and Confederate cavalries, their contributions to the war effort, and profiles such important cavalry leaders as Major-General James Ewell Brown Stuart, Major-General George Armstrong Custer, and Lieutenant-General Wade Hampton, C.S.A.

By the 1860s the camera was on its way to becoming an important medium for communication. The method used during this period was known as dagguereotype, named after its inventor Frenchman Louis Jacques Mandé Daguerre. By using this wet-plate process, however, the Civil War photographer was unable to capture action shots. Yet this disadvantage did not prevent him from capturing on film the human and material wreckage created by the war—the wistful face of the dying young soldier or the sabotaged railroad. The Battle of Bull Run marked the beginning of American military photography.

The Civil War photographers risked constant danger of battle and worked under the most difficult conditions—the bitter cold during the winters of 1862 and 1863 and the blistering heat in the summer. Important Civil War photographers—including Mathew B. Brady, Timothy O'Sullivan and Alexander Gardner as well as other combat photographers—provided the American people with an inside look at this war through their work. These poignant photographs stirred the hearts of Americans on both sides of the Mason-Dixon line then and will continue to do so today.

K.M.B.

"SIR—THE GUARD IS FORMED!"

This picture of guard-mounting is one of the earliest Civil War cavalry photographs. It was taken in 1861 at the Cavalry School of Practice and Recruiting Depot, at Carlisle barracks, Pennsylvania. The guard wears full-dress uniform. The adjutant is presenting it to the new Officer of the Day, on the right.

PREFACE

TO the public at large, the volume prepared by General Rodenbough and his associates will be not only instructive but decidedly novel in its view-point. In the popular conception the cavalryman figures as the most dashing and care-free among soldiers. He is associated primarily with charges at a gallop to the sound of clashing sabers and bugle calls, and with thrilling rescues on the field.

Adventurous, indeed, are the exploits of "Jeb" Stuart, Custer, and others recounted in the pages that follow, together with the typical reminiscences from Dr. Wyeth.

The characteristic that stands dominant, however, throughout this volume shows that the soldiers in the cavalry branch were peculiarly responsible. Not only must they maintain a highly trained militant organization, ready to fight with equal efficiency either mounted or on foot, but to them fell the care of valuable, and frequently scarce, animals, the protection of the armies' supplies, the transmission of important messages, and dozens more special duties which must usually be performed on the cavalryman's own initiative. On such detached duty there was lacking the shoulder to shoulder comradeship that large masses of troops enjoy. Confronted by darkness, distance, and danger, the trooper must carry out his orders with few companions, or alone.

The discussion of organization and equipment is most important to an understanding of the cavalryman as he actually worked. The Federal methods, described at length in this volume, naturally involved a larger system and a more elaborate growth than those of the South with its waning resources. In other respects, however, the Confederate organization differed from that of the Union. The feeling for locality in the South manifested itself at the beginning of the war through the formation of companies and regiments on a geographical basis, and the election of officers by the men of the companies themselves. Thus, in spite of the want of military arms and ordnance stores, and the later disastrous scarcity of horses, the Confederates "hung together" in a manner that recalls the English yeomen archers who fought so sturdily, county by county.

Altogether it was a gallant and devoted part that the American cavalryman, Federal or Confederate, played on his hard-riding raids and his outpost duty, as well as his better-known battles and charges, from 1861 to 1865.

CHAPTER ONE

THE EVOLUTION
OF THE
AMERICAN CAVALRYMAN

THE FIRST EXPERIMENT

The men on dress parade here, in 1862, are much smarter, with their band and white gloves, their immaculate uniforms and horses all of one color, than the troopers in the field a year later. It was not known at that time how important a part the cavalry was to play in the great war. The organization of this three months' regiment was reluctantly authorized by the War Department in Washington. These are the Seventh New York Cavalry, the "Black Horse," organized at Troy, mustered in November 6, 1861, and mustered out

SEVENTH NEW YORK CAVALRY, 1862

March 31, 1862. They were designated by the State authorities Second Regiment Cavalry on November 18, 1861, but the designation was changed by the War Department to the Seventh New York Cavalry. The seven companies left for Washington, D. C., November 23, 1861, and remained on duty there till the following March. The regiment was honorably discharged, and many of its members saw real service later. General I. N. Palmer, appears in the foreground with his staff, third from the left.

CAVALRY OF THE CIVIL WAR
ITS EVOLUTION AND INFLUENCE

By Theo. F. Rodenbough
Brigadier-General, United States Army (Retired)

IT may surprise non-military readers to learn that the United States, unprepared as it is for war, and unmilitary as are its people, has yet become a model for the most powerful armies of Europe, at least in one respect. The leading generals and teachers in the art and science of war now admit that our grand struggle of 1861–65 was rich in examples of the varied use of mounted troops in the field, which are worthy of imitation.

Lieutenant-General von Pelet-Narbonne, in a lecture before the Royal United Service Institution of Great Britain, emphatically maintains that "in any case one must remember that, from the days of Napoleon until the present time, in no single campaign has cavalry exercised so vast an influence over the operations as they did in this war, wherein, of a truth, the personality of the leaders has been very striking; such men as, in the South, the God-inspired Stuart, and later the redoubtable Fitzhugh Lee, and on the Northern side, Sheridan and Pleasonton."

For a long time after our Civil War, except as to its political or commercial bearing, that conflict attracted but little attention abroad. A great German strategist was reported to have said that "the war between the States was largely an affair of armed mobs"—a report, by the way, unverified, but which doubtless had its effect upon military students. In the meantime other wars came to pass in succession—Austro-Prussian (1866), Franco-German (1870), Russo-Turkish (1877), and later the Boer War and that between Russia and Japan.

THE AMERICAN CAVALRYMAN—1864

The type of American cavalryman developed by the conditions during the war fought equally well on foot and on horseback. In fact, he found during the latter part of the war that his horse was chiefly useful in carrying him expeditiously from one part of the battlefield to the other. Except when a mounted charge was ordered, the horses were far too valuable to be exposed to the enemy's fire, be he Confederate or Federal. It was only when cavalry was fighting cavalry that the trooper kept continually mounted. The Federal sabers issued at the beginning of the war were of long, straight Prussian pattern, but these were afterward replaced by a light cavalry saber with curved blade. A carbine and revolver completed the Federal trooper's equipment.

In none of these campaigns were the cavalry operations conspicuous for originality or importance as auxiliary to the main forces engaged.

Meanwhile, the literature of the American war—official and personal—began to be studied, and its campaigns were made subjects for text-books and monographs by British authors, which found ready publishers. Nevertheless, the American cavalry method has not gained ground abroad without a struggle. On the one hand, the failure of cavalry in recent European wars to achieve success has been made use of by one class of critics, who hold that " the cavalry has had its day "; that " the improved rifle has made cavalry charges impracticable "; that it has degenerated into mere mounted infantry, and that its value as an arm of service has been greatly impaired.

On the other hand it is held by the principal cavalry leaders who have seen service in the field—Field-Marshal Lord Roberts, Generals French, Hamilton, and Baden-Powell (of Boer War fame), De Negrier and Langlois of France, and Von Bernhardi of Germany, and others, (1) that while the method of using modern cavalry has changed, the arm itself is more important in war than ever; (2) that its scope is broadened; (3) that its duties require a higher order of intelligence and training of its personnel—officers and men, and (4), above all, that it is quite possible to turn out a modern horse-soldier, armed with saber and rifle, who will be equally efficient, mounted or dismounted.

Still the battle of the pens goes merrily on— the champions of the *arme blanche* or of the rifle alone, on the one side, and the defenders of the combination of those weapons on the other. The next great war will demonstrate, beyond peradventure, the practical value of " the American idea," as it is sometimes called.

A glance at the conditions affecting the use of mounted troops in this country prior to our Civil War may be instructive;

THE *ARME BLANCHE* OR THE RIFLE

The eternal question that has confronted cavalry experts ever since long-range firearms became effective, is whether the modern cavalry-man should use the saber—the *arme blanche*—or the rifle, or both the arms together.   The failure of cavalry to achieve success in recent European wars has been used by one class of critics to prove that "the cavalry has had its day" and that "the improved rifle had made cavalry charges impracticable."   On the other hand, many of the experienced cavalry leaders of the present day hold that it is quite possible to turn out a modern horse-soldier, armed with saber and rifle, who will be equally efficient, mounted or dismounted.   In 1911 an American board of officers recommended, however, that the United States troopers should give up their revolvers on the principle that two arms suffice—the carbine for long distance, the saber for hand-to-hand fighting.

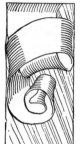

it will show that eighty-five years of great and small wars, Indian fighting, and frontier service, proved to be a training school in which the methods followed by Sheridan, Stuart, Forrest, and others of their time had been really initiated by their famous predecessors—Marion, the "Swamp Fox," and "Light Horse Harry" Lee of the War for Independence, Charlie May and Phil Kearny of the Mexican War, and those old-time dragoons and Indian fighters, Harney and Cooke.

Before the Revolution of 1776, the colonists were generally armed with, and proficient in the use of, the rifle—of long barrel and generous bore—and familiarity with the broken and wooded surface of the country made them formidable opponents of the British from the start, who both in tactical methods and armament were very inferior to the American patriots. Fortescue, an English writer, records the fact that "at the time of the Lexington fight there was not a rifle in the whole of the British army, whereas there were plenty in the hands of the Americans, who understood perfectly how to use them."

In the mountains of Kentucky and Tennessee, bodies of horsemen, similarly armed, were readily formed, who, if ignorant of cavalry maneuvers, yet with little preparation became the finest mounted infantry the world has ever seen; distinguishing themselves in numerous affairs, notably at King's Mountain, South Carolina, September 25, 1780, where two thousand sturdy "Mountain Men," hastily assembled under Colonels Sevier, Shelby, and Campbell, surrounded and almost annihilated a force of twelve hundred men (one hundred and twenty being regulars) under Major Ferguson, of the British army. Marion, the partisan, led a small brigade of mounted infantry, who generally fought on foot, although at times charging and firing from the saddle. There were also small bodies of cavalry proper, using the saber and pistol, with effect, against the British cavalry in many dashing combats.

The War of 1812 was not conspicuous for mounted operations, but the irregular warfare which preceded and followed

[20]

GRADUATES OF "THE ROUGH SCHOOL OF WAR"

The photograph reproduced above through the courtesy of Captain Noble D. Preston, who served with the Tenth New York Cavalry here represented, shows to what stage the troopers had progressed in the rough school of war by the winter of 1862–3. The Tenth New York was organized at Elmira, N. Y., September 27, 1861, and moved to Gettysburg, Penn., December 24th, where it remained till March, 1862. It took part in the battle of Fredericksburg in December, 1862, and participated in the famous "mud march," January, 1863, about the time this photograph was taken. The men had ample time for schooling and training in the Middle Department, in Maryland and the vicinity of Washington. They proved their efficiency in Stoneman's raid in April, 1863, and at Brandy Station and Warrenton. Later they accompanied Sheridan on his Richmond raid in May, 1864, in the course of which Stuart met his death, and they were still "on duty" with Grant at Appomattox.

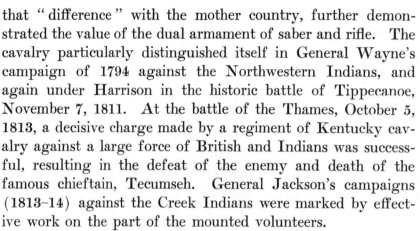

that "difference" with the mother country, further demonstrated the value of the dual armament of saber and rifle. The cavalry particularly distinguished itself in General Wayne's campaign of 1794 against the Northwestern Indians, and again under Harrison in the historic battle of Tippecanoe, November 7, 1811. At the battle of the Thames, October 5, 1813, a decisive charge made by a regiment of Kentucky cavalry against a large force of British and Indians was successful, resulting in the defeat of the enemy and death of the famous chieftain, Tecumseh. General Jackson's campaigns (1813–14) against the Creek Indians were marked by effective work on the part of the mounted volunteers.

In 1833, Congress reorganized the regular cavalry by creating one regiment, followed in 1836 by another, called respectively, the First and Second United States Dragoons. The First Dragoons were sent to the Southwest to watch the Pawnees and Comanches. On this expedition, it was accompanied by Catlin, the artist, who made many of his Indian sketches then. These regiments have been in continuous service ever since.

The first service of the Second Dragoons was against the Seminole Indians, in Florida, and for seven years the regiment illustrated the adaptability of the American soldier to service in the field under the most trying circumstances. "There was at one time to be seen in the Everglades, the dragoon (dismounted) in water from three to four feet deep; the sailor and marine wading in the mud in the midst of cypress stumps; and the infantry and artillery alternately on the land, in the water, or in boats." Here again, the combined mounted and dismounted action of cavalry was tested in many sharp encounters with the Indians.

It was but a step from the close of the Florida war to the war with Mexico, 1846–47. The available American cavalry comprised the two regiments of dragoons and seven new regiments of volunteers. The regular regiments were in splendid

THE FIRST UNITED STATES REGULAR CAVALRY

The sturdy self-reliance of these *sabreurs*, standing at ease though without a trace of slouchiness, stamps them as the direct successors of Marion, the "Swamp Fox," and of "Light-Horse Harry" Lee of the War for Independence. The regiment has been in continuous service from 1833 to the present day. Organized as the First Dragoons and sent to the southwest to watch the Pawnees and Comanches at the time it began its existence, the regiment had its name changed to the First United States Regular Cavalry on July 27, 1861, when McClellan assumed command of the Eastern army. This photograph was taken at Brandy Station in February, 1864. The regiment at this time was attached to the Reserve Brigade under General Wesley Merritt. The troopers took part in the first battle of Bull Run, were at the siege of Yorktown, fought at Gaines' Mill and Beverly Ford, served under Merritt on the right at Gettysburg, and did their duty at Yellow Tavern, Trevilian Station, and in the Shenandoah Valley under Sheridan; and they were present at Appomattox.

condition. The most brilliant exploit was the charge made by May's squadron of the Second Dragoons upon a Mexican light battery at Resaca de la Palma, May 9, 1846, which resulted in the capture of the battery and of General La Vega, of the Mexican artillery. This dashing affair was afterward to be repeated many times in the great struggle between the North and South.

The sphere of action, however, which had the most direct bearing upon the cavalry operations of the war was that known as "the Plains." The experience gained in the twelve years from 1848 to 1860, in frequent encounters with the restless Indian tribes of the Southwest, the long marches over arid wastes, the handling of supply trains, the construction of military roads, the exercise of command, the treatment of cavalry horses and draught animals, and the numerous other duties falling to officers at frontier posts, far distant from railroad or telegraph, all tended to temper and sharpen the blades that were to point the "path of glory" to thousands destined to ride under the war-guidons of Sheridan, Stuart, Buford, Pleasonton, Fitzhugh Lee, Stanley, Wilson, Merritt, Gregg, and others—all graduates of the service school of "the Plains."

At the outbreak of the Civil War, the military conditions in the two sections were very unequal. The South began the struggle under a commander-in-chief who was a graduate of West Point, had seen service in the regular army, had been a Secretary of War (possessing much inside information as to the disposition of the United States forces) and who, in the beginning at least, was supreme in the selection of his military lieutenants and in all matters relating to the organization and equipment of the Confederate troops.

On the other hand the North lacked similar advantages. Its new President was without military training, embarrassed rather than aided by a cabinet of lawyers and politicians as military advisers, captains of the pen rather than of the sword, and "blind leading the blind." Mr. Lincoln found himself

[24]

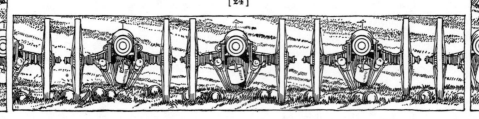

AMERICAN LANCERS—THE SIXTH PENNSYLVANIA

Few people have heard that there was an American regiment of lancers in '61–'63. Colonel Richard Rush's regiment, the Sixth Pennsylvania, attempted to fight in this European fashion during the great conflict in which so much was discovered about the art of war. The Pennsylvanians carried the lance from December, 1861, until May, 1863, when it was discarded for the carbine, as being unsuited to the wooded country of Virginia through which the command operated. The regiment was organized in Philadelphia by Colonel Richard H. Rush, August to October, 1861, and was composed of the best blood in that aristocratic city. The usual armament of Federal volunteer cavalry regiments at the outset of the war consisted of a saber and a revolver. At least two squadrons, consisting of four troops of from eighty-two to a hundred men, were armed with rifles and carbines. Later, all cavalry regiments were supplied with single-shot carbines, the decreased length and weight of the shorter arm being a decided advantage to a soldier on horseback.

surrounded by office-seekers—especially those claiming high military command as a reward for political services. It is true that the Federal Government possessed a small, well-trained army, with a large proportion of the officers and nearly all of the enlisted men loyal to their colors, which, together with a few thousand organized militia, would have formed a valuable nucleus for war had it been properly utilized at the start. From its ranks some were selected who achieved distinction as leaders when not hampered by association with incompetent "generals." For at least one year, the inexhaustible resources of the North were wasted for want of competent military direction and training.

If these field conditions marked the genesis of the Civil War in all arms of service, they were especially true of the mounted troops. In 1860, the "athletic wave" had not made its appearance in the United States, and out-of-door amusements had not become popular above the Mason and Dixon line. In the more thickly settled North, the young men of cities and towns took rather to commercial and indoor pursuits; in the South, the sports of a country life appealed to young and middle-aged alike, and the rifle and the saddle furnished particular attractions to a large majority. So it happened that the Confederates (their President an erstwhile dragoon) had only to mobilize the cavalry companies of the militia scattered through the seceding States, and muster, arm, and equip the thousands of young horsemen, each bringing his own horse and eager to serve the Confederacy.

The trials of many of the newly recruited organizations, until the beginning of the third year of the war, are illustrated in the following extract from a typical regimental history:* Captain Vanderbilt describes in graphic terms his first experience in escort duty (December 10, 1862):

Please remember that my company had been mustered into the service only about six weeks before, and had received horses less than a

* "History of the Tenth New York Cavalry."   (Preston, N. Y.)

VOLUNTEERS AT DRILL—A NEW YORK REGIMENT

It was New York State that furnished the first volunteer cavalry regiment to the Union—Autumn, 1861. The fleet horsemen of the Confederacy soon taught the North the need of improving that arm of the service. But it requires time to train an efficient trooper, and the Union cavalrymen were helpless at first when opposed to the natural horsemen of the South. After a purgatory of training they were hurried into the field, often to fall victims to some roving body of Confederates who welcomed the opportunity to appropriate superior arms and equipment. The regiment in this photograph is the Thirteenth New York Cavalry at Prospect Hill, Virginia. They are no longer raw troopers but have become the "eyes" of Washington and its chief protection against the swift-riding Mosby and his men. The troopers were drilled on foot as well as mounted.

month prior to this march; and in the issue we drew everything on the list—watering-bridles, lariat ropes, and pins—in fact, there was nothing on the printed list of supplies that we did not get. Many men had extra blankets, nice large quilts presented by some fond mother or maiden aunt (dear souls), sabers and belts, together with the straps that pass over the shoulders, carbines and slings, pockets full of cartridges, nose bags and extra little bags for carrying oats, haversacks, canteens, and spurs—some of them of the Mexican pattern as large as small wind-mills, and more in the way than the spurs of a young rooster, catching in the grass when they walked, carrying up briers, vines, and weeds, and catching their pants, and in the way generally—curry-combs, brushes, ponchos, button tents, overcoats, frying-pans, cups, coffee-pots, etc. Now the old companies had become used to these things and had got down to light-marching condition gradually, had learned how to wear the uniform, saber, carbine, etc.; but my company had hardly time to get into proper shape when "the general" was sounded, "boots and saddles" blown.

Such a rattling, jingling, jerking, scrabbling, cursing, I never heard before. Green horses—some of them had never been ridden—turned round and round, backed against each other, jumped up or stood up like trained circus-horses. Some of the boys had a pile in front on their saddles, and one in the rear, so high and heavy it took two men to saddle one horse and two men to help the fellow into his place. The horses sheered out, going sidewise, pushing the well-disposed animals out of position, etc. Some of the boys had never ridden anything since they galloped on a hobby horse, and they clasped their legs close together, thus unconsciously sticking the spurs into their horses' sides.

Well, this was the crowd I commanded to mount on the morning I was ordered by General Smith to follow him. We got in line near headquarters, and when we got ready to start we started all over. He left no doubt about his starting! He went like greased lightning! In less than ten minutes Tenth New York cavalrymen might have been seen on every hill for two miles rearward. Poor fellows! I wanted to help them, but the general was "On to Richmond"; and I hardly dared look back for fear of losing him. I didn't have the remotest idea where he was going, and didn't know but he was going to keep it up all day. It was my first Virginia ride as a warrior in the field. My uneasi-

[28]

A CAVALRY LEADER AT GETTYSBURG—GENERAL DAVID McM. GREGG AND STAFF

The Federal army at Gettysburg owed much to the cavalry. As Gettysburg was the turning-point in the fortunes of the Union army, it also marked an epoch in the development of the cavalry, trained in methods which were evolved from no foreign text-books, but from stern experience on the battlefields of America. The Second Cavalry Division under Gregg patrolled the right flank of the Federal army, with occasional skirmishing, until Stuart's arrival July 3d with the Confederate horse. Gregg's division and Custer's brigade were then on the right of the line. The ensuing cavalry battle was one of the fiercest of the war. W. H. F. Lee's brigade made the first charge for Stuart, as did the First Michigan Cavalry for Gregg. Countercharge followed upon charge. In a dash for a Confederate battleflag, Captain Newhall was received by its bearer upon the point of the spear-head and hurled to the ground. Finally the Confederate brigades withdrew behind their artillery, and the danger that Stuart would strike the rear of the Union army simultaneously with Pickett's charge was passed. This photograph shows Gregg with the officers of his staff.

ness may be imagined. I was wondering what in the mischief I should say to the general when we halted and none of the company there but me. He was the first real live general I had seen who was going out to fight. Talk about the Flying Dutchman! Blankets slipped from under saddles and hung from one corner; saddles slipped back until they were on the rumps of horses; others turned and were on the under side of the animals; horses running and kicking; tin pans, mess-kettles, patent sheet-iron stoves the boys had seen advertised in the illustrated papers and sold by the sutlers of Alexandria—about as useful as a piano or folding bed—flying through the air; and all I could do was to give a hasty glance to the rear and sing out at the top of my voice, "C-l-o-s-e u-p!" But they couldn't "close." Poor boys! Their eyes stuck out like those of maniacs. We went only a few miles, but the boys didn't all get up till noon.

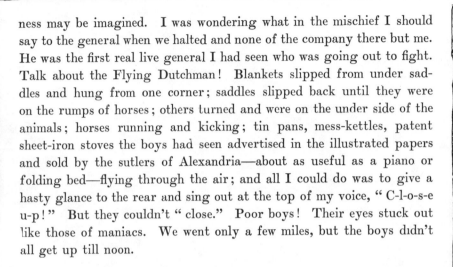

It was not until May, 1861, that the War Department at Washington reluctantly authorized the organization of a regiment of volunteer cavalry from New York with the proviso that the men furnish the horses, an allowance being made for use and maintenance. This system applied in the South, but was soon abandoned in the North. The door once open, other regiments were speedily formed, containing at least the crude elements of efficient cavalry. As a rule, the men regarded the horses with mingled curiosity and respect, and passed through a purgatory of training—"breaking in," it was sometimes called—before they had acquired the requisite confidence in themselves, plus horses and arms. All too soon they were "pitchforked" into the field, often to fall victims to some roving body of Confederates who were eager to appropriate the superior arms and equipment of the Federals.

Within a year in the rough school of war, these same helpless recruits became fairly efficient cavalry, at home in the saddle, able to deliver telling blows with the saber, and to ride boot-to-boot in battle charges. During the first two years of the war the Confederate cavalry exercised a tremendous moral effect. Beginning with the cry of "The Black Horse

THIRTEENTH NEW YORK CAVALRY—RESERVES AT GETTYSBURG

These were some of the few men who would have stood between Lee and the Northern Capital if the tide of battle which hung in the balance three days at Gettysburg had rolled with the line in gray. The organization of the Thirteenth New York Cavalry was not completed till June 20, 1863, ten days before Gettysburg. Six companies left New York State for Washington on June 23d, and took their part in patrolling the rear of the Army of the Potomac during the three fateful days. They were more than raw recruits; the regiment had been made up by the consolidation of several incomplete organizations. Had the troopers arrived a few days earlier they probably would have been brigaded with Pleasonton's cavalry. A week after Gettysburg they were back in New York quelling the draft riots. Thereafter they spent their time guarding Washington, when this photograph was taken, and scouting near the armies in the Virginia hills.

Cavalry," at the First Bull Run, so terrible to the panic-stricken Federal troops in their race to Washington and safety; Mosby's frequent dashes at poorly guarded Union trains and careless outposts; and Stuart's picturesque and gallant promenade around McClellan's unguarded encampment on the Chickahominy, in 1862, the war record of the Southern horse notwithstanding its subsequent decline and the final disasters of 1864–65 will always illumine one of the brightest pages of cavalry history.

The Gettysburg campaign, June 1 to July 4, 1863, was exceptionally full of examples of the effective use of mounted troops. They began with the great combat of Beverly Ford, Virginia, June 9th, in which for twelve hours, eighteen thousand of the flower of the horsemen of the armies of the Potomac and Northern Virginia, in nearly equal proportions, struggled for supremacy, with many casualties,* parting by mutual consent at the close of the day. This was followed by a series of daily skirmishes during the remainder of the month, in efforts to penetrate the cavalry screen which protected each army in its northward progress, culminating on the first day of July at Gettysburg in the masterly handling of two small brigades of cavalry.

It was here that General Buford delayed the advance of a division of Confederate infantry for more than two hours, winning for himself, in the opinion of a foreign military critic,† the honor of having " with the inspiration of a cavalry officer and a true soldier selected the battlefield where the two armies were about to measure their strength." The important actions on the third day comprised that in which Gregg prevented Stuart from penetrating the right rear of the Union line (largely a mounted combat with saber and pistol), and the affair on the Emmittsburg Road on the same day where

*The Second U. S. Cavalry alone losing 57 per cent. killed and wounded of its officers engaged.

†The Comte de Paris in "The Civil War in America."

STABLES FOR SIX THOUSAND HORSES

GIESBORO—ONE OF THE BUSIEST SPOTS OF THE WAR

The cavalry depot at Giesboro, D. C., established in July, 1863, was the place where remounts were furnished to the cavalry and artillery of the Army of the Potomac during the last two years of the war. The tents in the lower photograph are those of the officers in charge of that immense establishment, where they received and issued thousands of horses. Convalescents who had lost their mounts, with men to be remounted, were drawn upon to help take care of the horses, until their departure for the front. This photograph was taken in May, 1864, when Grant and Lee were grappling in the Wilderness and at Spottsylvania, only seventy miles distant. The inspection of horses for remounting was made by experienced cavalry officers, while the purchasing was under the Quartermaster's Department.

Merritt and Farnsworth menaced the Confederate left and, according to General Law,* neutralized the action of Hood's infantry division of Longstreet's corps by bold use of mounted and dismounted men, contributing in no small degree to the Federal success.

In the West, during the same period, the cavalry conditions were not unlike those in the East, except that the field of operations extended over five States instead of two and that numerous bands of independent cavalry or mounted riflemen under enterprising leaders like Forrest, Morgan, Wharton, Chalmers, and Wheeler of the Confederate army, for two years had their own way. The Union generals, Lyon, Sigel, Pope, Rosecrans, and others, loudly called for more cavalry, or in lieu thereof, for horses to mount infantry. Otherwise, they agreed, "it was difficult to oppose the frequent raids of the enemy on communications and supply trains."

Ultimately, Generals Grant and Rosecrans initiated a system of cavalry concentration under Granger and Stanley, and greater efficiency became manifest. About the time of the battle of Stone's River, or Murfreesboro, the Federal horse began to show confidence in itself, and in numerous encounters with the Confederates—mounted and dismounted—acquitted itself with credit, fairly dividing the honors of the campaign. The names of Grierson, Streight, Wilder, and Minty became famous not only as raiders but as important factors in great battles, as at Chickamauga, where the " obstinate stand of two brigades of [Rosecrans'] cavalry against the Confederate infantry gave time for the formation of the Union lines."

The most conspicuous cavalry operations of the war were those of 1864–65: Sheridan's Richmond raid, in which the South lost the brilliant and resourceful Stuart, and the harassing flank attacks on Lee's army in advance of Grant's infantry, which, ending in the campaign at Appomattox, simultaneously with Wilson's successful Selma raid, marked

* "Battles and Leaders of the Civil War."

THE CAVALRY DEPOT IN THE DISTRICT OF COLUMBIA

This photograph of the cavalry depot at Giesboro is peaceful and orderly enough with the Stars and Stripes drooping lazily in the wind, but it does not betray the hectic activity "behind the scenes." Not long after the depot was established the entire Second United States Cavalry was sent there to be remounted, recruited, and refitted. This operation took about a month, and they were ordered to rejoin the army in October, 1863. Every company had a special color of horse at the outset, but this effect was speedily lost in the field, except for the grays. "These were easily recruited," said an old cavalryman, "because nobody wanted grays. They were too conspicuous. No, I don't mean that they attracted the enemy's fire, but a gray horse that lies down in muddy places is very apt to get dirty. If you were coming in from a night of picket duty, would you rather take a rest, or spend your time getting your horse ready for inspection? The dark-coated animals did not show the dirt so much."

EVER–BUSY TROOPERS AT DRILL

The swiftly moving Confederate troopers, under dashing leaders like Stuart and Wheeler, allowed the heads of the Union cavalry not a moment of peace. When infantry went into winter quarters they could live in comparative comfort and freedom from actual campaigning until the roads became passable again for their heavy wagon-trains in the spring. But Confederate raiders knew neither times nor seasons, and there were many points when the damage they might do would be incalculable. So the Federal cavalry's winter task

UNION CAVALRY IN WINTER QUARTERS

was to discover, if possible, the Confederates' next move, and to forestall it.   This photograph shows three troops drilling on the plain beside their winter quarters.   The stark trees and absence of grass indicate clearly the time of the year, and the long shadows show as truly as a watch that the time of day was late afternoon. A swift night-march may be in store for the troopers on the plain, or they may return to the shelter of their wooden huts.   It is probable, however, that they cannot enjoy their comfort for more than a week or two.

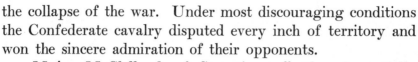

the collapse of the war. Under most discouraging conditions the Confederate cavalry disputed every inch of territory and won the sincere admiration of their opponents.

Major McClelland, of Stuart's staff, thus impartially summarizes the situation: *

"During the last two years no branch of the Army of the Potomac contributed so much to the overthrow of Lee's army as the cavalry, both that which operated in the Valley of Virginia and that which remained at Petersburg. But for the efficiency of this force it is safe to say that the war would have been indefinitely prolonged. From the time that the cavalry was concentrated into a corps until the close of the war, a steady progress was made in discipline. Nothing was spared to render this arm complete. Breech-loading arms of the most approved pattern were provided; horses and accouterments were never wanting, and during the last year of the war Sheridan commanded as fine a body of troops as ever drew sabers.

"On the other hand, two causes contributed steadily to diminish the numbers and efficiency of the Confederate cavalry. The Government committed the fatal error of allowing the men to own their horses, paying them a *per diem* for their use, and the muster valuation in cases where they were killed in action; but giving no compensation for horses lost by any other casualties of a campaign. . . . Toward the close of the war many were unable to remount themselves, and hundreds of such dismounted men were collected in a useless crowd, which was dubbed 'Company Q.' The second cause was the failure or inability of the Government to supply good arms and accouterments. Our breech-loading arms were nearly all captured from the enemy and the same may be said of the best of our saddles and bridles. From these causes, which were beyond the power of any commander to remedy, there was a steady decline in the numbers of the Confederate cavalry and, as compared with the Federal cavalry, a decline in efficiency."

* "Life and Campaigns of Major-General J. E. B. Stuart."

CHAPTER
TWO

———

THE FEDERAL CAVALRY
ITS ORGANIZATION
AND EQUIPMENT

———

"BOOTS AND SADDLES"—THIRD DIVISION, CAVALRY
CORPS, ARMY OF THE POTOMAC, 1864

A SPREADING SECTION OF THE FEDERAL CAVALRY ORGANIZATION IN 1864

At Belle Plain Landing on the Potomac lay a chief base of supplies for Grant's armies in the spring of 1864. On April 4th Sheridan had been given charge of all the cavalry. He had found the corps much run down and the horses in poor condition. In a month he had effected a decided change for the better in the condition and *morale* of his ten thousand men, and was begging to be allowed to use them as an independent corps to fight the Confederate cavalry. Though they had been relieved of much of the arduous picket duty that they formerly performed, they were still considered as auxiliaries, to protect the flanks and front of the infantry. On May 7th Grant's army advanced with a view to taking Spotsylvania Court House.

CAVALRY IN CLOVER AT THE BELLE PLAIN LANDING

Thus was precipitated the cavalry battle at Todd's Tavern, and in part at least Sheridan's earnest desire became fulfilled. The battle was between Hampton's and Fitzhugh Lee's commands of Stuart's cavalry and Gregg's division, assisted by two brigades of Torbert's division under the command of General Merritt. After a severe engagement the Confederate cavalry broke and were pursued almost to Spotsylvania Court House. This photograph shows some of the Federal horses recuperating at Belle Plain Landing before this cavalry engagement on a large scale. The cavalry were in clover here near the tents and ships that meant a good supply of forage. There was no such loafing for horses and men a little later in that decisive year.

THE BELLE PLAIN CAVALRY

A CLOSER VIEW

This photograph brings the eye a little nearer to the cavalry at Belle Plain landing than the picture preceding. One can see the horses grazing by the side of the beautiful river. A group of cavalrymen have ridden their mounts into the water. The test of the efficient trooper was his skill in caring for his horse. Under ordinary circumstances, in a quiet camp like the above, it might be safe to turn horses out to graze and let them drink their fill at the river. But when on the march a staggering animal with parched throat and fast-glazing eyes whinnied eagerly at the smell of water, it was the trooper who had to judge its proper allowance. One swallow too many for a heated horse on a long march, multiplied by the number of troopers still ignorant of horsemanship, meant millions of dollars loss to the Union Government in the early stages of the war. Comparatively few horses were destroyed by wounds on the battlefield as compared with those lost through the ignorance of the troopers as to the proper methods of resting a horse, and as to the science of how, when, and what to feed him, and when to allow him to drink his fill. The Southern horsemen, as a rule more experienced, needed no such training, and their superior knowledge enabled the Confederate cavalry, with little "organization" in the strict sense of the word, to prove nevertheless a mighty weapon for their cause.

NEARER STILL

AT THE RIVER'S BRINK

This view brings us to the very edge of the water, where Sheridan's troopers were getting their mounts into shape for the arduous duties of the summer and fall. They are sitting at ease on the barebacked horses which have walked out into the cool river to slake their thirst. The wagon with the four-mule team bears the insignia of the Sixth Army Corps, commanded by Sedgwick. The canvas top is somewhat wrinkled, so it is impossible to see the entire device, which was in the shape of a Greek cross. It was during the campaign which followed these preparations that Sheridan had his famous interview with Meade, in which the former told his senior that he could whip Stuart if allowed to do so. General Grant determined to give Sheridan the opportunity that he sought, and on the very day of the interview Meade directed that the cavalry be immediately concentrated and that Sheridan proceed against the Confederate cavalry. On May 9th the expedition started with a column thirteen miles long. Stuart, however, was nothing loth to try conclusions with the Federal cavalry once more. He finally overtook it on May 11th at Yellow Tavern. The Confederate horse, depleted in numbers and equipment alike, was no longer its former brilliant self, and in this engagement the Confederacy lost James B. Gordon and Stuart, the leader without a peer.

WITH THE FARRIERS

OF THE

FEDERAL CAVALRY

These photographs were made at the headquarters of the Army of the Potomac in August, 1863, the month following the battle of Gettysburg, where the cavalry had fully demonstrated its value as an essential and efficient branch of the service. Every company of cavalry had its own farrier, enlisted as such. These men not only had to know all about the shoeing of horses, but also had to be skilled veterinary surgeons, such as each regiment has at the present day, coming next in pay to a second lieutenant. Plainly visible are the small portable anvil on an overturned bucket and the business-like leather aprons of the men. An army "marches upon its stomach," but cavalry marches upon its horses' feet, which must be cared for. In the larger photograph the men have evidently just become aware that their pictures are being taken. In the smaller exposure in the corner, the man holding the horse on the right has faced about to show off his horse to the best advantage; the horse holder on the left is facing the camera, arms akimbo, and a cavalryman in the rear has led up his white-faced mount to insure his inclusion in the picture.

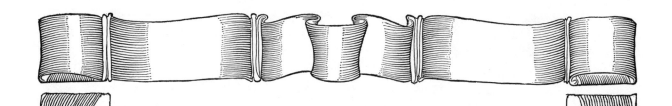

THE FEDERAL CAVALRY
ITS ORGANIZATION AND EQUIPMENT

By Charles D. Rhodes

Captain, General Staff, United States Army

AT the outbreak of the great Civil War in America, the regular cavalry at the disposal of the Federal Government consisted of the First and Second Regiments of Dragoons, one regiment of Mounted Rifles, and the First and Second Regiments of Cavalry. Early in the year 1861, the Third Cavalry was added to the others, and soon after, all six regiments were designated as cavalry and numbered serially from one to six.

The old regiments had been composed of ten troops, subdivided into five squadrons of two troops each, but the organization of the Sixth Cavalry Regiment called for twelve troops. In July, 1861, this organization was extended to all regular regiments, and in September of the same year the volunteer regiments, which had started out with ten troops each, were organized in a like manner. As the war progressed, the squadron organization was abandoned. When a regiment was subdivided for detached service, it was usually into battalions of four troops each.

The early war organization of cavalry troops called for one hundred enlisted men to a troop, officered by a captain, a first lieutenant, a second lieutenant, and a supernumerary second lieutenant. But in 1863, troops were given an elastic strength, varying between eighty-two and one hundred enlisted men, and the supernumerary lieutenant was dropped. Each regiment, commanded by a colonel, had a lieutenant-colonel and three majors, with a regimental commissioned and

[46]

THE FIRST EXTENSIVE FEDERAL CAVALRY CAMP—1862

This photograph shows the cavalry camp at Cumberland Landing just before McClellan advanced up the Peninsula. The entire strength of the cavalry the previous autumn had aggregated 8,125 men, of which but 4,753 are reported as "present for duty, equipped." It was constantly drilled during the fall and winter of 1861, with enough scouting and outpost duty in the Virginia hills to give the cavalry regiments a foretaste of actual service. In the lower photograph we get a bird's-eye view of Cumberland Landing where McClellan's forces were concentrated after the siege of Yorktown and the affair at Williamsburgh, preparatory to moving on Richmond. The cavalry reserve with the Peninsular army under that veteran horseman Philip St. George Cooke, was organized as two brigades under General Emry and Colonel Blake, and consisted of six regiments. Emry's brigade comprised the Fifth United States Cavalry, Sixth United States Cavalry, and Rush's Lancers—the Sixth Pennsylvania Cavalry. Blake's brigade consisted of the First United States Cavalry, the Eighth Pennsylvania Cavalry, and Barker's squadron of Illinois Cavalry.

AT CUMBERLAND LANDING

non-commissioned staff, which included two regimental surgeons, an adjutant, quartermaster, commissary, and their subordinates.

Owing, however, to losses by reason of casualities in action, sickness, and detached service, and through the lack of an efficient system of recruiting, whereby losses could be promptly and automatically made good with trained men, the cavalry strength, in common with that of other arms, always showed an absurd and oftentimes alarming discrepancy between the troopers actually in ranks and the theoretical organization provided by the existing law. Again, the losses in horse-flesh were so tremendous in the first years of the war, and the channels for replacing those losses were so inadequate and unsystematized, that regiments oftentimes represented a mixed force of mounted and unmounted men. Although the value of the dismounted action of cavalry was one of the greatest developments of the war, its most valuable asset, mobility, was wholly lacking when its horses were dead or disabled.

Cavalry is a most difficult force to organize, arm, equip, and instruct at the outbreak of war. Not only must men be found who have some knowledge of the use and handling of horses, but the horses themselves must be selected, inspected, purchased, and assembled. Then, after all the delays usually attending the organizing, arming, and equipping of a mounted force, many months of patient training, dismounted and mounted, are necessary before cavalry is qualified to take the field as an efficient arm. It is an invariable rule in militant Europe to keep cavalry at all times at war strength, for it is the first force needed to invade or to repel invasion, and, except perhaps the light artillery, the slowest to "lick into shape" after war has begun. In the regular cavalry service, it was a common statement that a cavalryman was of little real value until he had had two years of service.

It is, therefore, small wonder that during the first two years of the great struggle, the Federal cavalry made only a

BEEF FOR THE CAVALRY AT COMMISSARY HEADQUARTERS

So seldom did the cavalry get a chance to enjoy the luxuries to be had at commissary headquarters that they took advantage of every opportunity. It is February, 1864, and the cavalry officer in the picture can look forward to a month or two more of fresh beef for his men. Then he will find his troop pounding by the desolate farmhouses and war-ridden fields, as the army advances on Richmond under Grant. While the infantry lay snug in winter-quarters, the troopers were busy scouring the Virginia hills for signs of the Confederates, or raiding their lines of communication and destroying their supplies. It took a large part of the time of the Northern and Southern infantry to repair the damage done by the cavalry. The cavalry often had to live by foraging, or go without food. Miles of railroad destroyed, bridges burned, telegraph wires cut, a sudden cessation of the source of supplies caused hundreds of miles of marching and counter-marching, beside the actual work of repairing by the engineering corps. It was Van Dorn's capture of **Holly Springs** that forced Grant to abandon his overland march against Vicksburg and return to Memphis in December, 1862.

poor showing. The regular cavalry was but a handful, and when President Lincoln issued his call for volunteers, little or no cavalry was accepted. Even when need for it was forced on the North, it took the Federal War Department a long time to realize that an efficient cavalry ready for field service could not be extemporized in a day.

Strange as it may now seem, the Federal authorities intended, in the beginning, to limit the cavalry force of the Union army to the six regular regiments; and even such a veteran soldier as General Scott gave it as his opinion that, owing to the broken and wooded character of the field of operations between the North and South, and the improvements in rifled cannon, the duties of cavalry would be unimportant and secondary.

Only seven troops of regular cavalry were available for the first battle of Bull Run, in 1861, but the firm front which they displayed in covering the confused and precipitate retreat of the Federal army, probably saved a large part of the main body from capture; but they never received the recognition that was deserved. However, the importance of cavalry was not altogether unappreciated, for we find, at Gettysburg, the Union cavalry of the Army of the Potomac aggregating nearly thirteen thousand officers and men. The close of the war saw Sheridan at Appomattox with fifteen thousand cavalrymen, while Wilson, in the South, was sweeping Mississippi and Alabama with an army of horsemen. But the evolution of this vast host from insignificant beginnings was a slow process, fraught with tremendous labor.

In the South, lack of good highways forced the Southerner to ride from boyhood, while contemporaneously the Northerner, with his improved roads, employed wheeled vehicles as a means of transportation. But aside from this positive advantage to Southern organization, the Confederate leaders seemed, from the very beginning of the Civil War, to appraise cavalry and its uses at its true valuation; while the Northern

AT THE BUSY OFFICE OF A CAVALRY QUARTERMASTER

This photograph was taken at Brandy Station in the spring of 1864. The sign on the wooden door of the little tent tells where "A. Q. M." held forth. The cavalrymen are evidently at ease. They have not yet met Stuart in the Wilderness. The quartermaster of a cavalry corps was the nearest approach to perpetual motion discovered during the war. His wagon-train could receive only the most general directions. He could never be certain where the men he was to supply with food could be found at any given time. He had to go exploring for his own regiments, and watch vigilantly that he did not incidentally feed the Confederates. He had to give precedence to ammunition-trains; dark often found his wagons struggling and floundering in the wake of their vanished friends. The quartermaster was responsible for their movements and arrivals. Besides carrying a map of the country in his head, he assumed immense responsibilities.

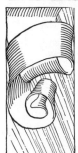

cavalry, even when finally mounted and equipped, was so mis-used and mishandled by those in control of military operations, that it was almost always at a disadvantage.

One of the first efforts of the War Department looking to the organization of Federal cavalry, is seen in the following circular letter, addressed by the Secretary of War to the Governors of the States:

WAR DEPARTMENT, WASHINGTON,
May 1, 1861.

To the Governors of the Several States,
And All Whom it may Concern:

I have authorized Colonel Carl Schurz to raise and organize a volunteer regiment of cavalry. For the purpose of rendering it as efficient as possible, he is instructed to enlist principally such men as have served in the same arm before. The Government will provide the regiment with arms, but cannot provide the horses and equipments. For these necessaries we rely upon the patriotism of the States and the citizens, and for this purpose I take the liberty of requesting you to afford Colonel Schurz your aid in the execution of this plan.

(Signed)   SIMON CAMERON,
Secretary of War.

Yet, in his report of preliminary operations in the first year of the war, General McClellan says:

Cavalry was absolutely refused, but the governors of the States complied with my request and organized a few companies, which were finally mustered into the United States service and proved very useful.

The armament of the volunteer cavalry regiments, organized with some show of interest after the battle of Bull Run, was along the same general lines as that of the regular regiments. Though suffering from a general deficiency in the number which could be purchased from private manufacturers —there being no reserve stock on hand—each trooper was armed with a saber and a revolver as soon as circumstances permitted. At least two squadrons (four troops) in each regi-

A WELL–EQUIPPED HORSE OF THE FIRST MASSACHUSETTS CAVALRY—1864

The saddle-bags and hooded stirrup of Captain E. A. Flint's horse shown in this photograph are "regulation," but the outfit of a regular cavalry horse did not call for a breast-strap. It was more apt to be used among the volunteers. The regulars as a rule preferred a single rein, curb bit, and no breast-strap or martingale. No breast-straps were issued, but they were found useful when cavalry was pounding up a slope, leaping fences, walls, and ditches, and otherwise putting unusual strain on the belly-band. The hooded stirrup was useful both to keep out rain and to keep the foot warm in winter. The saddle and blanket equipment in the photograph also conform to regulations. This is one of the horses and men that charged Stuart's cavalry so fiercely on the night of the third day at Gettysburg. The First Massachusetts was in the second division, under General David McM. Gregg. The photograph was taken in November, 1864, at the headquarters of the Army of the Potomac, then thoroughly in touch with its ample "supply trains."

JUST BEFORE SHERIDAN CAME, 1864

This photograph shows the Eighteenth Pennsylvania in winter-quarters near Brandy Station in March, 1864, a month before the most important event in the history of the Federal cavalry—the unifying of the cavalry branch under the aggressive Sheridan. After Kilpatrick's raid on Richmond, ending the 2d of March, these troopers rested in camp until Sheridan left for his Richmond raid on May 9th. A month in camp is a long time for cavalry, and here one has a good opportunity to see with what rapidity and ease a trooper had learned to make himself comfortable. Barrels have been placed upon the chimneys in order to

THE EIGHTEENTH PENNSYLVANIA CAVALRY

increase their draft. Light enclosures of poles have been thrown up for the horses, and fodder has been stacked up on the hill. With stumps and cross-pieces the McClellan saddles are kept out of the wet and mud. The saddles were covered with rawhide instead of leather, and were more uncomfortable when they split than an ill-fitting shoe. The troopers themselves look fairly contented, and some of them are not so lean and angular as in the days of scouting and hard riding. There is plenty of work ahead of them, however, nearer Richmond, which will quickly enable them to rid themselves of any superfluous flesh.

ment were armed with rifles or carbines. Later, all cavalry regiments were supplied with single-shot carbines, the decreased length and weight of the shorter arm being a decided advantage to a soldier on horseback. One volunteer regiment, the Sixth Pennsylvania Cavalry (Rush's Lancers), was armed with the lance in addition to the pistol, twelve carbines being afterwards added to the equipment of each troop for picket and scouting duty. But in May, 1863, all the lances were discarded for carbines as being unsuited for the heavily wooded battle-grounds of Virginia.

The carbines issued were of various pattern—the Sharp's carbine being succeeded by the Spencer, which fired seven rounds with more or less rapidity but which was difficult to reload quickly. In the later years of the war, certain regiments were armed with the Henry rifle, an improved weapon firing sixteen shots with great accuracy. A Colt's rifle, firing six rounds, and a light, simple carbine called the Howard, were also in evidence among cavalry regiments at the close of the war. Previous to, and during the first year of the war, the Burnside was favorably thought of by the Federal officers. This carbine was the invention of General Ambrose E. Burnside, and was manufactured in Bristol, Rhode Island. Its chief value lay in its strength and the waterproof cartridges used. But its chief objection also lay in the high cost and the difficulty in obtaining this cartridge, which was manufactured of sheet brass, an expensive metal at that time. Another arm, similar to Burnside's and made with a tapering steel barrel, was the Maynard, which was manufactured by the Maynard's Arms Company, Washington, District of Columbia.

At the beginning, the sabers issued were of the long, straight, Prussian pattern, but these were afterwards replaced by a light cavalry saber with curved blade. Many of these were fitted with attachments so as to be fastened to the end of the carbines in the form of a bayonet. There also was an ordinary saber handle which allowed of their being carried at the

CAVALRY STABLES AT GRANT'S HEADQUARTERS, CITY POINT, IN 1864

City Point was Grant's base of supplies during the operations about Petersburg, in 1864. Sheridan at last was handling his cavalry as a separate command, and was soon to go to the Shenandoah. Brigadier-General David McM. Gregg was in command of the cavalry which remained with Grant. The First Massachusetts, First New Jersey, Tenth New York, Sixth Ohio, and Twenty-first Pennsylvania formed the First Brigade, and the First Maine, Second Pennsylvania, Fourth Pennsylvania, Eighth Pennsylvania, Thirteenth Pennsylvania, and Sixteenth Pennsylvania were the Second Brigade. Some of these men had been on Sheridan's Richmond and Trevilian raids. This shows the comparative comfort of City Point. To the left is a grindstone, where sabers might be made keen.

hip, as a side-arm, for which purpose it was well adapted, having a curved edge with a sharp point.

The standard pistol was the Colt's revolver, army or navy pattern, loaded with powder and ball and fired with percussion caps. Within its limitations, it was a very efficient weapon.

The saddle was the McClellan, so-called because adopted through recommendations made by General McClellan after his official European tour, in 1860, although it was in reality a modification of the Mexican or Texan tree. It was an excellent saddle, and in an improved pattern is, after fifty years of trial, still the standard saddle of the United States regular cavalry. In its original form it was covered with rawhide instead of leather, and when this covering split, the seat became very uncomfortable for the rider.

Although the original recruiting regulations required cavalry troopers to furnish their own horses and equipments, this requirement was later modified, and the Government furnished everything to the recruit, in volunteer as well as in regular regiments. Many troopers sold their private horses to the Government and then rode them in ranks. It was argued by some cavalry officers of that period that this system was eminently successful in securing men for the cavalry who could ride and who would care for horses.

As is usual in a country weak in trained cavalry and utterly unprepared for war, vexatious delays occurred in receiving the equipment of newly organized cavalry regiments. Long after the Western regiments were organized, they were kept inactive from lack of equipment, for which the Federal Government had made no provision in the way of reserve supplies. In some instances months elapsed before saddles were received, and in several cases arms were even longer in putting in an appearance. The interim was employed by the commanders in teaching their men to ride and drill, to use their arms, and to care for their horses. In the absence of saddles,

THE FAR-REACHING FEDERAL CAVALRY ORGANIZATION—WATER-TANK AT THE LOUISIANA DEPOT

Water—that word alone spells half the miseries and difficulties of the cavalry, especially in the parched Southern country. Although an infantry column could camp beside a little spring, cavalry horses had to plod wearily on till they reached a river, a stream, or at least a fair-sized pool. Even then, some officer grown wise in war might pronounce the water unfit for drinking, and the troopers must rein up their thirsty, impatient steeds, wild to plunge their noses in the cool morass, and ride patiently on again till good water was found. The place is Green- ville in Louisiana, where one of the six great Union cavalry depots was located. The site of the camp was selected by General Richard Arnold, Chief of Cavalry, Department of the Gulf. On June 8, 1864, from New Orleans, he requested permission to move his camping ground. "Present camping-ground of the First and Fifth Brigades of my command near Banks is entirely unsuitable, and I ask permission to move to this side of the river, at or near Greenville. I can find no more suitable place on either side of the river within twenty miles of the city." Permission to move was granted June 14, 1864.

various makeshifts were used on the horses' backs, and the troopers were even drilled bareback.

This probationary period was a wearisome one for the cavalry recruit. A trooper must perforce learn much of what his comrade of the infantry knows, and in addition must be taught all that pertains to horses and horsemanship. Those who had been fascinated by the glamour and dash of the cavalry life doubtless wished many times, during those laborious days, that they had the more frequent hours of recreation granted their neighbors of the infantry. The reward of the Federal cavalry came in those later days when, after painstaking and unremitting instruction covering many months and enlightening experiences in the field, they gained that confidence in themselves and their leaders, which resulted in the ultimate destruction of the opposing cavalry, and the decisive triumph of the Federal arms.

But good cavalry cannot be made in a month, or even in a year. The first year of the war saw the Confederate cavalry plainly superior in every way, and there were humiliating instances of the capture by the *corps d'élite* of the South, of whole squadrons of Northern horsemen. The second year of the tremendous struggle passed with much improvement in the Federal cavalry, but with a still marked lack of confidence in itself. It was not until the third year of its organization and training that the Union cavalry really found itself, and was able to vindicate its reputation in the eyes of those who in the preceding period were wont to sneeringly remark that " no one ever sees a dead cavalryman!

The drill regulations of the period, called tactics in those days, were the " '41 Tactics " or " Poinsett Tactics," authorized for dragoon regiments in the year 1841, by the Honorable J. R. Poinsett, Secretary of War. These drill regulations were in the main a translation from the French, and although occasional attempts were made to improve them, they continued in use by the Eastern cavalry of the Union armies throughout the

WELL-GROOMED OFFICERS OF THE THIRTEENTH NEW YORK CAVALRY

Many of the Federal cavalry officers were extremely precise in the matter of dress, paying equal attention to their horses' equipment, in order to set a good example to their men. Custer was a notable example. This photograph shows full dress, fatigue dress, a properly equipped charger, an orderly, sentry, cavalry sabres and the short cavalry carbine. Except for the absence of revolvers, it is an epitome of the dress and equipment which the Federal Government supplied lavishly to its troopers during the latter half of the war. At the outset, the volunteer cavalrymen were required to supply their own horses, a proper allowance being made for food and maintenance. In 1861, the Confederate cavalry had no Colt's revolvers, no Chicopee sabers, and no carbines that were worth carrying. Their arms were of the homeliest type and of infinite variety. This photograph was taken in July, 1865, when Washington no longer needed watching.

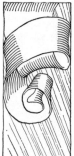

war. The Western cavalry used the "'41 Tactics" until late in the year 1864, and thereafter a system of drill formulated by General Philip St. George Cooke, which was published in 1862 by the War Department and prescribed a single-rank formation for the cavalry.

After all the months of drill, how different were those days of actual service in the field—weary marches in mud, rain, and even snow; short rations for men and for horses when the trains were delayed or when there were no trains; bivouacs on the soggy ground with saddles for pillows; gruesome night rides when troopers threw reins on the necks of horses and slept in their saddles; nerve-racking picket duty in contact with the foe's lines, where the whinny of a horse meant the wicked "ping" of a hostile bullet.

Like all soldiers new to the rigors of actual service in war, the Union volunteer cavalry, in those early days, loaded themselves and their horses with an amount of superfluous baggage which provoked sarcasm from the seasoned soldier and which later experience taught them wholly to discard. Some articles were absolutely necessary; much was entirely useless and oftentimes unauthorized.

In addition to his arms, which weighed not a little, the volunteer cavalryman carried a huge box of cartridges and another of percussion caps; from his shoulder depended a haversack filled with rations, and to which was often attached not only a tin cup but a coffee-pot. A canteen of water, a nose-bag of corn, a shelter tent, a lariat and picket pin, extra horseshoes and nails, a curry-comb and brush, a set of gun-tools and cleaning materials, and saddle-bags filled with extra clothing brought the weight of the trooper and his kit to a figure which was burdensome to an animal in even the best of condition. When to these articles of equipment were added an overcoat, extra blankets, additional boots, and the odds and ends of luxuries, which the recruit is wont to stow away surreptitiously, the result was a lame and broken-down horse, hundreds of troopers

BREAD AND COFFEE FOR THE CAVALRYMAN

The mess-house for cavalry ordered to Washington.—In the field the cavalrymen were glad when they could get the regular rations—bacon and hard bread. During the winter, in permanent camp, they occasionally enjoyed the luxury of soft bread. But they were kept so constantly employed, reconnoitering the enemy's position, watching the fords of the Rappahannock, and engaged in almost constant skirmishing, even in severe winter weather while the infantry was being made comfortable in winter-quarters, that this mess-house was regarded as a sort of Mecca by the troopers sent to Washington to be organized and remounted. Soft bread was not the only luxury here, and when they rejoined their commands their comrades would listen with bated breath to their thrilling stories of soup and eggs and other Lucullan delicacies. There was an army saying that it takes a good trooper to appreciate a good meal.

afoot, and the whole cavalry service rendered inefficient and almost useless.

As an evidence of the lack of discipline and of the ignorance of things military, which marked those early days of the cavalry service, it may be mentioned that many credulous troopers purchased so-called invulnerable vests, formed of thin steel plates and warranted by the makers to ward off a saber stroke or stop a leaden bullet. Dents in the armor were pointed out as evidence of this remarkable quality. Of course the vests were sooner or later discarded, but while retained they added about ten pounds to the burden of the already overloaded horse.

It is stated that the first time the Confederate cavalrymen, who rode light, met some of these remarkably equipped troopers, they wondered with amazement whether the Union horsemen were lifted into the saddle after the latter was packed, or whether the riders mounted first, and then had the numberless odds and ends of their equipment packed around them.

An anecdote is related of a humane Irish recruit, who, when he found his horse was unable to carry the heavy load allotted him, decided as an act of mercy to share the load with his charger. So, unloading nearly a hundred pounds from the horse, he strapped the mass to his own broad shoulders; and remounting his steed, rode off, quite jubilant over his act of unselfishness.

But it did not take long for cavalrymen in the field to learn with how little equipment the soldier may live and fight efficiently, and with how much greater zest the horses can withstand the long marches when the load is cut down to the limit of actual needs. There was danger then of the opposite extreme, and that absolutely necessary articles would be conveniently dropped and reported as " lost in action " or as " stolen." The net result, however, was that after one or two campaigns, the Federal cavalrymen learned to travel light, and, better than anything else, learned that quality of discipline

THE HAY BUSINESS OF THE GOVERNMENT

The matter of proper feed for cavalry horses was a constant perplexity to the Federal Government until the men had learned how to care for their mounts. During the first two years of the war two hundred and eighty-four thousand horses were furnished to the cavalry, although the maximum number of cavalrymen in the field at any time during this period did not exceed sixty thousand. The enormous number of casualties among the horses was due to many causes, among which were poor horsemanship on the part of the raw troopers mustered in at the beginning of the war, and the ignorance and gross inefficiency on the part of many officers and men as to the condition of the horses' backs and feet, care as to food and cleanliness, and the proper treatment of the many diseases to which horses on active service are subject. In such a tremendous machine as the quartermaster's department of the Army of the Potomac, containing at the beginning of the war many officers with absolutely no experience as quartermasters, there were necessarily many vexatious delays in purchasing and forwarding supplies, and many disappointments in the quality of supplies, furnished too often by scheming contractors. By the time the photograph above reproduced was taken, 1864, the business of transporting hay to the army in the field had been thoroughly systematized, as the swarming laborers in the picture attest.

AT THE HAY WHARF, ALEXANDRIA

GOVERNMENT HAY-WHARF AT ALEXANDRIA, VIRGINIA

The army which McClellan took to the Peninsula had to be created from the very foundation. The regular army was too small to furnish more than a portion of the general officers and a very small portion of the staff, so that the staff departments and staff officers had to be fashioned out of perfectly raw material. Artillery, small-arms, and ammunition were to be manufactured, or purchased from abroad; wagons, ambulances, bridge-trains, camp equipage, hospital stores, and all the vast impedimenta and material indispensable for an army in the field were to be manufactured. The tardiness with which cavalry remounts were forwarded to the regiments was a frequent subject of complaint. General McClellan complained that many of the horses furnished were "totally unfitted for the service and should never have been re-

SENTRY GUARDING FEED FOR FEDERAL HORSES, 1864

ceived." General Pope had in fact reported that "our cavalry numbered on paper about four thousand men, but their horses were completely broken down, and there were not five hundred men, all told, capable of doing such service as should be expected of cavalry." The demand for horses was so great that in many cases they were sent on active service before recovering sufficiently from the fatigue incident to a long railway journey. One case was reported of horses left on the cars fifty hours without food or water, and then being taken out, issued, and used for immediate service. Aside, too, from the ordinary diseases to which horses are subject, the Virginia soil seemed to be particularly productive of diseases of the feet. That known as "scratches" disabled thousands of horses during the Peninsula campaign and the march of Pope.

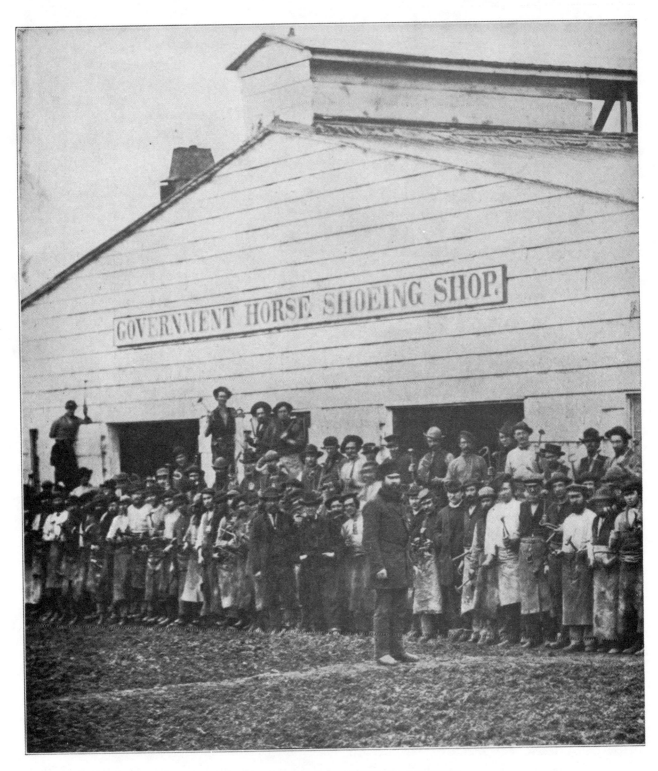

MEN WHO SHOD A MILLION HORSES

This photograph presents another aspect of the gigantic system whereby the Union cavalry became organized and equipped so as to prove irresistible after 1863. In the fiscal year 1864 the Union Government bought and captured nearly 210,000 horses. The army in the field required about 500 new horses every day. Sheridan's force alone required 150 new horses a day during the Shenandoah campaign. At Giesboro, the big remount depot near Washington, they handled 170,622 horses in 1864, and in June, 1866, they had

PART OF THE GIGANTIC ORGANIZATION OF THE FEDERAL CAVALRY

only 32 left.   This was exclusive of 12,000 or 13,000 artillery horses handled at the same depot.   All these animals had to be shod.   This photograph shows some of the men who did it, with the implements of their trade.   The army in the field kept this army at home busy supplying its manifold needs.   The Southerners' only array of men was at the front.   At home, they had only an army of women, knitting, weaving, and sewing for the ragged soldiers in the field.   The men wholesale had left their businesses and enlisted.

which subordinates the comfort and pleasure of the individual to the greatest good of the greatest number.

The trouble was that upon the organization of so many regiments of volunteer cavalry, both officers and men were naturally uninstructed and therefore inefficient. Horses were overloaded, marches were prolonged beyond endurance and without proper halts for rest, forage was not always regularly provided, and troopers were not held down to those many little things which, whether in the saddle or in camp, make for the endurance of the horse and for the mobility of mounted troops.

Tactically, both officers and men of the newly made cavalry had everything to learn. In spite of the splendid natural material which was attracted to the mounted service, and the lavish expenditures of the Federal Government in its behalf, the first period of the war only emphasized the fact that, given unlimited resources in the way of men, horses, and equipment, efficient cavalry cannot be developed inside of two years or more.

To be fully prepared at the outbreak of war, regular cavalry should be kept during peace at its war strength; while if reserves of militia cavalry cannot be conveniently maintained during peace, ample reserve supplies of arms and equipment should be laid by, and such encouragement given to the breeding and rearing of saddle-horses as will enable the Government to place cavalry in the field without all the vexatious and humiliating delays which attended the fitting out of the Federal cavalry force in 1861 and 1862.

CHAPTER
THREE

THE CONFEDERATE CAVALRY
IN THE EAST

GENERAL "JEB" STUART
LEADER OF
THE VIRGINIA CAVALRY

BRIGADIER–GENERAL
BEVERLY H. ROBERTSON
C.S.A.

SUCCESSOR TO ASHBY
AS COMMANDER OF
THE "VALLEY" CAVALRY
IN 1862

MAJOR–GENERAL
W. H. F. LEE,
C.S.A.

IN 1862 COLONEL OF
THE NINTH VIRGINIA CAVALRY
IN "FITZ" LEE'S BRIGADE
UNDER STUART

CONFEDERATE
CAVALRY
LEADERS

MAJOR–GENERAL
THOMAS L. ROSSER,
C.S.A.

IN 1862 COLONEL OF THE
FIFTH VIRGINIA CAVALRY
IN "FITZ" LEE'S BRIGADE
UNDER STUART

BRIGADIER–GENERAL
WILLIAM E. JONES,
C.S.A.

IN 1862 COLONEL OF
THE SEVENTH VIRGINIA
CAVALRY IN THE ARMY
OF THE VALLEY

**ACTIVE IN THE
EARLY VIRGINIA
CAMPAIGNS**

ONE OF THE REGIMENTS THAT STUART ELUDED

A glance at the gallant and hardy bearing of Rush's Lancers as they looked in 1862, and at their curious weapons, suggestive more of Continental than of American warfare, brings sufficient testimony to the high quality of the men who endeavored to curb the Confederate leader, Stuart, and the resources behind them. The usual armament of the Union volunteer cavalry regiments consisted of a saber, a revolver, and a single-shot carbine. The Sixth Pennsylvania was provided with lances in addition to the pistol, twelve carbines being afterwards added to the equipment of each troop for picket and scouting duty. A clean cut, smart-looking lot they are by the streaming pennants—the privates, recruited from the fashionable athletic set of the day in Philadelphia, no less than the officer, so intent upon the coffee that his orderly is pouring out. But it was vainly that in North or South, in Pennsylvania or in Virginia, in Federal territory or along the banks of the Chickahominy, the men of this crack Pennsylvania regiment tried to catch Stuart and his

LANCERS IN THE FEDERAL CAVALRY

fleet command. At Tunstall's Station, Virginia, they were two hours late; at Emmittsburg, Maryland, an hour early. On the occasion of Stuart's famous raid on Chambersburg, in October, 1862, General Pleasonton, irritated by the audacity of the daring Southerner, had made every disposition to head off the raiders before they reached the Potomac. General Pleasonton himself, with eight hundred men; Colonel Richard H. Rush, with his unique lancers, and General Stoneman, with his command, were all scouring the country in search of Stuart, who was encumbered with many captured horses, but was moving steadily toward the Potomac. A march of thirty-two miles from Chambersburg brought the wily Stuart to Emmittsburg about seven o'clock on the evening of the 11th. One hour before their arrival six companies of the Lancers, at that time attached to the Third Brigade, had passed through the town on their way to Gettysburg. But until the day of his death, Stuart often managed so that the Union cavalry came too early or too late.

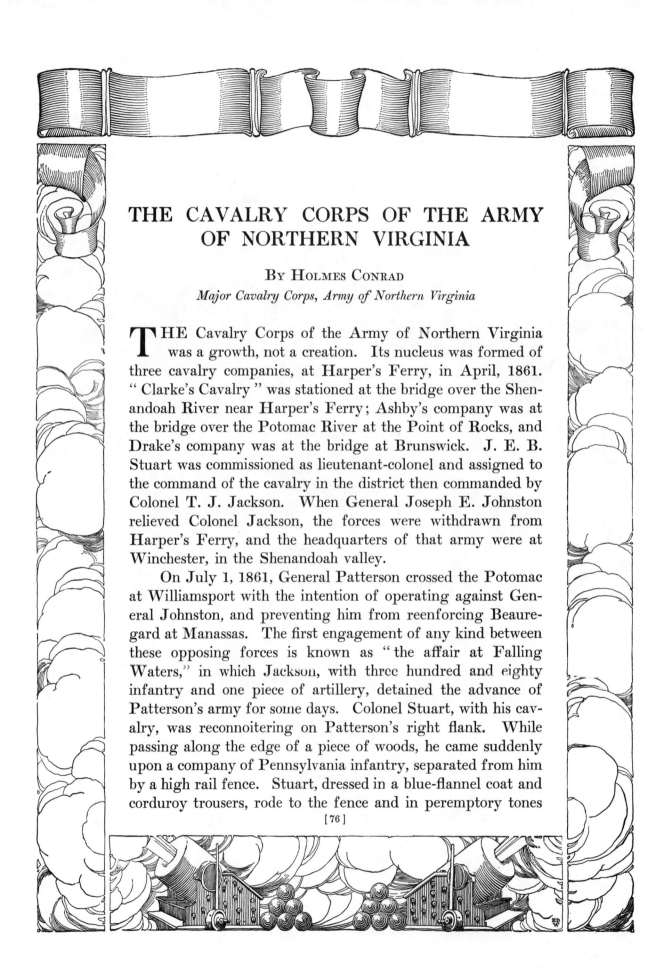

THE CAVALRY CORPS OF THE ARMY OF NORTHERN VIRGINIA

By Holmes Conrad
Major Cavalry Corps, Army of Northern Virginia

THE Cavalry Corps of the Army of Northern Virginia was a growth, not a creation. Its nucleus was formed of three cavalry companies, at Harper's Ferry, in April, 1861. "Clarke's Cavalry" was stationed at the bridge over the Shenandoah River near Harper's Ferry; Ashby's company was at the bridge over the Potomac River at the Point of Rocks, and Drake's company was at the bridge at Brunswick. J. E. B. Stuart was commissioned as lieutenant-colonel and assigned to the command of the cavalry in the district then commanded by Colonel T. J. Jackson. When General Joseph E. Johnston relieved Colonel Jackson, the forces were withdrawn from Harper's Ferry, and the headquarters of that army were at Winchester, in the Shenandoah valley.

On July 1, 1861, General Patterson crossed the Potomac at Williamsport with the intention of operating against General Johnston, and preventing him from reenforcing Beauregard at Manassas. The first engagement of any kind between these opposing forces is known as "the affair at Falling Waters," in which Jackson, with three hundred and eighty infantry and one piece of artillery, detained the advance of Patterson's army for some days. Colonel Stuart, with his cavalry, was reconnoitering on Patterson's right flank. While passing along the edge of a piece of woods, he came suddenly upon a company of Pennsylvania infantry, separated from him by a high rail fence. Stuart, dressed in a blue-flannel coat and corduroy trousers, rode to the fence and in peremptory tones

ONE OF THE EARLIEST CONFEDERATE CAVALRY EXPLOITS

A month before the first battle of Bull Run, the bridge at Berlin, Md., six miles below Harper's Ferry, was thoroughly destroyed in one of the first exploits of the Confederate cavalry. It was not yet organized. A few detached bands here and there—the Clarke company at the bridge over the Shenandoah River near Harper's Ferry, Ashby's company at the bridge over the Potomac River at the Point of Rocks, and Drake's company at the bridge at Brunswick—were operating along the first Confederate line of defense. But they had already begun to demonstrate their daring and effectiveness. This was the prelude to the bold rides of Stuart and Forrest, to the swift raids of Morgan and the terror-inspiring Mosby. It was acts like this that hampered the Union leaders, and detained an army between Washington and the Confederates. Not until the Union cavalry had learned to retaliate, and to meet and fight the exhausted Confederate horsemen on their own ground and in their own way, did the Union generals get complete possession of their infantry.

ordered the Federals to pull down the fence at once, which they did. The cavalry rode into their midst, and without the firing of a pistol took the entire company of thirty or forty men.

On the 18th of July, Johnston withdrew his army from Winchester, and moved toward Manassas. Stuart's entire command consisted of twenty-one officers and three hundred and thirteen men. All were well mounted and at home on horseback. Yet for arms they could muster but few sabers of regulation make and still fewer revolvers, although double-barreled shotguns and rifles were prevalent.

This command reached Manassas on the evening of the 20th of July, and went into camp. The next morning, at early dawn, it was aroused by the firing of a signal gun by the Federals. In the afternoon, General T. J. Jackson's brigade, while fully occupied in front, was threatened by the advance of a heavy attacking column on its left. Stuart was sent to its relief, and moving in column on Jackson's left, he soon came in view of a formidable line of Zouaves moving upon Jackson. The appearance of the head of Stuart's column arrested the movement of the opponents, attracted their fire, and finally caused their withdrawal, for which Jackson, in his report, made grateful acknowledgment.

During the summer and fall, the cavalry occupied and held Mason's and Munson's hills and picketed as far as Falls Church and at points along the Potomac. With the exception of an affair at Lewinsville, in September, the period was un-eventful and free from striking incidents. In September, 1861, Stuart was commissioned brigadier-general, and in December occurred the battle of Dranesville, in which he commanded the Confederate forces, but the result of the engagement afforded him no ground for congratulation.

In March, 1862, the Confederates evacuated Manassas, and moved below Richmond. The advance of McClellan up the Peninsula toward Williamsburg, afforded but little opportunity for cavalry operations other than protecting the flanks

FALLS CHURCH, ON THE CONFEDERATE PICKET LINE IN '61—NEARLY THREE
MILES FROM WASHINGTON

This typical cross-roads Virginia church, less than three miles from Washington, lay on the end of the line patroled by the Confederate cavalry pickets in the summer and fall of '61. Strange-looking soldiers were those riders in Colonel J. E. B. Stuart's command, without uniforms, armed with rifles and double-barreled shot-guns, with hardly a saber or a revolver. While McClellan was drilling his army in Washington and metamorphosing it from an "armed mob" into an efficient fighting machine, the Confederate horsemen occupied and held Mason's and Munson's Hill and picketed at points along the Potomac. With the exception of an affair at Lewinsville in September there was little actual fighting. In that month Stuart was commissioned brigadier-general, and in December occurred the battle of Dranesville, in which he commanded the Confederate forces, but failed to carry the day. Soon, however, he leaped into fame.

and rear of the army as it withdrew within the lines around Richmond. Toward the middle of June was effected that brilliant movement which so distinctly illustrates the daring and skill of Stuart and the unfailing endurance of his men. He passed around the entire Federal army, obtaining the information he sought and returning to camp with the substantial rewards of his prowess.

During the Seven Days' battles around Richmond, but little opportunity was afforded for cavalry operations beyond the ordinary work of obtaining information on the front and flanks, but in the latter part of June, Stuart reached White House, where a Federal gunboat had been seen on the Pamunkey. Seventy-five dismounted cavalrymen, armed with carbines and deployed as skirmishers, approached the vessel, whereupon a body of sharpshooters was landed from the gunboat and advanced to meet them. A single howitzer of the Stuart horse artillery opened on the war-ship from a position on which her guns could not be brought to bear. The shells from the howitzer greatly distressed her, and withdrawing her sharpshooters, she disappeared down the river.

On no occasion was the audacity of Stuart and the temper of his men more severely tested than in October, when there was carried through the movement to Chambersburg, Pennsylvania, which was reached on the 10th. The advance was bold and perilous enough, but it was tame in comparison with the return. The Union forces had been thoroughly aroused, and dispositions had been ordered, intended and calculated to head off the invaders before they could recross the Potomac. Leaving Chambersburg, a march of nearly thirty-two miles brought Stuart and his men to Emmittsburg at about seven o'clock on the evening of the 11th. One hour before their arrival, four companies of the Sixth Pennsylvania Cavalry had passed through the town on their way to Gettysburg. General Pleasonton with eight hundred men, Colonel Rush with his regiment, and General Stoneman with his command were scouring

A CONFEDERATE HORSE AT AN HISTORIC VIRGINIA SPOT, IN MAY, 1862

When '61 came, the young men in the North were to be found rather at commercial and indoor pursuits, as compared to those in the South. There the sports of country life appealed in preference, and the rifle and saddle were more familiar than the counting-house. Thus the Confederate cavalrymen saw nothing wrong in the proposition that they should furnish their own mounts throughout the war. The name of the beautiful horse in this photograph was "Secesh." Its upraised ears and alert expression of interest in the man who is waving his hat in the foreground, to make it look at the camera, proves it a "well-bred" animal. "Secesh" was captured by the Federals in 1862 at Yorktown, and the spot where the photograph was taken is historic. It is the cave excavated in the marl bluff by Cornwallis in 1781, for secret councils.

the country in search of Stuart, who was encumbered with many captured horses in his march toward the Potomac. Pleasonton had so interpreted Stuart's movements as to make it clear to his mind that Stuart must cross the river at the mouth of the Monocacy, but, as a matter of fact, White's Ferry was the point at which the Confederate purposed to get over. Colonel W. H. F. Lee commanded the advance, and as he approached the ferry, he found it guarded by a force of Federal infantry.

Lee had arranged his plan of attack upon these troops when it occurred to him to try a milder method. He sent a flag of truce to the Union commander and demanded the unconditional surrender of his men within fifteen minutes. To this there was no response, and Colonel Lee then opened with one gun, which fire was not returned. In a few moments the Union infantry quit their impregnable position and withdrew down the river. Stuart and his returning legions, with all their plunder, then crossed the Potomac in safety.

Several companies in the Virginia cavalry regiments were mounted on thoroughbred racers, sired by horses whose names are as household words in racing annals. One experience, in the summer of 1861, demonstrated their unfitness for cavalry service. After General Patterson had crossed the Potomac at Williamsport and occupied Martinsburg, the First Virginia Cavalry was in camp in an apple orchard, about two miles south of that town. A section of a Federal battery of two rifled guns advanced and took position a few hundred yards from the orchard, and threw some percussion shells over the cavalrymen. The missiles struck soft earth beyond and did not explode, but their screams, as they passed over the camp, were appalling. One of the companies, mounted on thoroughbreds, had no more control over their steeds than they had over the shells that frightened them. The commander of the company sought to divert attention from the noise by keeping the horses in motion, but no sooner were they brought into line than they broke and ran. A hundred yards distant was a fence, eight

A SOUTHERN ROADSTER IN 1862, AT THE SPOT WHERE STUART ON HIS FAMOUS
RAID ESCAPED FROM DANGER

The spring, the rangy endurance of this Virginia riding-horse, halted on the highway near Charles City
Court House, illustrates one factor in the dismay the Confederate cavalrymen were able to implant in the
hearts of their Northern opponents during the first two years of the war. This horse, by the way, is tread-
ing the very road where Stuart, two years before, had escaped across the Chickahominy from the vengeful
army riding in his wake after he had ridden completely around its rear. Such raids, until the North had
created an efficient cavalry force, destroyed millions of dollars' worth of Federal property and exercised a
tremendous moral effect. The cry of "The Black Horse Cavalry" terrified still further the panic-stricken
Federal troops at Bull Run; Mosby's brilliant dashes at poorly guarded Union wagon trains and careless
outposts taught the Northern leaders many a lesson, and Stuart's two raids around McClellan's army, on
the Peninsula and in Maryland, resulted in the systematic upbuilding of a Federal cavalry. In the
latter years of the war, when the South was exhausted of such horses, their cavalry became less efficient,
but nothing can dim the luster of their performances in those first two hopeful and momentous years.

rails high. They cleared this like deer, and moved to the north-west. The rifled guns returned to Martinsburg, and the regiment remained in the orchard, but it was two days before all those race-horses found their way back to the regiment. Blooded horses proved unfit for the service; they fretted and exhausted themselves on a quiet march, and proved to be unmanageable in field engagements.

June, 1863, witnessed the most spectacular tournament in which the cavalry of the opposing armies in Virginia ever engaged. The Army of Northern Virginia was entering upon the campaign that was to culminate in the three days' battle of Gettysburg, and the entire cavalry force had been assembled for review, at Brandy Station. General Pleasonton, commander of the Union Cavalry Corps, wished to cross the Rappahannock to ascertain the disposition of General Lee's army. Two fords led across the river in that vicinity, Beverly and Kelly's, and these were promptly approached by the inquisitive Northerners. The second and third divisions of cavalry and a brigade of infantry were ordered to cross at Kelly's Ford; the first cavalry division, with another brigade of infantry, was ordered to cross at Beverly Ford. Several batteries of artillery accompanied each column, and never were batteries more gallantly served or skilfully commanded. On the morning of the 9th of June, the Eighth New York Cavalry crossed at Beverly Ford. One company of the Sixth Virginia, under Captain Gibson, formed the picket at this point. Stuart's headquarters had been on Fleetwood Hill from which, however, he had, luckily, removed his baggage at an early hour.

General Buford's force of Federal cavalry which crossed at Beverly Ford was, in the opinion of all of us, quite enough to satisfy the wishes of reasonable men, and Stuart had not reckoned on a further assault on his rear. But General Gregg, with another division of Federal cavalry, crossed at Kelly's Ford, and thus had Fleetwood Hill, which was the key to the situation between the two hostile forces. A disabled

[84]

THE BANKS OF THE CHICKAHOMINY IN '62—WHEN STUART CROSSED IT IN THE
FIRST GREAT RAID OF THE WAR

This small but quick-rising little stream came nearer than the entire Union army to stopping Stuart in his famous "ride around McClellan" on the Peninsula, June 13–15, 1862. This was the first of the great Confederate raids that served to startle the Union into a recognition of the maladministration of its cavalry. After a brush with a squadron the Fifth United States Cavalry, commanded by Captain W. B. Royall, and a short halt at Old Church, he marched with only twelve hundred cavalrymen, by night, down through New Kent to Sycamore Ford on the Chickahominy, thence straight back to Richmond along the James River road. His entire loss was one man killed and a few wounded; yet he brought prisoners and plunder from under McClellan's very nose. Of most importance, he discovered the exact location of the Federal right wing, so that Jackson attacked it a few days later successfully. The cavalry gained confidence in itself, and the Confederacy rang with praises of its daring. The one really dangerous moment to the adventurous party came when the Chickahominy was reached on the homeward journey and was found to be swollen suddenly, and impassable even by swimming. Only Stuart's promptness in tearing down a mill and building a bridge with its timbers got his men across before the Federals hove in sight.

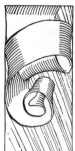

6-pounder howitzer had been left on Fleetwood Hill, under charge of Lieutenant Carter, and with this disabled gun and a very limited amount of ammunition, General Gregg was held in check until aid from General W. E. Jones' brigade could be sent. Gregg very naturally supposed that so important a position would not have been left unprotected, and that a stronger protection than one howitzer would have been afforded it. One dash by him with but a single regiment would have taken the position, and placed Stuart in a very uncomfortable situation.

From early morn till the stars arose did the battle of Brandy Station rage. The full cavalry forces of both armies were engaged, and neither could claim the advantage in gallantry or skill. The greater credit is due, perhaps, to the Federals, because they were the attacking party, and their assault had to be made by crossing a swollen river in the face of a cavalry corps that had the advantage of being on its own ground, and had the means of concentrating at each of the fords, which were the only ways the Federals had of getting access to the field. In no engagement between these two cavalry corps were sabers used so freely, or charges by regiments in line made so frequently and furiously.

General Lee was then advancing toward Pennsylvania; Stuart was screening this movement by keeping to the east of the Blue Ridge, and marching northward. The country was checkered with stone fences, strongly built and in good condition. Along the turnpike from Washington to Winchester, passing through Aldie, Middleburg, Upperville, and Paris there was continuous and severe fighting in which the cavalry alone participated. A Federal force, formed of the second cavalry division under General Gregg, with Kilpatrick's brigade and a battery of artillery, moved swiftly and with determination. Captain Reuben Boston had been placed with his Confederate squadron on the right of the road, with instructions to hold it. It appeared later that this little band had been

[86]

BRIGADIER–GENERAL THOMAS T. MUNFORD, C.S.A.

From the Peninsula to the last stand of the Confederate cavalry at Sailor's Creek, General Munford did his duty both gallantly and well. As colonel of the Second Virginia Cavalry he masked the placing of a battery of thirty-one field pieces upon the bluff at White Oak swamp, June 30, 1862. When the screen of cavalry was removed, the gunners opened up and drove a Union battery of artillery and a brigade of McClellan's infantry rear-guard from a large field just across the White Oak stream. His was the regiment which picketed the roads leading in the direction of the Federal forces upon the occasion of Jackson's famous raid around Pope's army to Manassas Junction. At Antietam he commanded a brigade of dismounted cavalry, comprising the Second and Twelfth Virginia regiments and eight guns, and he was with Longstreet and Hill at South Mountain. General Munford and General Rosser were two brigadiers of Fitzhugh Lee when the latter assumed command of all the cavalry of the Army of Northern Virginia in March, 1865. Munford's diminished brigade was swept before the Federal infantry fighting bravely at Five Forks, but with undiminished courage it drove back Crook on the north side of the Appomattox River only two days before Lee's surrender to Grant.

stationed too far to the front to receive aid from the rest of the regiment, and hence, after receiving and repulsing several attacks, Boston fell, with a remnant of his squadron, into the hands of the Sixth Ohio Cavalry.

Peremptory orders were frequently given without due consideration, and they were as frequently obeyed, even when the person so ordered knew that they were destructive. In this same campaign, Colonel Duffié, of the First Rhode Island Cavalry, was ordered to encamp at Middleburg on the night of June 17th, and his line of march was prescribed. He followed that line and it disclosed to him the presence of the Confederates at many points along its course. He reached Middleburg, and despatched an officer to General Kilpatrick, at Aldie, to advise him of the situation, but Kilpatrick's troops were too exhausted to go to Duffié's relief, and the latter's regiment was attacked in the morning by Robertson's Confederate brigade, and two hundred of his men fell into Robertson's hands.

Many brilliant incidents of the Gettysburg campaign testify to the efficiency of the cavalry on both sides. While Stuart was off on the left of the Confederate army, Robertson's brigade was on the right. General W. E. Jones was sent, with three regiments, to protect the wagon train near Fairfield. Near that place, the Sixth United States Cavalry, under Major Starr, met the Seventh Virginia, and decidedly worsted that gallant regiment; but the Sixth Virginia, under Major Flournoy, took its place, and the tide was turned. The Sixth United States was routed, its brave commander was wounded and captured, with one hundred and eighty-four of his command.

As Lee fell back from Gettysburg, the Potomac River was much swollen. From the 8th to the 11th of July, Stuart was engaged in guarding the front of the Confederate army, waiting for the waters to fall. Cavalry engagements, of more or less severity, with the divisions of Buford and Kilpatrick, took place at Boonesboro, Beaver Creek, Funkstown, and in

A RESTFUL SCENE AT GENERAL McDOWELL'S HEADQUARTERS—TAKEN WHILE
STUART'S CAVALRY WAS EXTREMELY BUSY

The Federals were camping in peaceful and luxurious fashion, August, 1862, quite unconscious that Jackson with Stuart's cavalry, was cutting in between them and Washington. It would have seemed madness to the Union generals in command of one hundred thousand men, with potential reinforcements of fifty thousand more, that the Confederate leaders should split their army of only fifty-five thousand and separate the parts by two days' march. It turned out that the Confederate generals were "mad," but that there was brilliant method in their madness. Twice they had attempted to turn the Federal right, when Pope lay across the Rappahannock waiting for McClellan's return from the Peninsula, and twice the watchful Pope had foiled the attempt. It was not until Jackson left Early's brigade in an exposed position across the hastily repaired bridge at Rappahannock Station that he managed to delude the Union general into accepting this point as his real objective. Leaving Early quite as mystified as his opponent, Jackson dispatched Stuart with all the cavalry to Catlett's Station, on the Orange & Alexandria Railroad, where Pope's supply trains were parked. The night of August 23d was pitchy black, and the rain was descending in torrents, when the Confederate horsemen burst into Pope's camp. A few hours later they rode away with the Federal general's uniform and horses, his treasure-chest and personal effects, a member of his staff, and some three hundred prisoners, leaving the blazing camp behind them. The retreat of the cavalry was the final indication that there would be no more efforts to turn his right. Two days later Jackson, with twenty thousand men, marched around the Union right and, joined by Stuart's cavalry, captured the immense supply-department depot at Manassas Junction.

REPAIRING AFTER STUART'S RAID

In a single night Stuart's cavalry, falling upon the Orange & Alexandria Railroad at Catlett's Station, thirty-five miles from Washington, had done damage to Pope's railroad connection which it took days to repair. This was on August 22d, and only the heavy rainstorm prevented the burning of a large quantity of army stores at Catlett's. Stuart's troopers got away with two hundred and twenty horses from the wagon trains and all the personal baggage of General Pope and his staff. The superior railroad facilities of the Federals were in this instance turned into a means of danger and delay, necessitating the detachment of a large repair force and enabling Lee's army to seize advantage elsewhere.

A MILITARY TRAIN UPSET BY CONFEDERATES

This is part of the result of General Pope's too rapid advance to head off Lee's army south of the Rappahannock River. Although overtaking the advance of the Confederates at Cedar Mountain, Pope had arrived too late to close the river passes against them. Meanwhile he had left the Orange & Alexandria Railroad uncovered, and Jackson pushed a large force under General Ewell forward across the Bull Run Mountains. On the night of August 26, 1862, Ewell's forces captured Manassas Junction, while four miles above the Confederate cavalry fell upon an empty railroad train returning from the transfer of Federal troops. The train was destroyed. Here we see how well the work was done.

front of Sharpsburg. Thus was the advance of Meade's army delayed until the Confederates had recrossed the river.

In September, 1863, the Cavalry Corps of the Army of Northern Virginia was reorganized, and Stuart's headquarters were at Culpeper Court House. On the 18th, Kilpatrick's division crossed the Rappahannock, and pressing its way with celerity and vigor toward Culpeper, captured three guns of the Confederate horse artillery. On the 22d, Buford encountered Stuart at Jack's shop, in Madison County, and a fierce engagement occupied the divisions of both Buford and Kilpatrick, with the result that Stuart withdrew across the Rapidan.

In October, General Lee entered upon what is known as the Bristoe campaign, which aimed at turning the right flank of the Federal army in Culpeper County. To cover this movement, Stuart distributed his command over a wide extent of country and along the Rapidan. On the 10th, Stuart was ordered to make a reconnaissance toward Catlett's Station. He sent Lomax forward, who moved to Auburn, and there learned that the Federals were in force at Warrenton Junction. He further discovered that the entire Federal wagon train was parked in a position easy of access. It was most desirable that its commissary supplies should be so applied as to appease the hunger of his half-starved cavalrymen. Stuart consequently moved in that direction, and on reaching a piece of woods there was plainly seen, about half a mile beyond, the vast park of wagons. Stuart gazed long and ardently at this coveted prize, but as he gazed, the hopeful expression on his countenance faded away and was succeeded by one of vexation and disappointment. Beyond the park of wagons, his practised eye discerned a moving cloud of dust, which appeared to be passing on the left of the wagons. It was growing dusk; tidings from his rear seemed to disconcert him, and he appeared to those who were near to be anxiously awaiting something. He rearranged his column; some pieces of artillery were put in front, and behind these a medical transport wagon, and then

THE TRAIN "STONEWALL" JACKSON AND STUART STOPPED AT BRISTOE

By a move of unparalleled boldness, "Stonewall" Jackson, with twenty thousand men, captured the immense Union supplies at Manassas Junction, August 26, 1862. His was a perilous position. Washington lay one day's march to the north; Warrenton, Pope's headquarters, but twelve miles distant to the southwest; and along the Rappahannock, between "Stonewall" Jackson and Lee, stood the tents of another host which outnumbered the whole Confederate army. "Stonewall" Jackson had seized Bristoe Station in order to break down the railway bridge over Broad Run, and to proceed at his leisure with the destruction of the stores. A train returning empty from Warrenton Junction to Alexandria darted through the station under heavy fire. The line was promptly torn up. Two trains which followed in the same direction as the first went crashing down a high embankment. The report received at Alexandria from the train which escaped ran as fol-

lows: "No. 6 train, engine Secretary, was fired into at Bristoe by a party of cavalry some five hundred strong. They had piled ties on the track, but the engine threw them off. Secretary is completely riddled by bullets." It was a full day before the Federals realized that "Stonewall" Jackson was really there with a large force. Here, in abundance, was all that had been absent for some time; besides commissary stores of all sorts, there were two trains loaded with new clothing, to say nothing of sutler's stores, replete with "extras" not enumerated in the regulations, and also the camp of a cavalry regiment which had vacated in favor of Jackson's men. It was an interesting sight to see the hungry, travel-worn men attacking this profusion and rewarding themselves for all their fatigues and deprivations of the preceding few days, and their enjoyment of it and of the day's rest allowed them. There was a great deal of difficulty for a time in finding what each man needed most, but this was overcome through a crude barter of belongings as the day wore on.

the cavalry. Thus formed, he moved to the front, leaving wagons and moving dust far to our right.

At some distance ahead, there rose from the plain a wooded ridge, extending northeast and southwest. Toward the end nearest to us we headed, and began its ascent, in the order in which we were formed. The front of the column reached the top and moved on to the further end, from which the ridge fell with more precipitousness than the end which we had ascended. When the last file of the rear regiment was well up on the ridge and protected by the trees, no room remained for more. We were dismounted and lay down, holding the bridle-reins in our hands.

In less than an hour a heavy column of infantry approached the ridge from the direction in which we had come. It passed to the left and moved along very close to the ridge and toward its further end. Almost at once, another column, like unto the first and moving by its side, passed to the right of the ridge, and at about the same distance from it, in a parallel line toward the same end of the ridge. So near were these moving columns, and so still were we, that all night long we could hear the conversation carried on among our foemen on either side of us.

The hours seemed interminable, but those marching columns seemed even longer. Daylight came, but still they marched. Should sunrise find us still so beleaguered, our chances of escape would be small. As the earliest rays of the sun routed the mists, the long-hoped-for rear of these columns went by, and halted but a few rods beyond the further end of our ridge. During the night, Stuart had sent messengers to General Lee, telling him of our situation and asking for relief. That relief was sent, but it miscarried. As the sun rose higher, Stuart opened on the rear of these two columns, which had halted for breakfast, had made their fires, and were boiling their coffee. The four guns did some execution, and the Federals, startled by this " bolt from the blue," ran—not, as we hoped,

MANASSAS JUNCTION, WHERE THE FEDERAL WAR DEPARTMENT ENTERTAINED
UNEXPECTED GUESTS

"Stonewall" Jackson and twenty thousand men were the unexpected guests of the North
at Manassas Junction on August 26, 1862. The ragged and famished Confederates, who
had marched over fifty miles in the last two days, had such a feast as they never knew
before. The North had been lavish in its expenditures for the army. No effort had
been spared to feed, clothe, and equip them, and for the comfort of the individual soldier
the purse-strings of the nation were freely loosed. Streets of warehouses, crammed to the
doors, a line of freight cars two miles in length, thousands of barrels of flour, pork, and
biscuit, ambulances, field-wagons, and pyramids of shot and shell, met the wondering
gaze of the Confederate soldiery. The sutlers' stores contained a wealth of plunder.
"Here," says General George H. Gordon, describing the scene that followed, "a long,
yellow-haired, barefooted son of the South claimed as prizes a tooth-brush, a box of
candies, and a barrel of coffee, while another, whose butternut homespun hung round him
in tatters, crammed himself with lobster salad, sardines, potted game, and sweetmeats,
and washed them down with Rhenish wine. Nor was the outer man neglected. From
piles of new clothing, the Southerners arrayed themselves in the blue uniforms of the
Federals. The naked were clad, the barefooted were shod, and the sick provided with
luxuries to which they had long been strangers." All unportable stores were destroyed.

from the danger that presented itself, but ran, and with intrepid force, toward us. They charged the steep ascent, struck
down the commander of a North Carolina regiment, and only
desisted when the fire from our guns repelled them. Stuart
withdrew from the ridge. He had extricated himself in safety,
and what would have been stigmatized as his folly, had we
been routed, became a proof of his genius and heroic courage.

The object of the Bristoe campaign was accomplished as
far as such objects are generally accomplished, but, on the 18th
of October, Stuart was at Buckland, with Kilpatrick in front
of him. A device suggested by Fitzhugh Lee proved successful. Stuart withdrew and Kilpatrick followed him hopefully,
but Fitzhugh Lee had taken a position which threw him in Kilpatrick's rear. Upon an agreed signal, Stuart turned on Kilpatrick in front and Lee struck his rear, and a rout ensued in
which Davies' brigade bore the brunt. It ran, and the race
extended over five miles. Custer, however, saved his artillery
and crossed Broad Run in safety.

On the 28th of February following, Custer made a brilliant, and in the main successful, foray from Madison Court
House into Charlottesville, with about fifteen hundred cavalry.
Near Charlottesville were four battalions of artillery, resting
in fond security in winter quarters. The guns were all saved
but horses were taken, and some of the quarters were burned,
with the loss of clothing and blankets.

Kilpatrick was moving on Richmond with about thirty-
five hundred cavalry. Colonel Ulric Dahlgren and about four
hundred and fifty men were pushed rapidly toward the Virginia Central Railroad, which they struck at Frederick's Hall,
where they captured eight officers who were sitting on a court
martial, and moved toward the James River. Thence they
moved down on the north side of the James to Richmond,
where they attacked the outer entrenchments. Hampton attacked Kilpatrick's camp and drove him from it, compelling
his return to Fredericksburg. Colonel Dahlgren made a wide

OUT OF REACH

OF THE

CONFEDERATE CAVALRY

U. S. MILITARY

ENGINES STORED

IN ALEXANDRIA, 1863

By the middle of 1863 the Federal generals had learned the wisdom of storing in a safe place, under a heavy guard, anything they wanted to keep. Of especial value was the rolling stock of the military railroads, which when not in use was ordered out of the danger zone. General J. E. B. Stuart with his tireless troopers had proved himself so ignorant of the meaning of the words "danger" or "distance" that the Federals had lost their confidence of the previous year, when they believed that the mere interposition of an army of a hundred thousand men was sufficient to protect a base of supplies. This photograph was taken about the time the battle of Gettysburg was raging, and Stuart was causing a diversion by throwing shells near Washington. It was not until the Army of the Potomac returned to Virginia, with headquarters established at Brandy Station, that any great number of these iron horses were allowed out of their stables. By that time the Union cavalry had received the experience and equipment to meet the Confederate troopers in their own way, and threatened the railroads running into Richmond. Organization and numbers had begun to tell.

circuit, crossing the Pamunkey and the Mattapony, but at length he fell into an ambuscade near King and Queen Court House where he lost his life, as did many of his command.

We have reached now, in the order of time, the Wilderness campaign which opened May 4, 1864. General Grant's object was to interpose his army between Lee and Richmond. Sheridan, with about ten thousand cavalry and several batteries, had moved to Hamilton's Crossing and thence toward Richmond, on the Telegraph road. General Wickham, with his brigade, followed in pursuit. Near Mitchell's shop he was joined by Fitzhugh Lee, with about five thousand cavalry. Stuart, now in command, moved toward Yellow Tavern, which he reached before the appearance of Sheridan's troopers. They did appear, however, and attempted to drive Stuart from the Telegraph road. A severe fight ensued, in which Stuart lost heavily in officers, but maintained his position.

About four o'clock in the afternoon, a brigade of Federal cavalry attacked Stuart's extreme left, and he, after his fashion, hurried to the point of danger. One company of the First Virginia Cavalry was bearing the entire burden. Stuart joined himself to this little band and attacked the flank of the Union cavalry. The First Virginia drove the Federals back. Many of the latter, having lost their horses in the fight, were keeping up on foot. One of these dismounted men turned, as he ran, and firing at the general with his pistol, inflicted the wound from which he shortly afterward died.

Now, to turn back, when General Johnston, on the 18th of July, 1861, moved from the Shenandoah valley to Manassas, he left a body of cavalry, under Colonel McDonald, scattered throughout the country between the Shenandoah River and the North Mountains. In this body was a company from Fauquier County, commanded by Turner Ashby. Later on, this company was organized into a huge regiment of which McDonald was colonel; Turner Ashby, lieutenant-colonel, and Oliver Funsten, major. The duty assigned to this regiment

COVERING LEE'S RETREAT FROM PENNSYLVANIA

This photograph is an excellent illustration of the cavalry's method of destroying the railroads between the two capitals. The light rails were placed across piles of ties. The ties were lighted and the rails heated until of their own weight they bent out of shape. Mile upon mile of railroad could thus be destroyed in a day. New rails had to be brought before it was possible to rebuild the line. Note the tangle of telegraph wires. The telegraph lines were also destroyed wherever the Confederate position was known and it was therefore impossible to tap them and read the Union leaders' messages. The Army of Northern Virginia and the Army of the Potomac spent the month of October, 1863, when this photograph was taken, maneuvering for position along the Rappahannock. On October 20th the Army of the Potomac was occupying Warrenton and Lee had retired to the north bank of the Rappahannock, having destroyed the Orange and Alexandria Railroad from Bristoe Station to the river, and by the 22d, both armies were again in camp.

THE PRIZE THAT IMPERILLED STUART ON HIS DARING RAID INTO THE
FEDERAL LINES

In this striking photograph of 1863 appears the prize at which General J. E. B. Stuart gazed long and ardently during his reconnaissance to Warrenton Station on the 10th of October, 1863, after Lee's Bristoe campaign. His half-starved cavalrymen urgently needed just such a wagon-train as that. But, as they peered from their ambush, the hopeful expressions faded away. Beyond the park of wagons Stuart's practiced eye had discerned a moving cloud of dust. That night he was confined to a little ridge, with the Union columns moving to the right and left of his isolated force. By dawn the rear of the passing columns were cooking their breakfasts at the foot of the ridge. By the bold device of firing into them and

PART OF THE "VAST PARK OF WAGONS" ON WHICH THE CONFEDERATES GAZED
FROM AMBUSH, OCTOBER 10, 1863

repelling their first attack, Stuart disconcerted the pursuit and made good his escape. This view of the wagons "in park," or gathered in one large body in an open field, represents a train of the Sixth Corps, Army of the Potomac, near Brandy Station, during the autumn days of 1863, after the Gettysburg campaign. The wagons in the foreground are ambulances, while immediately in their rear stand the large army wagons used for subsistence and quartermaster's stores. The horses are harnessed to the vehicles preparatory to the forward movement. It took this train across the Rappahannock River toward Culpeper and the Rapidan, where history indicates that they formed part of those upon which Stuart gazed so covetously.

was the guarding of the Potomac River on a line nearly one hundred and twenty-five miles in length. No more striking and picturesque figure than Ashby ever won the confidence and affections of his followers. Since his boyhood he had been famed as a horseman, even in that land of centaurs. Throughout all those marvelous campaigns in the Valley, which have made Jackson immortal, Turner Ashby, as brigadier-general, commanded the cavalry that formed an impenetrable screen between Jackson and the Federal armies in his front.

In May and June, 1862, Jackson moved up the Shenandoah valley, Generals Banks and Saxton following with fourteen thousand troops. General Fremont, with his army, was approaching Strasburg from the direction of Moorefield, while General Shields, who had crossed the Blue Ridge from the east, was moving up Luray Valley on Jackson's left flank, with still another division. Jackson waited at Strasburg nearly twenty-four hours for one of his regiments, which he had left below him, to rejoin his command. Meanwhile Fremont approached within ten miles, was met by General Richard Taylor, and held in check until Jackson, starting his wagon trains off before him, had followed in a leisurely manner, while Ashby, with his cavalry, kept back Fremont, who was pressing Jackson's rear. Shields was moving rapidly in the hope of intercepting Jackson before he could cross the Blue Ridge, which Shields supposed he' was striving to do. A few miles south of Harrisonburg, Jackson turned toward Port Republic, encountered Fremont's cavalry, under Colonel Percy Wyndham, which Ashby quickly routed, capturing Colonel Wyndham and a large part of his command. Fremont sent forward General Bayard and his command, which met the Fifty-eighth Virginia, near Cross Keys. General Ashby dismounted, and placing himself at the head of this infantry regiment, received the bullet which ended his career.

His former regiment, with certain additions, was organized into a brigade consisting of the Second, Sixth, Seventh,

A SAD SIGHT FOR THE CAVALRYMAN

This pitiful scene after the battle of Gettysburg illustrates the losses of mounts after each engagement, which told heaviest on the Southern cavalry. Up to the next winter, 1863–4, it was well organized and had proved its efficiency on many fields. But from that period its weakness increased rapidly. The sources of supplies of both men and horses had been exhausted simultaneously; many of the best and bravest of men and officers had fallen in battle. From then onward it was a struggle for bare existence, until at Appomattox the large-hearted Lee pointed out to Grant that the only mounts left to the Confederacy were those that his men were actually riding. Be it recorded to the Northern general's credit that he gave immediate instructions that every Confederate who owned his horse should be allowed to take it home for plowing and putting in his crop. This photograph shows staff officers' horses killed at Gettysburg.

and Twelfth Virginia regiments, and the Seventeenth Battalion which soon afterward became the Eleventh Virginia Cavalry. After Ashby's death, this brigade was, for a time, commanded by Colonel Munford. General Shields reached the village of Port Republic, where Jackson encountered him and drove him back down Luray Valley, and thus ended the Valley campaign of that year.

General Beverly Robertson was now assigned to the command of the old Ashby brigade. On the 2d of August, a sharp hand-to-hand encounter took place in the streets of Orange Court House, between the Seventh Virginia, and the Fifth New York and First Vermont, both commanded by General Crawford, in which Colonel Jones and Lieutenant-Colonel Marshall, of the Seventh Virginia, were wounded. The Sixth Virginia coming up, the Federals reluctantly gave way, and were pursued as far as Rapidan Station.

On December 29th, 1862, General W. E. Jones was assigned to the command of the Valley District, and in March, 1863, he moved to Moorefield Valley, with the view of gathering much-needed supplies of food, and also with the intention of destroying the Cheat River viaduct, on the Baltimore and Ohio Railroad. The south branch, at Petersburg in Hardy County, West Virginia, was high, and the fords were almost impassable. The artillery and the loaded wagon trains were sent back to Harrisonburg, and Jones, with his cavalry alone, undertook the invasion of West Virginia. At Greenland Gap, on the summit of the Alleghany Mountains, a body of Federal infantry held a blockhouse, strongly built and gallantly defended. This was taken only after the loss of several men, and the wounding of Colonel Dulany of the Seventh Virginia. It was repeatedly charged by the dismounted cavalry, and was finally taken by stratagem rather than assault.

The Cheat River viaduct was reached on the 26th of April, and found to be guarded by three hundred infantry entrenched in a blockhouse, too strong to be taken in a moment, and time

HORSES KILLED IN BATTLE—A SERIOUS LOSS

The number of horses killed in battle was, after all, but a small fraction of those destroyed by exhaustion, starvation, and disease during the Civil War. When Lee's army marched into Pennsylvania he had issued stringent orders against plundering. The orders were almost implicitly obeyed except when it came to the question of horses. The quartermasters, especially of artillery battalions, could seldom report their commands completely equipped. The Confederacy had no great cavalry depots like Giesboro, or those at St. Louis or Greenville in Louisiana. When a mount was exhausted he had to be replaced. Some of the farmers actually concealed their horses in their own houses, but a horseless trooper was a veritable sleuth in running down a horse, whether concealed in the parlor or in the attic. The Confederates offered to pay for the horses, but in Confederate currency. The owners occasionally accepted it on the principle that it was "better than nothing." The animals thus impressed in Pennsylvania were for the most part great, clumsy, flabby Percherons and Conestogas, which required more than twice the feed of the compact, hard-muscled little Virginia horses. It was pitiable to see these great brutes suffer when they were compelled to dash off at full gallop with a field-piece after pasturing on dry broom-sedge and eating a quarter of a feed of weevil-infested corn.

A CAVALRY HORSE PICKETED
AT THE EVENING BIVOUAC

did not allow of tarrying. On April 28th, the command reached Morgantown, where it crossed on a suspension bridge to the west side of the Monongahela, and after dark moved on Fairmont. Here the Federals were found in considerable force, which, after some fighting, was dispersed, and the object of the visit to that point being the destruction of the fine iron bridge, of three spans of three hundred feet each, that work was entered upon and continued until the bridge was destroyed.

Oiltown, near Elizabeth Court House, on the Little Kanawha River, was owned mainly by Southern men who had first engaged in the oil industry. There were found thousands of gallons of oil, in barrels, tanks, and in deep flatboats then on the water. All was burned, and Dante might have gained some new impressions of the regions described by him, from the scenes that presented themselves to the destroyers. The dense, black smoke rose to the heights of hundreds of feet; the intense heat caused by the burning oil excited a breeze, and the flatboats filled with burning oil, floated down the river toward Elizabeth. After thirty days incessant marching, without supplies of food, save what was taken from the people, without artillery or wagons of any kind, the expedition returned with seven hundred prisoners, one thousand cattle and twelve hundred horses, and with a loss of ten killed and forty-two wounded.

Jones was back in the Valley the last week of May, and, by crossing the mountains, joined Stuart near Culpeper Court House. A little later he took conspicuous part in the battle of Brandy Station and the ensuing campaign. The events and incidents of that and the following campaigns to the death of General Stuart, have been already related.

General Thomas L. Rosser had been assigned to the command of the old Ashby brigade, and soon proved himself a most efficient cavalry commander. In January, 1864, then under General Early in the Valley District, he was in command of the cavalry. On January 29th, Rosser crossed the

A SECOND "ARMY" OPPOSED TO THE CONFEDERATE CAVALRY—A FEDERAL CAVALRY MESS-HOUSE

The Confederate cavalry, like the Confederacy itself, was hastened to its fall because of the exhaustion of resources. While horseflesh was growing scarcer and poorer in quality in Virginia, and proper fodder had become little but a memory since Sheridan's devastation of the Shenandoah Valley, the Union Government, with its immense resources, was able to systematize the handling of supplies for its cavalry corps, establishing half a dozen huge cavalry remount depots, and devoting the proper amount of attention to every branch of the work. This photograph shows the mess-house at the Government stables in Washington. The Confederacy barely supplied food for the troopers themselves, while the Union Government was able to build mess-houses for those who were engaged in caring for the troopers' wants.

mountains to Moorefield, in Hardy County, West Virginia, and there learning that a large wagon train of supplies was moving from New Creek to Petersburg, moved forward to take it. He found parked at Medley a train of ninety-five wagons, guarded by three hundred infantry and a small body of cavalry. He moved one regiment toward the rear of this body, placed others on the flank, and then opened with one gun on its front. The effect was to stampede the teamsters, and the infantry were unable to withstand the attack by dismounted cavalry, so that in a short time the wagons, with some prisoners, fell into Rosser's hands. On the 1st of February, moving upon the Baltimore and Ohio Railroad, at Patterson's Creek, he captured the guard there, and brought out about twelve hundred cattle and some sheep.

On the 7th of June, Sheridan was sent with two divisions to communicate with Hunter, and to break up the Virginia Central Railroad and the James River Canal. He started on this mission with eighty-nine hundred cavalry. On the morning of the 8th, Hampton, who had succeeded Stuart in the command of the Cavalry Corps of the Army of Northern Virginia, moved with two divisions and some batteries of horse artillery to look after this movement. His first step was to intercept Sheridan before he reached the railroad. On the night of the 10th, he had reached Green Spring Valley, three miles from Trevilian Station, and there encamped. At this time General Fitzhugh Lee was at Louisa Court House, and Custer, with his characteristic boldness, took an unguarded road around Hampton's right and essayed to reach Trevilian. He captured ambulances, caissons, and many led horses. Near at hand was Thompson's battery, wholly unmindful of danger, and this Custer essayed to take. But Colonel Chew, commander of the battalion of artillery to which this belonged, deployed a South Carolina regiment to hold Custer in check until he could get another battery into position. This he soon did, and Rosser, coming up with his brigade at the moment,

A WAR–TIME VIEW OF STUART'S GRAVE

"Gen'l Stuart—wounded May 11, 1864—died May 12, 1864." This simple head-slab on its wooded hill near Richmond toward the close of the war spelt a heavy blow to the Confederate cause. In that struggle against heavier and heavier odds, every man counted. And when destroying Fate chose for its victim the leader whose spirit had never fallen, whose courage had never failed, no matter how dangerous the raid, how fierce the charge and countercharge—well might the Confederacy mourn. To the memory of this American chevalier, tributes came not only from comrades but from opponents. One of these, Theophilus F. Rodenbough—a Federal captain at the time of Stuart's death, later a cavalry historian and a contributor to other pages of this volume—wrote, twenty years after the tragedy, this fitting epitaph: "Deep in the hearts of all true cavalrymen, North and South, will ever burn a sentiment of admiration mingled with regret for this knightly soldier and generous man."

compelled Custer to relinquish his well-earned gains and betake himself to flight, while all his plunder fell into Rosser's hands.

Custer, however, remained that night near Trevilian, from which Rosser strove to drive him, but his reward was a severe wound which disabled him from further action that day. Desperately did Sheridan endeavor to drive Hampton from his path, and the fight continued through three days, but the result was the withdrawal of Sheridan's forces, and his rejoining Grant. General Grant, in his "Memoirs," states of this withdrawal that "Sheridan went back because the enemy had taken possession of a crossing by which he proposed to go west, and because he heard that Hunter was not at Charlottesville."

In September, Lee's army was sorely in need of beef. Scouts reported at Coggin's Point a large but well-guarded herd of cattle, and on the morning of the 11th, Hampton, with his cavalry, started to capture it. Notice of this movement had got abroad, and near Sycamore Church a regiment of Federal cavalry was awaiting the assault. The cattle were protected by a strong abatis, through which cavalry could not pass, and a deliberate attack was required. Accordingly the Seventh Virginia was dismounted and moved forward, while other regiments were sent around the obstruction. The herders then broke down the fence of the corral, and tried by firing pistols to stampede the cattle, and thus get them beyond Hampton's reach. But Hampton's cavalry were born cowboys, and, heading off the frightened cattle, soon rounded them up, so that the expedition returned with twenty-five hundred cattle to Lee's starving soldiers. On the 17th, General B. F. Butler informed General Grant that "three brigades of Hampton's cavalry turned our left and captured about two thousand cattle, and our telegraph construction party."

Rosser returned to the Valley with his brigade, and on November 27th started on the "New Creek raid," so called from a village on the Baltimore and Ohio Railroad, about

BRIGADIER–GENERAL JAMES B. GORDON, C.S.A.

KILLED DURING SHERIDAN'S RAID ON RICHMOND, MAY 11, 1864

MAJOR–GENERAL LENSFORD L. LOMAX, C.S.A.

WITH THE CONFEDERATE CAVALRY IN THE SHENANDOAH

twenty-two miles west from Cumberland. A Federal scouting party had been sent out from New Creek on the 26th, and Rosser, marching all night, arrived within six miles of New Creek at daylight on the morning of the 27th. The village was strongly fortified, with one heavy gun enfilading the road on which Rosser was moving toward it. General W. H. Payne's brigade was put in front, with about twenty men in blue overcoats. The column moved slowly toward its object, and citizens along the road, and travelers at that early hour thought it was the returning party that had gone out the night before on a scout. Less than a mile from the two, the first picket was reached. These men jocularly mocked the empty-handed returning party, but they were silently surrounded and taken along with the column. New Creek was reached and entered. On the left was a high hill, not steep, on which an infantry force of twelve hundred men was encamped. The Federal troops were engaged in drying their blankets and preparing their breakfast, when the mounted column of Confederates, suddenly breaking into line, charged the hill, and, without the loss of a single life, took eight hundred of these infantry. The Confederates then proceeded to destroy the railroad bridge, and gather as much as they could carry away of the large supplies they found stored at that point. Rosser, encumbered with many hundred cattle and sheep, and a long train of captured stores, turned his column homeward.

At Beverly, a village seventy-five miles west from Staunton, there were stored large supplies, guarded by a Federal garrison that did not exceed one thousand men. Rosser, learning of this fact, took three hundred men from the several brigades and started before daylight from Swoope's Depot, on January 10th. He spent that night, or a part of it, on a mountainside, without fires. The snow was deep, and the weather bitterly cold. Before daylight on the morning of the 11th, he was on a hill west of Beverly, overlooking the garrison of Federal infantry in their wooden huts on the plain below. The moon

M. C. Butler
Maj Genl. C. S. A.

BRIGADIER–GENERAL M. C. BUTLER, C. S. A.

General Butler was a leader under Wade Hampton, who played an important part in the defeat of Sheridan with eight thousand men at Trevilian Station, June 12, 1864, just one month after the death of Stuart. Between 2 P.M. and dark, Butler, in command of Hampton's division of cavalry, repulsed seven determined assaults of Sheridan's men. During the day Butler was unable to keep his batteries in exposed positions entirely manned, but between sunset and dark, when the Federal cavalrymen made their last desperate effort, the howitzers were remanned and double-shotted with canister. The Federals emerged from the woods a stone's throw from the Confederate lines, and the canister tore great holes in their lines. It was at this engagement that General Butler lost his leg.

was full and shining brilliantly on snow over a foot in depth. Dismounting a part of his command, and moving them in line in front, with the mounted men behind, Rosser moved upon the sleeping host. Had they remained in their strong huts and used their rifles, the disaster might have been averted, but as the result, five hundred and eighty prisoners, and ten thousand rations fell into the hands of the invaders.

On the morning of February 21, 1865, a portion of McNeill's command, under Lieutenant Jesse McNeill, entered the city of Cumberland, Maryland, an hour before daylight. Major-General Crook, the commander of the Department of West Virginia, and Brigadier-General Kelley, his able lieutenant, were quietly sleeping, the one at the St. Nicholas Hotel, and the other at the Revere House. Six thousand troops, of all arms, occupied the city. Sergeant Vandiver called on General Crook, while some other member of the command performed the like civility to General Kelley. These two officers were persuaded to accompany their ill-timed callers on their return to Dixie, and were entertained in Richmond at an official hostelry there. Rosser and his command were present at Appomattox, but did not participate in the surrender, but while that ceremony was in progress, this command passed on to Lynchburg, and dissolved into their individual elements.

Up to the winter of 1863–64, the Confederate cavalry was well organized and had proven its efficiency on many fields, but its weakness from that period grew rapidly. The sources of supplies of both men and horses had been exhausted, and the best and the bravest of men and officers had fallen in battle.

On the other hand, when General Sheridan took command of the Federal cavalry, a new and far more vigorous life was imparted to it. Armed with repeating carbines and fighting on foot, as well as mounted, it became the most formidable arm of the Federal service. When the war ended, it was but reasonable to aver that the cavalry of the Army of the Potomac was the most efficient body of soldiers on earth.

CHAPTER

FOUR

——————

RAIDS OF THE
FEDERAL CAVALRY

——————

WELL-CONDITIONED MOUNTS, EQUIPPED FOR A LONG RAID
1862

FEDERAL CAVALRY LEAVING CAMP

The well-filled bags before and behind each trooper indicate a long and hard trip in store. Both the Confederate and Federal cavalry distinguished themselves by their endurance on their arduous and brilliant raids. The amount of destruction accomplished by this arm of the service was well-nigh incalculable. Stuart, Mosby, Forrest on one side—Sheridan, Grierson, Kilpatrick on the other—each in turn upset the opponents' calculations and forced them to change their plans. It was Van Dorn's capture at Holly Springs that caused Grant's first failure against Vicksburg. It was not until after the surrender at Appomattox that Lee learned

THE ARM THAT DEALT A FINAL BLOW TO THE CONFEDERACY

the final crushing blow—that the rations destined for his men had been captured by Sheridan.   Up and down the Rappahannock the cavalry rode and scouted and fought by day and by night, sometimes saddled for sixty hours, often sleeping by regiments on the slowly moving columns of horses.   It was Grierson who reported, after his ride from Vicksburg to Baton Rouge, that the Confederacy was but a hollow shell—all of its men were on the battle-line.   It was Stuart who twice circled McClellan's army, on the Peninsula and in Maryland, and who caused Lincoln to recall the schoolboy game: " Three times round and out."

REPAIRING CONFEDERATE DAMAGE

The busy Federal engineers are rebuilding the railroad bridge across Cedar Run, near Catlett's Station, destroyed by the Confederates on the previous day, October 13th, when they fell back before the Army of the Potomac under General Meade.   The fall of 1863 was a period of small cavalry battles.   On September 16th the Army of the Potomac crossed the Rappahannock and took position near Culpeper Court House.   During the next few weeks the cavalry was actively engaged in reconnoitering duty.   On October 10th General John Buford was sent across the Rappahannock with the First Cavalry Division (consisting of the Eighth Illinois, Twelfth Illinois, four companies Third Indiana, six companies Eighth New York, Sixth New York, Ninth New York, Seventeenth Pennsylvania, and

FEDERAL ENGINEERS AT WORK OCTOBER 14, 1863

Third West Virginia, two companies) to uncover, if possible, the upper fords of the river. Buford forced a passage over the Germanna Ford, and bivouacked that night at Morton's Ford, where he recrossed the Rapidan and engaged a body of the enemy. At daylight on October 14th, the Confederates attacked Gregg's Second Cavalry Division, but he held his position tenaciously while General Warren got the Second Corps across Cedar Run. It seldom took over a few hours to rebuild one of these bridges. Sometimes the troops tore down the nearest wooden houses to get boards and timber. This wrecking of houses was very arduous work. The trees in the foreground have been sacrificed for construction purposes.

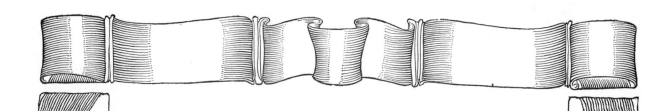

FEDERAL RAIDS AND EXPEDITIONS IN THE EAST

By Charles D. Rhodes
Captain, General Staff, United States Army

CAVALRY operations known as raids, were a distinct product of the Civil War, and although many other tactical and strategical lessons have since been deduced by European experts from this great war, it was the raid which first excited comment abroad and created interest, as something new in the handling of mounted men.

As early as June, 1862, General " Jeb " Stuart had demonstrated to both armies the possibilities of independent operations by well-mounted cavalry boldly handled by a resourceful leader, when, with twelve hundred Confederate troopers, he rode entirely around the Federal army on the Peninsula of Virginia. And again, in October of the same year, his raid into Pennsylvania proved that good cavalry can move with impunity through a well-supplied hostile country. This raid had the effect of causing consternation in the National capital, and of drawing off many Federal troops for the protection of Washington.

Stuart's successful raids caused some modification of the previous short-sighted policy of always attaching Union cavalry to infantry commands, and although until Sheridan's time, the raids made by the Federal cavalry in the East were not remarkably successful and the time for their initiation not well chosen, the Federal cavalry constantly increased in powers of mobility and independence of action.

Early in 1863, General Hooker detached Stoneman with the Cavalry Corps from the main operations of the Army of

COLONEL ULRIC DAHL-
GREN, WHO MET HIS
DEATH IN THE RAID
UPON RICHMOND

As Stuart threatened Washington, so Kilpatrick in turn
threatened the Capital of the
South. He was accompanied
by Colonel Ulric Dahlgren
who was to leave him near
Spotsylvania with five hundred picked men, to cross the
James, enter Richmond on
the south side, after liberating
the prisoners at Belle Isle,
and unite with Kilpatrick's
main force March 1, 1864.
The latter left Stevensburg
with four thousand cavalry
and a battery of horse artillery
on the night of Sunday, the
28th of February, crossed the
Rapidan at Ely's Ford, surprised and captured the
picket there, and marched
rapidly toward Richmond.
On March 1st the column was
within five miles of the
city. Failing to connect with
Dahlgren, Kilpatrick finally
withdrew, but not until he
had driven in the force
sent to oppose him to the
inner lines of the Richmond
defenses. This was the nearest that any body of Union
troops got to Richmond before its fall. Colonel Dahlgren met his death upon this
raid, and part of his command was captured, the rest
escaping to Kilpatrick, March
2d, at Tunstall's Station,
near White House.

UNION CAVALRYMEN IN RICHMOND—NOT UNTIL 1865

the Potomac, with orders to cross the Rappahannock for a raid on the communications with Richmond—turning Lee's left flank and inflicting on him every possible injury.

During Stoneman's absence the sanguinary battle of Chancellorsville was fought by the Army of the Potomac, and as the success of the raid depended in great measure upon a Federal victory at Chancellorsville, it was not, strategically at least, a success. The detachment of the Union troopers deprived General Hooker of cavalry at a time when he particularly needed a screening force to conceal his movements by the right flank; and it is probable that if Stoneman's cavalry had been present with the Army of the Potomac, it would have given ample warning of "Stonewall" Jackson's secret concentration opposite the Union right, which well nigh caused a decisive defeat for the Union army.

But Stoneman's raid destroyed millions of dollars' worth of Confederate property, and although it cut Lee's communications for a short time only, its moral effect was considerable, as shown by the Confederate correspondence since published.

The Stoneman raid was followed in February, 1864, by the famous raid of General Judson Kilpatrick, having as its objective the taking of the city of Richmond and the liberation of the Union prisoners confined therein. General Meade assisted the raid by demonstrations against Lee's left and by sending Custer on a minor raid into Albemarle County. It was supposed, at the time, that Richmond was comparatively defenseless, and that Kilpatrick's force might take the city before reenforcements from either Petersburg or Lee's army on the Rapidan could reach it.

Kilpatrick's force consisted of nearly four thousand men. Near Spotsylvania, about five hundred men under Colonel Ulric Dahlgren were detached for the purpose of crossing the James River, and, after liberating the Union prisoners at Belle Isle, attacking Richmond from the south.

Dahlgren's little command destroyed considerable

TROOPERS OF THE FIRST MASSACHUSETTS JUST AFTER THEIR ATTEMPT TO RAID RICHMOND IN 1864

A GROUP OF OFFICERS, FIRST MASSACHUSETTS CAVALRY

The officers and men of the First Massachusetts Cavalry formed part of General Judson Kilpatrick's force in his Richmond raid. The men look gaunt and hungry because they are down to "fighting weight." Starvation, fatigue, exposure, and nights in the saddle soon disposed of any superfluous flesh a trooper might carry. These men heard the laugh of the Confederate sentries inside the fortifications of the Southern Capital, and turned back only when success seemed impossible. Kilpatrick's object had been to move past the Confederate right flank, enter Richmond, and release the Union captives in its military prisons. This bold project had grown out of President Lincoln's desire to have his proclamation of amnesty circulated within the Confederate lines. The plan included also a raid upon communications and supplies. A joint expedition, under Dahlgren, met defeat, and Kilpatrick, not hearing from it, turned back.

Confederate property, but through the alleged treachery of a guide, the raiders were led out of their course. A portion of the command became separated; Dahlgren, with about one hundred and fifty troopers, was ambushed near Walkerton, and the leader killed and most of his force captured. The remainder of Dahlgren's command, under Captain Mitchell, managed to rejoin Kilpatrick, who had meanwhile threatened Richmond from the north, and who, finding the city prepared for his attack, finally withdrew across the Chickahominy and joined General Butler on the Peninsula, March 3, 1864.

The Kilpatrick raid failed in its main object, but that it might easily have succeeded seems evident from Confederate correspondence, which shows that the interception of a despatch from Dahlgren to Kilpatrick, asking what hour the latter had fixed for a simultaneous attack upon Richmond, alone made it possible for the Confederates successfully to defend the city.

When, early in 1864, General Grant gave Sheridan the long hoped for opportunity to "whip Stuart," and until the final end at Appomattox, this peerless cavalry leader never missed an opportunity to cut loose from the main army, drawing off from Grant's flanks and rear the enterprising and oftentimes dangerous Confederate cavalry, cutting Lee's communications with the South and Southwest time and again, and destroying immense quantities of the precious and carefully husbanded supplies of the Army of Northern Virginia.

Sheridan's Richmond raid, probably the most daring and sensational of these more or less independent operations, had for its object, not so much the destruction of Confederate property, as to draw Stuart and his cavalry away from the Union army's long lines of supply-trains, and then to defeat the great Confederate trooper.

In May, 1864, Sheridan's splendid body of horsemen, ten thousand in number and forming a column thirteen miles in length, moved out from the vicinity of Spotsylvania, through Chilesburg and Glen Allen Station. At Yellow Tavern the

A STILL SMOKING WRECK ON THE PATH OF THE FEDERAL RAIDERS

This photograph shows the ruins of the bridge over the North Anna, which were still smoking when the photographer arrived with the Union troops at the end of Sheridan's raid. He had ridden nearer to Richmond than any other Union leader before its fall. On the night of May 11, 1864, his column of cavalry could see the lights of the city and hear the dogs barking, and the following day an enterprising newsboy slipped through the lines and sold copies of the Richmond *Inquirer*. Sheridan declared that he could have taken Richmond, but that he couldn't hold it. The prisoners told him that every house was loopholed and the streets barricaded, and he did not think it worth the sacrifice in men. But in the death of Stuart at Yellow Tavern, Sheridan had dealt a blow severer than a raid into the Capital would have been.

decisive conflict which Sheridan had sought with the Confederate cavalry took place. The latter were driven back upon Richmond; the gallant and knightly Stuart received his mortal wound, and the Union cavalry gained complete control of the highway leading to the Confederate capital. The casualties on both sides were severe.

Pushing on rapidly by way of the Meadow Bridge, Sheridan actually found himself and his force within the outer fortifications of the city of Richmond, and in imminent peril of annihilation. In fact, a portion of the command was in such close proximity to the city proper, that officers could plainly discern its lights and hear the dogs barking a warning to the city's defenders of the presence of an army of invaders.

But with his usual genius for overcoming difficulties, Sheridan quickly extricated his command from its hazardous and uncomfortable position, and pressing on over Bottom's Bridge and past Malvern Hill successfully reached Haxall's Landing on the James River, where the command was furnished much needed supplies. On May 17th, the raiding force began its retrograde movement to rejoin Grant, which was successfully accomplished on the 24th near Chesterfield Station, Virginia. Sheridan's casualties suffered on the raid were six hundred and twenty-five men killed, wounded, and captured, and three hundred horses.

General Grant describes the results attained in this famous raid as follows:

Sheridan, in this memorable raid, passed entirely around Lee's army, encountered his cavalry in four engagements, and defeated them in all; recaptured four hundred Union prisoners, and killed and captured many of the enemy; destroyed miles of railroad and telegraph, and freed us from annoyance by the cavalry for more than two weeks.

This brilliant success by the Cavalry Corps of the Army of the Potomac, was followed in June by one scarcely less important in its moral and material effect upon the Confederacy

THE RETURN OF SHERIDAN'S TROOPERS—MAY 25, 1864

After their ride of sixteen days to the very gates of Richmond, Sheridan and his men rejoined Grant near Chesterfield Station. The photographer caught the returning column just as they were riding over the Chesterfield bridge. On the 21st they had crossed the Pamunkey near White House on the ruins of the railroad bridge, which they took only six hours to repair. Two regiments at a time, working as pioneers, wrecked a neighboring house, and with its timbers soon had the bridge ready to bear the weight of horses and artillery. The only mishap was the fall of a pack-mule from the bridge into the water thirty feet below. It takes much, however, to disturb the equanimity of an army mule. It turned a somersault in the air, struck an abutment, disappeared under water, came up, and swam tranquilly ashore without disturbing its pack. This speaks well for the ability as saddle-packers of Sheridan's men. The total results of this important raid were the destruction of an immense quantity of supplies, damage to Confederate communications, the death of Stuart, and the saving to the Union Government of the subsistence of ten thousand horses and men for three weeks. It perfected the *morale* of the cavalry corps, with incalculable benefit to the Union cause. The casualties on the raid were six hundred and twenty-five men killed and wounded.

—Sheridan's Trevilian raid, in which, at Trevilian Station, the Confederate cavalry was again seriously defeated.

The purpose of the raid was to injure Lee's lines of supply, and to draw off the Southern cavalry during Grant's movement forward by the left flank, following his unsuccessful attempt to take the strong Confederate position at Cold Harbor by direct assault.

Sheridan started on June 7, 1864, with about eight thousand cavalrymen, the trains and supplies being cut down to the absolute minimum. Wilson's division remained with the Army of the Potomac. By June 11th, the command was in the vicinity of Trevilian Station, where the enemy was encountered. Here, Torbert's division, pressing back the Confederate's pickets, found the foe in force about three miles from Trevilian, posted behind heavy timber. At about the same time, Custer was sent by a wood road to destroy Trevilian Station, where he captured the Confederate wagons, caissons, and led horses.

Assured of Custer's position, Sheridan dismounted Torbert's two remaining brigades, and aided by one of Gregg's, carried the Confederate works, driving Hampton's division back on Custer, and even through his lines. Gregg's other brigade had meanwhile attacked Fitzhugh Lee, causing the entire opposing cavalry to retire on Gordonsville.

Following this victory, Sheridan continued his raid and finally reached White House on the Pamunkey, on June 20th, where he found orders directing him to break up the supply depot there and conduct the nine hundred wagons to Petersburg. This was successfully accomplished.

It is interesting to note that in this period of great activity for the Cavalry Corps (May 5th to August 1, 1864) the casualties in the corps were nearly forty-nine hundred men, and the loss in horses from all causes about fifteen hundred. The captures by the cavalry exceeded two thousand men and five hundred horses, besides many guns and colors.

[128]

CHAPTER
FIVE

———

FEDERAL RAIDS
IN THE WEST

———

A BLOCKHOUSE ON THE TENNESSEE

SIX HUNDRED MILES IN SIXTEEN DAYS

Seventeen hundred men who marched 600 miles in sixteen days, from Vicksburg to Baton Rouge. On April 17, 1863, Grant despatched Grierson on a raid from LaGrange, Tennessee, southward as a means of diverting attention from his own movements against Vicksburg, and to disturb the Confederate line of supplies from the East. Grierson destroyed sixty miles of tracks and telegraph, numberless stores and munitions of war, and brought his command safely through to Baton Rouge. These two pictures by Lytle, the Confederate Secret Service agent at Baton Rouge, form one of the most remarkable feats of wet-plate photography. The action continued as he moved his camera a trifle to the right, and the result is a veritable "moving picture." In the photograph on the left-hand page, only the first troop is dismounted and unsaddled. In the photo-

HOW GRIERSON'S RAIDERS LOOKED TO THE CONFEDERATE SECRET SERVICE CAMERA

graph on the right-hand page two troops are already on foot.   Note the officers in front of their troops.   The photograph was evidently a long time exposure, as is shown by the progress of the covered wagon which has driven into the picture on the left-hand page.   It was at the conclusion of this remarkable raid that Grierson reported that "the Confederacy was a hollow shell."   All of its population able to carry arms was on the line of defense.   Captain John A. Wyeth, the veteran Confederate cavalryman who contributes to other pages of this volume, wrote when he saw these photographs: "I knew General Grierson personally, and have always had the highest regard for his skill and courage as shown more particularly in this raid than in anything else that he did, although he was always doing well."

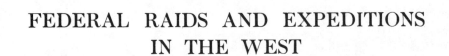

FEDERAL RAIDS AND EXPEDITIONS IN THE WEST

By Charles D. Rhodes
Captain, General Staff, United States Army

THE military operations of the Union armies in the South and West were not lacking in famous raids, having for their main objects the destruction of the supply centers of the Confederacy, the cutting of railroads and lines of communication between these centers and the Southern troops, and the drawing away from important strategic operations of large bodies of the foe. One of the most famous of these raids was that made by Colonel B. H. Grierson in the spring of 1863.

Starting from La Grange, Tennessee, on April 17th, with three cavalry regiments of about seventeen hundred men, Grierson made a wonderful march through the State of Mississippi, and finally reached the Union lines at Baton Rouge, Louisiana, on May 2d.

On April 21st, Grierson had detached a regiment under Colonel Hatch, Second Iowa Cavalry, to destroy the railroad bridge between Columbus and Macon, and then return to La Grange. At Palo Alto, Hatch had a sharp fight with Confederate troops under General Gholson, defeating them without the loss of a man. Much of Hatch's success during his entire raid was due to the fact that his regiment was armed with Colt's revolving rifles. Hatch then retreated along the railroad, destroying it at Okolona and Tupelo, and arriving at La Grange on April 26th, with the loss of but ten troopers. The principal object of his movement—to decoy the Confederate troops to the east, and thus give Grierson ample opportunity to get well under way, was fully attained.

GRIERSON—THE RAIDER WHO PUZZLED PEMBERTON

To the enterprise of Lytle, the Confederate Secret Service photographer, we owe this portrait of Colonel B. H. Grierson, at rest after his famous raid. He sits chin in hand among his officers, justly proud of having executed one of the most thoroughly successful feats in the entire war. It was highly important, if Grant was to carry out his maneuver of crossing the Mississippi at Grand Gulf and advance upon Vicksburg from the south, that Pemberton's attention should be distracted in other directions. The morning after Admiral Porter ran the batteries, Grierson left La Grange, Tennessee, to penetrate the heart of the Confederacy, sweeping entirely through Mississippi from north to south, and reaching Baton Rouge on May 2d. Exaggerated reports flowed in on Pemberton as to Grierson's numbers and whereabouts. The Confederate defender of Vicksburg was obliged to send out expeditions in all directions to try to intercept him. This was one of the numerous instances where a small body of cavalry interfered with the movements of a much larger force. It was Van Dorn, the Confederate cavalryman, who had upset Grant's calculations four months before.

Meanwhile Grierson had continued his raid with less than one thousand horsemen, breaking the Southern Mississippi, and the New Orleans, Jackson, and Great Northern railroads. Near Newton the raiders burned several bridges, and destroyed engines and cars loaded with commissary stores, guns, and ammunition; at Hazelhurst, cars and ammunition; and at Brookhaven, the railroad depot and cars.

Having no cavalry available to watch Grierson's movements, the Confederates were kept in a state of excitement and alarm. Rumors exaggerated his numbers, and he was reported in many different places at the same time. Several brigades of Confederate infantry were detached to intercept him, but he evaded them all.

In sixteen days, Grierson marched six hundred miles— nearly thirty-eight miles a day—destroying miles of railroad, telegraph, and other property; but most of all, he distracted the Confederates' attention from Grant's operations against Vicksburg at the critical time when the latter was preparing to cross the Mississippi River near Grand Gulf. In its entirety, the Grierson raid was probably the most successful operation of its kind during the Civil War.

The appearance of Morgan's men on the north bank of the Ohio River (July, 1863) created great consternation in Indiana and Ohio. The Governor of Indiana called out the "Home Guards" to the number of fifty thousand, and as Morgan's advance turned toward Ohio, the Governor of the "Buckeye State" called out fifty thousand "Home Guards" from his State. At Corydon, Indiana, the "Home Guards" gave the invaders a brisk little battle, and delayed their advance for a brief time.

On July 1, 1864, General A. J. Smith assembled a large force at La Grange, Tennessee, for a raid on Tupelo, Mississippi, in which a cavalry division under General Grierson took a prominent part in defeating the formidable General Forrest as he had probably never been defeated before. The raid

A FEDERAL CAVALRY CAMP AT BATON ROUGE

This photograph of an Illinois regiment's camp at Baton Rouge was taken in 1863, just before the Port Hudson campaign upon which Grierson and his men accompanied General Banks. The troopers have found fairly comfortable quarters. The smoke rising from their camp-fires lends a peaceful touch to the scene. A cavalry camp ccupied more space than an infantry camp. The horses are tethered in long lines between the tents, about the width of a street-way. They are plainly visible in this photograph, tethered in this fashion, a few of them grazing about the plain. In the foreground by the officers' quarters, a charger stands saddled, ready for his master. This is an excellent illustration of a camp laid out according to Federal army regulations.

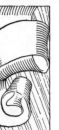

resulted in the burning of all bridges and trestles north and south of Tupelo, and the destruction of the railroad.

During the raid, a portion of the cavalry division was newly armed with seven-shot Spencer carbines, capable of firing fourteen shots per minute. The Confederates were astonished and dismayed by the tremendous amount of lead poured into their ranks, and after the Tupelo fight one of the Confederate prisoners wonderingly asked a cavalryman, " Say, do you all load those guns you all fight with on Sunday, and then fire 'em all the week? "

In the spring of the following year, 1865, General James H. Wilson, who had commanded a division in Sheridan's Army of the Shenandoah, began, under the direction of General Thomas, an important demonstration against Selma and Tuscaloosa, Alabama, in favor of General Canby's operations against Mobile and central Alabama. This great raid, which severed the main arteries supplying life-blood to the Confederacy, was destined to be the culminating blow by the Federal cavalry inflicted on the already tottering military structure of the Southern Confederacy.

Starting on March 22, 1865, and marching in three separate columns on a wide front, because of the devastated condition of the country, Wilson began his movement by keeping the Confederate leaders completely in ignorance as to whether Columbus, Selma, or Tuscaloosa, was his real objective. At Selma, April 2d, a division of Wilson's dismounted cavalry, facing odds in position, gallantly carried the Confederate semipermanent works surrounding the city, in an assault which swept all before it.

General Wilson's report says:

The fortifications assaulted and carried consisted of a bastioned line, on a radius of nearly three miles, extending from the Alabama River below to the same above the city. The part west of the city is covered by a miry, deep, and almost impassable creek; that on the east side by a swamp, extending from the river almost to the Summerfield

[136]

A DESTRUCTIVE RAID IN MISSISSIPPI

The burning of all bridges and trestles north and south of Tupelo and the destruction of the rail-road was the result of General A. J. Smith's raid on that point in 1864. General Smith started from Lagrange, Tenn., on July 1st, accompanied by a cavalry division under General Grierson, who took a prominent part in defeating the formidable General Forrest as he had probably never been defeated before. The Union cavalry raids in the West were more uniformly successful than the raids of the cavalry with the Army of the Potomac. The greater part of the Confederate cavalry was busy attacking the supply-trains of the armies in the North or striking at the long lines of communication. The story of the campaigns in the West, where there were fewer photographers and communication was slower is not so well-known as that of the more immediate East, but the deeds performed there were of quite equal dash and daring and importance to the result.

GENERAL A. J. SMITH

road, and entirely impracticable for mounted men at all times. General Upton ascertained by a personal reconnaissance that dismounted men might with great difficulty work through it on the left of the Range Line road. The profile of that part of the line assaulted is as follows: Height of parapet, six to eight feet; thickness, eight feet; depth of ditch, five feet; width, from ten to fifteen feet; height of stockade on the glacis, five feet; sunk into the earth, four feet. . . . The distance which the troops charged, exposed to the fire of artillery and musketry, was six hundred yards. . . . General Long's report states . . . that the number actually engaged in the charge was 1550 officers and men. The portion of the line assaulted was manned by Armstrong's brigade, regarded as the best in Forrest's corps, and reported by him at more than 1500 men. The loss from Long's division was 40 killed, 260 wounded, and 7 missing. . . . The immediate fruits of our victory were 31 field-guns, and one 30-pounder Parrott, which had been used against us; 2700 prisoners, including 150 officers; a number of colors and immense quantities of stores of every kind. . . . I estimate the entire garrison, including the militia of the city and surrounding country, at 7000 men. The entire force under my command, engaged and in supporting distance, was 9000 men and eight guns.

On April 8th and 9th, Wilson's entire cavalry corps, excepting Croxton's brigade, crossed the Alabama River, and having rendered Selma practically valueless to the Confederacy by his thorough destruction of its railroads and supplies, Wilson marched into Georgia by way of Montgomery. On April 12th, the mayor of Montgomery surrendered that city to the cavalry advance guard, and after destroying great quantities of military stores, small arms, and cotton, the cavalry corps moved, on April 14th, with General Upton in advance, and on the 16th captured the cities of Columbus and West Point.

The capture of Columbus lost to the South 1200 prisoners, fifty-two field-guns, the ram *Jackson* (six 7-inch guns), nearly ready for sea, together with such tremendously valuable aids in prolonging the war as fifteen locomotives and two hundred and fifty cars, one hundred and fifteen thousand bales of cot-

FLEET STEAMING UP THE ALABAMA RIVER IN WAR-TIME

The sight of the stern-wheelers splashing up the Alabama River into the heart of the threatened Confederacy has been preserved by a curious chance. This photograph was secured by a Scotch visitor to the States on his wedding-trip in 1865. He took it home. A generation later his son came to America, bringing his father's collection of pictures. He settled in New Orleans. An editor of the PHOTOGRAPHIC HISTORY, traveling in search of photographs to round out the collection, perceived this to be unique as a war-time scene on the river where Wilson and Forrest were making history. The Alabama River was not only one of the great arteries of the South along which it conveyed its supplies, but it was also the scene of much of its naval construction which the blockade precluded on the coast. Wilson's raid resulted in the capture at Columbus of the Confederate ram *Jackson* with six 7-inch guns, when she was nearly ready for the sea. Just a year previous, in April, 1864, the hull of the Confederate iron-clad ram *Tennessee* was constructed on the Alabama River, just above Selma. Admiral Buchanan sent James M. Johnston, C. S. N., with two steamers to tow her down to Mobile. The work was all done at high pressure for fear of just such a raid as Wilson's. The incident is somewhat similar to the saving of Admiral Porter's Red River fleet in May, 1864.

ton, four cotton factories, a navy yard, arms and ammunition factories, three paper-mills, over one hundred thousand rounds of artillery ammunition, besides immense stores of which no account was taken.

This great and decisive blow to the material resources of the Confederacy, was followed by the surrender of the cities of Macon and Tuscaloosa, and other successes, until, on April 21st, Wilson's victorious progress was ordered suspended by General Sherman, pending the result of peace negotiations between the Federal and Confederate Governments.

This great movement was made in a hostile country which had been stripped of supplies except at railroad centers, and in which no aid or assistance could be expected from the inhabitants of the country. As an evidence of some of the hardships attending the operations of separate columns composing Wilson's corps, General Croxton states in an official report that from Elyton (March 30th) through Trion and Tuscaloosa, Alabama, to Carrollton, Georgia (April 25th), his command marched six hundred and fifty-three miles through a mountainous country so destitute of supplies that the troops could only be subsisted and foraged with the greatest effort. The brigade swam four rivers and destroyed five large iron works (the last remaining in the cotton States), three factories, numerous mills, and quantities of supplies. The losses of the brigade during this important movement, were but four officers and one hundred and sixty-eight men, half of whom were made prisoners by the Confederates while straggling from the command.

CHAPTER
SIX

CONFEDERATE RAIDS
IN THE WEST

THE PRIZE OF THE CONFEDERATE RAIDER—
A FEDERAL COMMISSARY CAMP
ON THE TENNESSEE

CAMP IN THE TENNESSEE MOUNTAINS, 1863

The soldiers leaning on their sabers by the mountain path would have smiled in grim amusement at the suggestion that a life like theirs in "the merry greenwood" must be as care-free, picturesque, and delightful as the career of Robin Hood, according to old English ballads. These raiders of 1863 could have drawn sharp contrasts between the beauty of the scene in this photograph—the bright sunshine dappling the trees, the mountain wind murmuring through the leaves, the horse with his box of fodder, the troopers at ease in the shade—and the hardships that became every-day matters with the cavalry commands whose paths led them up and down the arduous western frontier. On such a pleasant summer day the Civil War photographer was able to make an exposure.

A PLEASANT INTERLUDE FOR THE WESTERN CAVALRYMAN

But the cavalryman's duty called at all hours and at all seasons; and the photographer could not portray the dreary night rides over rocks made slippery with rain, through forests hanging like a damp pall over the troopers rocking with sleep in their saddles, every moment likely to be awakened by the bark of the enemy's carbines. It is undoubtedly true that there is something more dashing about the lot of a cavalryman, but on account of his greater mobility he was ordered over more territory and ran more frequent if not greater risks than the infantryman. But this was the sort of day the cavalryman laughed and sang. Though the storm-clouds and war-clouds, the cloud of death itself, lay waiting, the trooper's popular song ran: "If you want to have a good time, jine the cavalry."

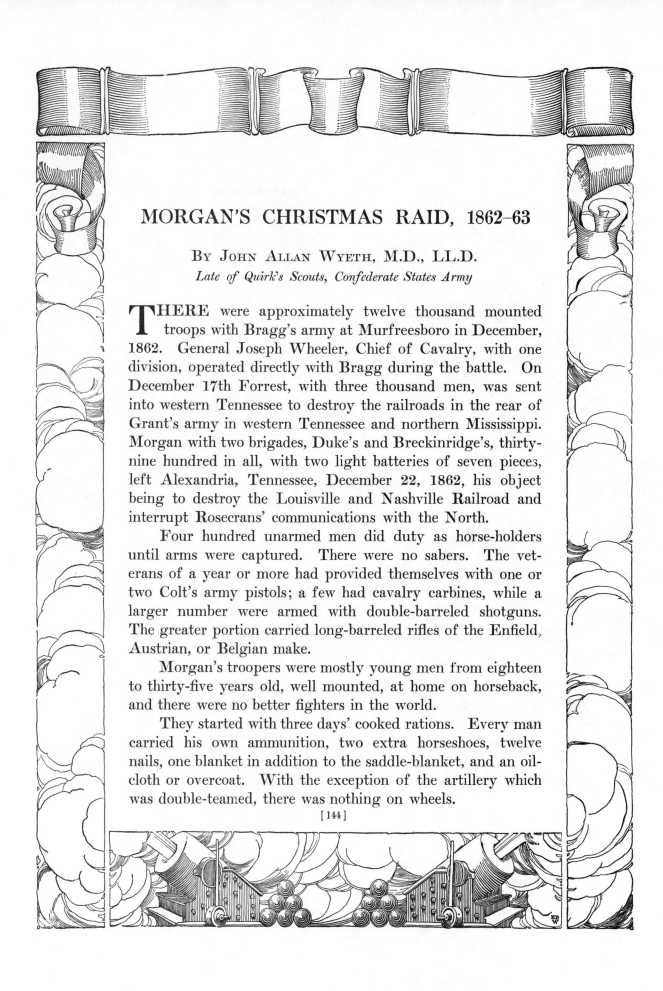

MORGAN'S CHRISTMAS RAID, 1862–63

By John Allan Wyeth, M.D., LL.D.
Late of Quirk's Scouts, Confederate States Army

THERE were approximately twelve thousand mounted troops with Bragg's army at Murfreesboro in December, 1862. General Joseph Wheeler, Chief of Cavalry, with one division, operated directly with Bragg during the battle. On December 17th Forrest, with three thousand men, was sent into western Tennessee to destroy the railroads in the rear of Grant's army in western Tennessee and northern Mississippi. Morgan with two brigades, Duke's and Breckinridge's, thirty-nine hundred in all, with two light batteries of seven pieces, left Alexandria, Tennessee, December 22, 1862, his object being to destroy the Louisville and Nashville Railroad and interrupt Rosecrans' communications with the North.

Four hundred unarmed men did duty as horse-holders until arms were captured. There were no sabers. The veterans of a year or more had provided themselves with one or two Colt's army pistols; a few had cavalry carbines, while a larger number were armed with double-barreled shotguns. The greater portion carried long-barreled rifles of the Enfield, Austrian, or Belgian make.

Morgan's troopers were mostly young men from eighteen to thirty-five years old, well mounted, at home on horseback, and there were no better fighters in the world.

They started with three days' cooked rations. Every man carried his own ammunition, two extra horseshoes, twelve nails, one blanket in addition to the saddle-blanket, and an oil-cloth or overcoat. With the exception of the artillery which was double-teamed, there was nothing on wheels.

[144]

A GROUP OF
CONFEDERATE CAVALRY
IN THE WEST

Old cavalrymen find this photograph absorbing; it brings to life again the varied equipment of the Confederate cavalrymen in the West. The only uniformity is found with respect to carbines, which are carried by all except the officers. Three of the men in the center have pistols thrust in their belts, ready for a fight at close quarters. Some have belts crossed over their chests, some a single belt, still others none at all. One of the single belts acts as a carbine sling, the other as a canteen strap. Horse holders have fallen out with the chargers visible behind the line of men. The Western photographers, Armstead & Carter, were the artists enterprising enough to secure this photograph. The territory their travels covered in Mississippi and Tennessee changed hands so frequently that fortunately for posterity an opportunity at last did come to photograph a troop of the swift-traveling and little interviewed warriors that composed the Confederate cavalry. They did important service in the West.

AN OFFICER

Under Forrest and Wheeler they helped Bragg to defeat Rosecrans at Chickamauga, and their swift raids were a constant menace to the Union supplies. This photograph was probably taken late in the war, as up to the third year the Confederate troopers could not boast equipments even so complete as shown in this photograph. In 1861 the Confederate cavalry had no Colt revolvers, no Chicopee sabers, and no carbines that were worth carrying. Their arms were of the homeliest type and of infinite variety. At the battle of Brandy Station, in 1863, every man was armed with at least one, and sometimes several, Army and Navy revolvers and excellent sabers. The civilian saddles had given place to McClellans, and that man was conspicuous who could not boast a complete outfit of saddle, bridle, blankets—woolen and rubber—and arms, all taken from the generous foe. The Confederate cavalry in the West failed to secure equally complete outfits, although they looked to the same source of supply.

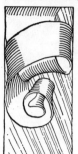

In three short winter days, over little-used highways through a rough and hilly country, they rode a distance of ninety miles to Glasgow, Kentucky, arriving at dark, December 24th. The order was to start at daylight, stop from eleven to twelve to feed, unsaddle, curry, and rest, then on until night. As the advance guard reached one corner of the public square, several companies of the Second Michigan Cavalry with no idea that Morgan's men were near, rode into sight a few yards away. In the *mêlée* which ensued, one Federal was killed and two wounded, and a Confederate captain and one soldier were mortally and one lieutenant slightly wounded. Twenty prisoners were captured, among them the adjutant of the regiment, whose equipment the writer appropriated. A number of Christmas turkeys which these excellent foragers had strapped to their saddles were also taken by us.

Ten miles north of Glasgow, on December 25th, with our company of fifty men a mile in advance of the main column, the vedette reported the Federals in line of battle in our front. We were ordered to load and cap our guns, and then rode briskly forward. When about two hundred yards from the Federal lines, Captain Quirk halted us, called off horse-holders, and we advanced on foot. Reaching the top of a rise in the lane with a high worm-fence on either side, the Federals gave us a lively volley, which we returned from the fence corners. The fight had scarcely opened, when a second detachment of Federals (Company C, Fifth Indiana), which had been in ambush to our right, charged to within a few yards of the road abreast of and in the rear of our position, and fired into us at practically muzzle range. Several of our men were wounded, our captain being twice hit. The fusillade stampeded the horses and horse-holders who fled in panic to the rear, leaving us on foot in the presence of a superior force. Five members of our company were captured. The rest of us scrambled over the opposite fence and ran for a scrub-oak thicket, one or two hundred yards across a field.

FEDERAL CAVALRY GUARDING THE CHATTANOOGA STATION

General Rosecrans looked narrowly to his line of communications when he set out from Nashville to attack General Braxton Bragg in the latter part of December, 1862. The Confederate cavalry leader, General Wheeler, was abroad. At daylight on December 30th he swooped down at Jefferson on Starkweather's brigade of Rousseau's division, in an attempt to destroy his wagon-train. From Jefferson, Wheeler proceeded to La Vergne, where he succeeded in capturing the immense supply trains of McCook's Corps. Seven hundred prisoners and nearly a million dollars' worth of property was the Union Government's penalty for not heeding the requests of the commanding general for more cavalry. A train at Rock Spring and another at Nolensville shared the same fate at Wheeler's hands, and at two o'clock on the morning of the 31st Wheeler completed the entire circuit of Rosecrans' army, having ridden in forty-eight hours.

By this time the leading regiment of the main column came in sight, caught our horses, and rescued us. We remounted at once, and joined in the charge which drove the Federals from the field. In the pursuit Captain Quirk, despite two scalp wounds, killed one of the Northerners with his pistol. Two others surrendered.

On the further march to Green River and Hammondsville that day, we captured a sutler's huge outfit, the contents of which were appropriated. That night we camped in the woods between Hammondsville and Upton Station on the Louisville and Nashville Railroad. We had had a merry Christmas.

Early December 26th, we struck the road at Upton, capturing a number of Union soldiers guarding the track. Here General Morgan overtook the scouts. Attached to his staff was a telegraph operator, a quick-witted young man named Ellsworth, better known by the nickname of "Lightning." After the wire was tapped, I sat within a few feet of General Morgan and heard him dictate messages to General Boyle, in Louisville, and other Federal commanders, making inquiries as to the disposition of the Federal forces, and telling some tall stories in regard to the large size of his own command and its movements. While thus engaged, a train with artillery and other material came in sight from the north, but the wary engineer saw us in time to reverse his engine and escape. Heavy cannonading was now heard at Bacon Creek Bridge stockade, which after a stout resistance surrendered, and the bridge was destroyed. That same afternoon before dark, the stockade at Nolin was taken by Duke and another bridge burned.

We camped that night, December 26th, a few miles from Elizabethtown, which place, guarded by eight companies of an Illinois regiment, six hundred and fifty-two men and officers, we captured on the 27th. A number of brick warehouses near the railroad station had been loopholed and otherwise strengthened for defense. The town was surrounded, the artillery

LIEUTENANT–GENERAL

JOSEPH WHEELER,

C. S. A.

After his exploits in Tennessee, and the days of Chickamauga, Chattanooga, and Knoxville, where his cavalry were a constant menace to the Union lines of communication, so much so that the railroads were guarded by blockhouses at vulnerable points, Wheeler joined Johnston with the remnant of his men. Their swift movements went far to make it possible for Johnston to pursue his Fabian policy of constantly striking and retreating before Sherman's superior force, harassing it to the point of desperation. Wheeler operated on Sherman's flank later in the Carolinas, but the power of the Confederate cavalry was on the wane, and the end was soon to come.

ONE OF THE BLOCKHOUSES ON THE NASHVILLE AND CHATTANOOGA RAILROAD IN 1864

brought up, and after the raiders fired a number of shells and solid shot, which knocked great holes in the houses, the garrison surrendered.

On the 28th, the two great trestles on the Louisville and Nashville Railroad at Muldraugh's Hill were destroyed. They were each from sixty to seventy-five feet high, and nine hundred feet long, constructed entirely of wood. They were guarded by two strong stockade forts, garrisoned by an Indiana regiment of infantry. Both strongholds were assailed at the same time, the artillery doing effective work, and in less than two hours, the two garrisons of seven hundred men were prisoners. They were armed with new Enfield rifles, one of the most effective weapons of that day.

After burning the trestles, the command moved to Rolling Fork River. The greater portion crossed that night and proceeded toward Bardstown. Five hundred men under Colonel Cluke, with one piece of artillery, attacked the stockade at the bridge over Rolling Fork River, but before it could be battered down, a column three thousand strong under Colonel Harlan (later a Justice of the Supreme Court), compelled his withdrawal. A sharp engagement between our rear guard and Harlan's command took place at Rolling Fork. Colonel Basil W. Duke recrossed to take command and led Cluke's five hundred men and Quirk's scouts in such a vigorous attack that the Federal commander hesitated to press his advantage.

At this moment, Duke was wounded by a fragment of a well-aimed shrapnel which struck him on the head and stunned him. The same shell killed several horses. Captain Quirk and two of the scouts placed Duke astride the pommel of the saddle on which our captain was seated, who, with one arm around the limp body, guided his faithful horse into the swollen stream. Quirk and Duke were both small in stature, and the powerful big bay carried his double load safely across. A carriage was impressed, filled with soft bedding, and in this our wounded colonel was placed, and carried safely along with the command.

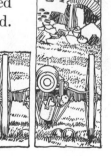

BLOCKHOUSES GARRISONED

AGAINST

WHEELER'S CAVALRY

In 1863 an attempt to supplement his lack of cavalry for the guarding of his line of communications was made by Rosecrans, through the building of blockhouses along the railroad, garrisoned by small forces of infantry. The attempt was not uniformly successful. The Confederate horsemen under Wheeler sometimes advanced on foot and succeeded in carrying the blockhouses and enforcing the surrender of its garrison. The cavalry were the real trouble-makers for the generals in the field who were attempting to victual their armies. The problem became less complex in the last two years of the war, when the Federal cavalry was trained to higher efficiency and the power of the Confederates had dwindled following the exhaustion of their supply of horses.

Colonel Harlan reported his loss as three killed and one wounded. We did not lose a man, and with the exception of Duke, our wounded rode out on their horses.

We reached Bardstown at dusk on the 29th. Between daylight and sunrise, December 30th, I witnessed one of the frequent incidents in all warfare—the pillaging of the largest general store in this town. The men who had crowded in through the doors they had battered down, found difficulty in getting out with their plunder through the surging crowd, which was pressing to get in before everything was gone. One trooper induced the others to let him out by holding an ax in front of him, cutting edge forward. His arm clasped a bundle of a dozen pairs of shoes and other plunder, while on his head was a pyramid of eight or ten soft hats, telescoped one into the other just as they had come out of the packing-box.

About midday a chilling rain set in, which soon turned into sleet. Reaching Springfield in the gloom of December 30th, we were ordered on to Lebanon, nine miles further, to drive in the pickets there and build fires in order to give the foe the impression that we were up in force and were only awaiting daylight to attack. We piled rails and made fires until late at night, while Morgan was making a detour along a narrow and little-used country road around Lebanon. Later we overtook the command, and acted as rear guard throughout that awful night. Between the bitter, penetrating cold, the fatigue, the overwhelming desire to sleep, so difficult to overcome and under the conditions we were experiencing so fatal if yielded to, the numerous halts to get the artillery out of bad places, the impenetrable darkness, and the inevitable confusion which attends the moving of troops and artillery along a narrow country road, we endured a night of misery never to be forgotten.

As morning neared, it became our chief duty to keep each other awake. All through the night the sleet pelted us unmercifully, and covered our coats and oilcloths with a sheet of ice. Time and time again we dismounted, and holding on to the

General Chalmers was the right-hand man of General Forrest. His first service was at Shiloh. During Bragg's invasion of Kentucky he attacked Munfordville, September 14, 1862, but was repulsed. He took part in a Confederate charge at Murfreesboro, December 31st of the same year, and was so severely wounded as to disqualify him for further duty on that field. He commanded two brigades on Forrest's expedition of April 12, 1864, when the latter captured Fort Pillow and was unable to restrain the massacre. He served with Forrest at Nashville and led Hood's cavalry at the battle of Franklin, delaying the Federal cavalry long enough to enable the Confederate army to make good its escape. He was with Forrest when the latter was defeated by Wilson on the famous

Wilson raid through Alabama and Georgia in the spring of 1865, and remained with the cavalry until it crumbled with the Confederacy to nothing. The lower photograph of the rails laid across the piles of ties shows how the Confederate cavalry, east and west, destroyed millions of dollars' worth of property. While Generals Lee and Bragg and Hood were wrestling with the Union armies, the Confederate cavalry were dealing blow after blow to the material resources of the North. But in vain; the magnificently equipped Union pioneer corps was able to lay rails nearly as fast as they were destroyed by the Confederates, and when the Army of Northern Virginia shot its weight in men from the ranks of Grant's army in the fearful campaign of 1864, the ranks were as constantly replenished.

BRIGADIER–GENERAL JAMES R. CHALMERS

IN THE WAKE OF THE RAIDERS

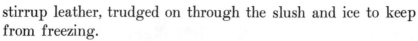

stirrup leather, trudged on through the slush and ice to keep from freezing.

Daylight found us several miles south of Lebanon and the strong Federal command concentrated there to catch us, but we kept on without halting, for another heavy column was reported moving out from Mumfordville and Glasgow to intercept us at Columbia or Burkesville, before we could recross the Cumberland River.

About ten o'clock on the morning of December 31st, as the rear guard was crossing Rolling Fork some five or six miles south of Lebanon, there occurred an incident of more than ordinary interest. Captain Alexander Tribble, Lieutenant George B. Eastin, and a private soldier were sent on a detour to New Market, four or five miles from the line of march, to secure a supply of shoes which were reported stored at that point. As they were returning to overtake the command, they were pursued by a squad of Federal cavalry. Being well mounted, the three kept a safe distance ahead of their pursuers. Glancing backward over a long, straight stretch of road, they observed, as the chase proceeded, that all but three of their pursuers had checked up, and they determined at the first favorable place to ride to one side and await the approach of their pursuers and attack them. The place selected was the ford at the river. At this point Eastin checked his horse and turned sharply to the right, concealing himself under the bank. Tribble continued into the middle of the stream, which here was about fifty yards wide, and stopped his horse where the water was about two feet deep. For reasons satisfactory to himself, the private soldier kept on, leaving the two officers to confront the three Federals, who now were in sight, coming at full speed toward the river and from fifty to one hundred yards apart. The leading Federal was Colonel Dennis J. Halisy of the Sixth Kentucky Cavalry. As he came near Eastin, the latter fired at him with his six-shooter, which fire Halisy returned. Both missed, and as Eastin now had the drop on his adversary,

[154]

THE RAILROAD BRIDGE ACROSS THE CUMBER-LAND, 1864

GATES READY TO BE SHUT AGAINST THE CONFED-ERATES

"By all means," telegraphed Grant to Thomas, "avoid a foot-race to see which, you or Hood, can beat to the Ohio." This was the voicing of the Union general's fear in December, 1864, that Hood would cross the Cumberland River in the vicinity of Nash-ville and repeat Bragg's march to the Ohio. A cavalry corps was stationed near the Louisville and Nashville Railroad fortified bridge, and a regiment of pickets kept guard along the banks of the stream, while on the water, gunboats, ironclads, and "tinclads" kept up a constant patrol. The year before the Confederate raider, John H. Morgan, had evaded the Union guards of the Cumberland and reached the border of Pennsylvania, before he was forced to surrender. On December 8th a widespread report had the Confederates across the Cumberland, but it proved that only a small detachment had been sent out to reconnoiter—sufficient, however, to occasion Grant's telegram. Note the huge gates at the end of the bridge ready to be rushed shut in a moment.

THE VALLEY OF THE CUMBERLAND, FROM THE TOP OF THE NASHVILLE MILITARY ACADEMY

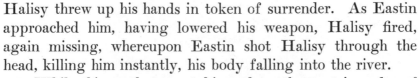

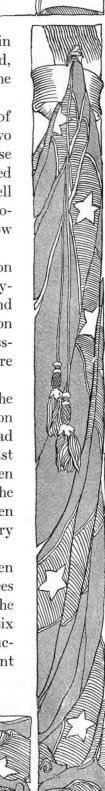

Halisy threw up his hands in token of surrender. As Eastin approached him, having lowered his weapon, Halisy fired, again missing, whereupon Eastin shot Halisy through the head, killing him instantly, his body falling into the river.

While this combat was taking place, the next in order of the Federals had closed with Captain Tribble. These two opened fire without effect when Tribble spurred his horse toward his adversary, threw his arm around him, and dragged him with himself from the saddle into the river. Tribble fell on top, and strangled his foe into surrendering. At this moment, the third Union trooper came on the scene, only to throw up his hands and deliver himself to the two Confederates.

Midday, December 31st, we rested an hour, and then on to Campbellsville where we arrived at dark, having been thirty-six hours in the saddle. That night we slept eight hours, and New Year's Day, 1863, left for Columbia, and thence on throughout the whole bitter cold night without stopping, passing through Burkesville on the morning of January 2d, where we recrossed the Cumberland.

This was Morgan's most successful expedition. The Louisville and Nashville Railroad was a wreck from Bacon Creek to Shepherdsville, a distance of sixty miles. We had captured about nineteen hundred prisoners, destroyed a vast amount of Government property, with a loss of only two men killed, twenty-four wounded, and sixty-four missing. The command returned well armed and better mounted than when it set out. The country had been stripped of horses. Every man in my company led out an extra mount.

During our absence the battle of Murfreesboro had been fought. The Confederates had captured twenty-eight pieces of artillery, and lost four—and although Bragg retreated, he had hammered his opponent so hard, that it was nearly six months before he was ready to advance. Morgan's destruction of the Louisville and Nashville Railroad was an important factor in this enforced delay.

RUINS OF SALTPETRE WORKS

IN TENNESSEE

1863

Saltpetre being one of the necessary ingredients of powder, it was inevitable that when cotton-mills, iron-works, and every useful industry were suffering destruction by the Union cavalry in Tennessee, the salt-petre factory should share the same fate. The works were foredoomed, whether by the Union cavalry or by the Confederate cavalry, in order to prevent them from falling into Union hands. The enterprising photographer seized a moment when the cavalry was at hand. A dejected charger is hanging his head by the side of the ruined mill. Two men are standing at the left of the house, of which nothing remains but the framework and chimney. The importance of destroying these works could hardly have been over-estimated. It was the case half a century later, as stated by Hudson Maxim and other military authori-ties, that collision between America and a foreign country with a powerful navy would bring, as that coun-try's first move, the cutting off of our saltpetre supply from South America and thus the crippling of our ability to manufacture powder.

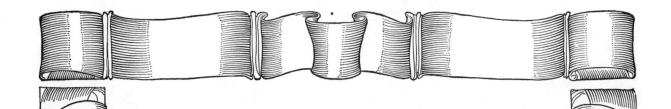

THE DESTRUCTION OF ROSECRANS' GREAT WAGON TRAIN

BY JOHN ALLAN WYETH, M.D., LL.D.
(Late of Quirk's Scouts, Confederate States Army)

THE Confederate cavalry was an important factor in Bragg's defeat of Rosecrans' army at Chickamauga. Forrest was in full command on the right, while Wheeler, six miles away, covered the Confederate left wing.

Bragg had placed them thus wide apart for the reason that Forrest had flatly refused to serve under his chief of cavalry. After Wheeler's disastrous assault on Fort Donelson, February 3, 1863, where Forrest had two horses shot under him, and his command lost heavily, he bluntly told his superior in rank he would never serve under him again, and he never did.

The records of these two days of slaughter at Chickamauga—for twenty-six per cent. of all engaged were either killed or wounded—show how these great soldiers acquitted themselves. Forrest's guns fired the first and last shots on this bloody field. It was Wheeler's vigilance and courage which checked every move and defeated every advance on the Federal right, and finally in his last great charge on Sunday, pursued the scattered legions of McCook and Crittenden through the cedar brakes and blackjack thickets in their wild flight toward Chattanooga. And it was this alert soldier who on Monday, September 21st, in the Chattanooga valley, five miles from the field of battle, made an additional capture of a train of ninety wagons and some four hundred prisoners. The success of his operations at Chickamauga may be judged from his official report:

THE PRECARIOUS MILITARY RAIL-
ROAD IN 1864

A close look down the line will convince the beholder that this is no modern railroad with rock-ballasted road-bed and heavy rails, but a precarious construction of the Civil War, with light, easily bent iron which hundreds of lives were sacrificed to keep approximately straight. In order to supply an army it is absolutely necessary to keep open the lines of communication. An extract from General Rosecrans' letter to General Halleck, written October 16, 1863, brings out this necessity most vividly: "Evidence increases that the enemy intend a desperate effort to destroy this army. They are bringing up troops to our front. They have prepared pontoons, and will probably operate on our left flank, either to cross the river and force us to quit this place and fight them, or lose our communication. They will thus separate us from Burnside. We cannot feed Hooker's troops on our left, nor can we spare them from our right depots and communications, nor has he transportation. . . . Had we the railroad from here to Bridgeport, the whole of Sherman's and Hooker's troops brought up, we should not probably outnumber the enemy. This army, with its back to the barren mountains, roads narrow and difficult, while the enemy has the railroad and the corn in his rear, is at much disadvantage." The railway repairs of Sherman's army in the Atlanta campaign were under the management of Colonel Wright, a civil engineer, with a corps of two thousand men. They often had to work under a galling fire until the Confederates had been driven away, but their efficiency and skill was beyond praise. The ordinary wooden railway bridges were reconstructed with a standard pattern of truss, of which the parts were interchangeable, safely in the rear.

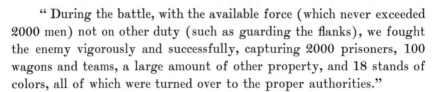

" During the battle, with the available force (which never exceeded 2000 men) not on other duty (such as guarding the flanks), we fought the enemy vigorously and successfully, capturing 2000 prisoners, 100 wagons and teams, a large amount of other property, and 18 stands of colors, all of which were turned over to the proper authorities."

After Rosecrans' army had sheltered itself behind the fortifications of Chattanooga, Forrest was ordered in the direction of Loudon and Knoxville to watch Burnside, whose corps occupied the latter place, while Wheeler remained in command of the cavalry with Bragg in front of Chattanooga.

When Bragg consulted Wheeler in regard to an expedition north of the Tennessee to break Rosecrans' lines of communications, Wheeler informed him that few of the horses were able to stand the strain of such an expedition. He was, however, ordered to do the best he could, and a few days after the battle all the best mounts were assembled for the raid.

We reached the Tennessee River on September 30th, at or near Cottonport, about forty miles east of Chattanooga, and although our crossing was opposed by some squadrons of the Fourth Ohio Cavalry, posted in the timber which lined the north bank, under cover of two 6-pounder Parrott guns, we succeeded in fording the river, which here was not more than two or three feet deep at this dry season of the year. From this point, without meeting with any material opposition, we made our way rapidly across Walden's Ridge and descending into the Sequatchie valley at Anderson's Cross Roads, early on the morning of October 2d, encountered the advance guard of an infantry escort to an enormous wagon train loaded with supplies for the army in Chattanooga. Parts of two regiments under Colonel John T. Morgan were ordered to charge the escort of the train, which they did, but were repulsed, and came back in disorder. I was standing near Colonel A. A. Russell who commanded the Fourth Alabama Cavalry, when General Wheeler rode up and ordered him to lead his regiment in. As soon as our line could be formed, we rode forward at

THE INADEQUATE REDOUBT

AT

JOHNSONVILLE

When, most unexpectedly, the Confederate General Nathan B. Forrest appeared on the bank opposite Johnsonville, Tennessee, November 4, 1864, and began firing across the Tennessee River, a distance of about four hundred yards, the fortifications of the post were quite inadequate. They consisted only of a redoubt for six guns on the spur of the hill overlooking the town and depot (seen clearly in the distance above), and two advanced batteries and rifle-pits. Three gunboats were in the river. Their commander, afraid of falling into the hands of the enemy, ordered his gunboats set afire and abandoned. The ranking officer of the troops ashore followed his example and ordered all transports and barges destroyed in the same way. A terrible conflagration which consumed between one and two million dollars' worth of Federal property ensued. On the 30th of November the few remaining stores not burned or captured by Forrest having been removed by railroad to Nashville, the post was evacuated.

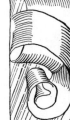

full speed, and receiving a volley at close quarters, were successful in riding over and capturing the entire escort within a few minutes. We found ourselves in possession of an enormous wagon train, and such a scene of panic and confusion I had never witnessed. Our appearance directly in the rear of Rosecrans' army, which was not more than twenty miles away, was wholly unexpected. As a matter of precaution, the Federal general had directed Colonel E. M. McCook with a division of cavalry, then near Bridgeport, to move up the Sequatchie valley, and be within supporting distance of this train, but he failed to be in position at the critical moment.

When the fighting with the escort began, the teamsters had turned about in the hope of escape in the direction of Bridgeport. As we came nearer, they became panic-stricken and took to their heels for safety, leaving their uncontrolled teams to run wild. Some of the wagons were overturned, blocking the road in places with anywhere from ten to fifty teams, some of the mules still standing, some fallen and tangled in the harness, and all in inextricable confusion. For six or eight miles we followed this line of wagons, with every half-mile or so a repetition of this scene. As we proceeded, men were detailed to set fire to the wagons and to kill the mules, since it was impossible to escape with the livestock. After a run of six or seven miles, I ventured to stop for a few minutes to help myself to a tempting piece of cheese and some crackers which I saw in one of the wagons. Filling my haversack, I was on the point of remounting, when General Wheeler rode up and ordered me to "get out of that wagon and go on after the enemy," which order I obeyed, and had the honor of riding side by side with my commander for some distance further among the captured wagons. As he turned back, he ordered the small squadron that was in advance, to go on until the last wagon had been destroyed, which order was fully executed.

By this time the smoke of the burning train was visible for many miles, and soon the explosions of fixed ammunition, with

THE EVACUATION OF JOHNSONVILLE AFTER FORREST'S SUCCESSFUL RAID

When General Forrest swooped down on Johnsonville the landings and banks, several acres in extent, were piled high with freight for Sherman's army. There were several boats and barges yet unloaded for want of room. Forrest captured *U. S. Gunboat 55* and three transports and barges. Owing to a misunderstanding of Forrest's orders to a prize-crew, two Union gunboats recaptured the transport *Venus*, loaded with stores which Forrest had transferred from the steamer *Mazeppa*, captured at Fort Heiman, and also some of Forrest's 20-pounder Parrott guns, which his exhausted horses could no longer draw. Colonel R. D. Mussey U. S. A., reports that the Thirteenth U. S. Colored Infantry and a section of Meig's battery stood their ground well. This was one of Forrest's swift raids which imperiled the stores of the Union armies.

which a number of wagons were loaded, sounded along the valley road, not unlike the firing of artillery in action. General Rosecrans expressed the opinion that the Confederates were bombarding his depot of supplies at Bridgeport.

General Rosecrans, in his official report, admitted the loss of five hundred wagons, so that there must have been from one to two thousand mules destroyed. While the wagons were still burning, and before those of us who had gone to the extreme limit of the train could return to the main column, Colonel McCook, in command of the Federal cavalry, arrived on the scene and formed his line of battle between us and our main column.

The capture and destruction of this immense train was one of the greatest achievements of General Wheeler's cavalry, and I was proud of the fact that the Fourth Alabama, unaided, did the fighting which took it. Its loss was keenly felt by the Federals, for it added to the precarious situation of the army in Chattanooga, and reduced rations to a cracker a day per man for several days in succession. General Wheeler reported:

"The number of wagons was variously estimated from eight hundred to fifteen hundred. . . . The quartermaster in charge of the train stated that there were eight hundred six-mule wagons, besides a great number of sutler's wagons. The train was guarded by a brigade of cavalry in front and a brigade of cavalry in rear, and on the flank, where we attacked, were stationed two regiments of infantry." General Rosecrans in a despatch to General Burnside dated October 5, 1863, said, "Your failure to close your troops down to our left has cost five hundred wagons loaded with essentials, the post of McMinnville, and heaven only knows where the mischief will end." From my own observation, I believe that five hundred would not be very far from correct. We missed about thirty wagons which had turned off in a narrow and little-used roadway, and were already partly toward Walden's Ridge.

CHAPTER
SEVEN

PARTISAN RANGERS
OF THE CONFEDERACY

AFTER A VISIT BY THE CONFEDERATE RAIDERS—ON THE FEDERAL
LINE OF COMMUNICATION IN VIRGINIA, 1862

COLONEL JOHN S. MOSBY AND SOME OF HIS MEN

Speaking likenesses of Colonel John S. Mosby, the famous Confederate independent leader and his followers—chiefly sons of gentlemen attracted to his standard by the daring nature of his operations. His almost uniform success, with the spirit of romance which surrounded his exploits, drew thousands of recruits to his leadership. Usually his detachments were small—twenty to eighty men. The names and locations in the group are as follows: Top row, left to right: Lee Herverson, Ben Palmer, John Puryear, Tom Booker, Norman Randolph, Frank Raham; second row: Parrott, John Troop, John W. Munson, Colonel John S. Mosby, Newell, Necly, Quarles; third row: Walter Gosden, Harry T. Sinnott, Butler, Gentry.

FAIRFAX COURT HOUSE, AFTER MOSBY'S CAPTURE OF STOUGHTON

If you had said "Mosby" to the Federal cavalrymen that this picture shows loitering before Fairfax Court House in June, 1863, they might have gnashed their teeth in mortification; for only a couple of months before, the daring Confederate partisan had entered the nearby headquarters of General Edwin H. Stoughton, and had "captured" him from the very midst of the army. When Lee retired behind the Blue Ridge and began to advance up the Shenandoah in the summer of 1863, Hooker's line was spread out from Fairfax Court House on the north to Culpeper on the south. Hooker followed up Lee closely on the other side of the Blue Ridge, leaving three corps, the Second, Fifth, and Twelfth, held in reserve at Fairfax Court House within twenty miles of Washington, for the protection of the Capital. The Federal cavalry sought and scouted in vain to locate the elusive partisan. It was at this time that Mosby performed one of the most audacious feats of his career. On March 8, 1863, with a small band of carefully picked men, he rode safely through the Union picket lines, where the sentries mistook him for their own scouts returning from one of their vain searches for himself. Upon reaching the vicinity of Fairfax Court House, Mosby entered the house used as headquarters by General Stoughton, woke the general and demanded his person. Believing that the town had surrendered, Stoughton made no resistance.

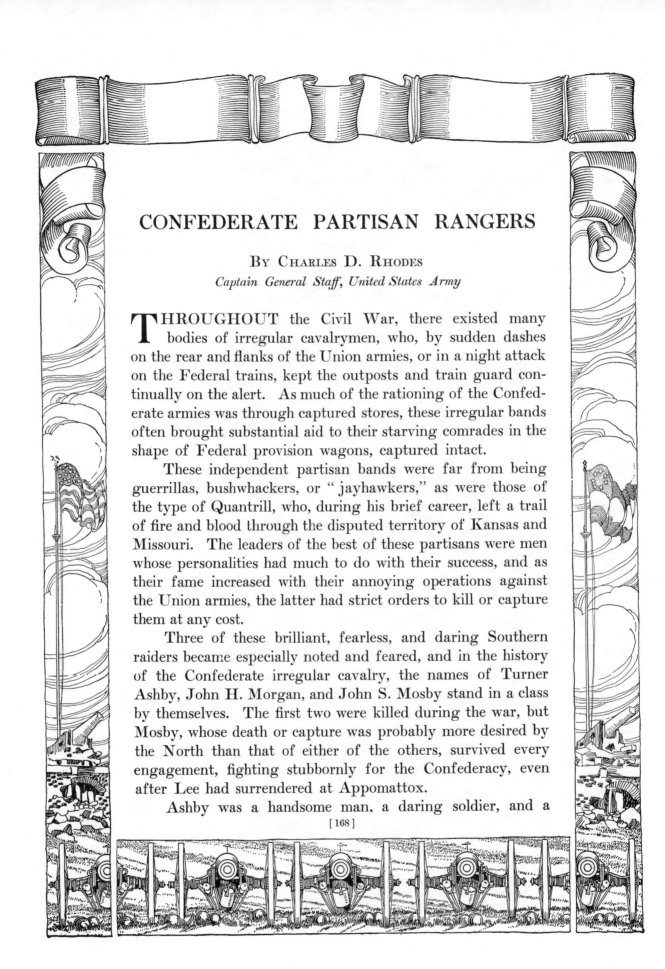

CONFEDERATE PARTISAN RANGERS

By Charles D. Rhodes
Captain General Staff, United States Army

THROUGHOUT the Civil War, there existed many bodies of irregular cavalrymen, who, by sudden dashes on the rear and flanks of the Union armies, or in a night attack on the Federal trains, kept the outposts and train guard continually on the alert. As much of the rationing of the Confederate armies was through captured stores, these irregular bands often brought substantial aid to their starving comrades in the shape of Federal provision wagons, captured intact.

These independent partisan bands were far from being guerrillas, bushwhackers, or "jayhawkers," as were those of the type of Quantrill, who, during his brief career, left a trail of fire and blood through the disputed territory of Kansas and Missouri. The leaders of the best of these partisans were men whose personalities had much to do with their success, and as their fame increased with their annoying operations against the Union armies, the latter had strict orders to kill or capture them at any cost.

Three of these brilliant, fearless, and daring Southern raiders became especially noted and feared, and in the history of the Confederate irregular cavalry, the names of Turner Ashby, John H. Morgan, and John S. Mosby stand in a class by themselves. The first two were killed during the war, but Mosby, whose death or capture was probably more desired by the North than that of either of the others, survived every engagement, fighting stubbornly for the Confederacy, even after Lee had surrendered at Appomattox.

Ashby was a handsome man, a daring soldier, and a

THE WORK OF THE RANGER—RAILROAD IRON ON THE FIRE

A pile of bent and twisted railroad iron across a heap of smouldering ties was often the only indication found by the Union soldiers that Mosby had paid them another visit. The daring Confederate ranger himself seemed to have a charmed life. Even after he became well-established as a partisan, his men were never organized as a tactical fighting body, and had no established camp. His expeditions often led him far within the Union lines, and when the command was nearly surrounded and the situation apparently hopeless, Mosby would give the word and the detachment would suddenly disintegrate, so that there was no longer any "Mosby and his band"—until the next time.

superb horseman. At the outbreak of the war, he received a commission as captain of a band of picked rangers, working in conjunction with the main operations of the Confederate armies, but unhampered by specific instructions from a superior. He was rapidly promoted. As colonel of a partisan band he was a continual menace to the Federal trains, and moved with such rapidity as oftentimes to create the impression that several bodies of mounted troops were in the field instead of but one. Falling upon an isolated column of army wagons at dawn, he would strike a Federal camp thirty miles away by twilight of the same day. His men were picked by their leader with great care, and although there is reason to believe that Southern writers surrounded these troopers with a halo of romance, there is no disputing that they were brave, daring, and self-sacrificing.

Ashby himself was looked upon by many officers and men in the Union armies as a purely mythical character. It was said that no such man existed, and that the feats accredited to Ashby's rangers were in reality the work of several separate forces. Much of the mystery surrounding this officer was due to his beautiful white horse, strong, swift, and a splendid jumper. He and his horse, standing alone on a hill or ridge, would draw the Union troops on. When the latter had reached a point where capture seemed assured, Ashby would slowly mount and canter leisurely out of sight. When his pursuers reached the spot where he had last been seen, Ashby and his white charger would again be observed on the crest of a still more distant hill.

Only once during his spectacular career in the Confederate army was Ashby outwitted and captured, but even then he made his escape before being taken a mile by his captors—a detachment of the First Michigan Cavalry.

The Confederate leader was surrounded before he was aware of the presence of the Union troops, and the latter were within fifty rods of him when he saw several of them pushing

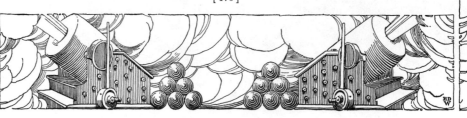

COLONEL JOHN SINGLETON MOSBY

It is hard to reconcile Mosby's peaceful profession of a lawyer at Bristol, Washington County, Louisiana, before the war with the series of exploits that subsequently made him one of the most famous of the partisan leaders in the war. After serving under General Joseph E. Johnston in the Shenandoah in 1861–62, he was appointed by General E. B. Stuart as an independent scout. His independent operations were chiefly in Virginia and Maryland. His most brilliant exploit was the capture in March, 1863, of Brigadier-General Stoughton at Fairfax Courthouse, far inside the Federal lines. He followed Lee's army into Pennsylvania in June, 1863, and worried the flanks of the Federal army as it moved southward after Gettysburg. In January, 1864, he was repulsed in a night attack on Harper's Ferry; in May he harassed the rear of Grant's army as it advanced on Fredericksburg; a little later he made a long raid into Maryland, and in August he surprised and captured Sheridan's entire supply-train near Berryville. In September he was wounded at Falls Church, but the following month he captured two Federal paymasters with $168,000, tore up the Baltimore & Ohio Railroad tracks, destroyed rolling-stock, and made a prisoner of Brigadier-General Alfred Duffié. In December, 1864, he was promoted to be a colonel, and at the close of the war was paroled by the intercession of no less a person than Grant himself.

along a cross-road which afforded the only avenue of escape. Nevertheless, Ashby made a dash for freedom. Vaulting into the saddle, the daring rider raced to beat the foremost Union trooper to the open road. Sergeant Pierson, who was in command of the little body of flankers, rode the only horse which could equal the speed of Ashby's fleet charger, and he and the Southerner reached the road crossing together—Pierson far in advance of his comrades. As Pierson neared Ashby, the latter fired at him with his revolver, but the Union trooper did not attempt to return the fire and Ashby himself replaced his weapon in the holster.

As the two men, magnificently mounted, came together, Ashby drew a large knife and raised it to strike. Pierson was a bigger and stronger man than Ashby, and reaching over, he seized Ashby's wrist with one hand while with the other he grasped the partisan leader's long black beard. Then, throwing himself from his horse, Pierson dragged the Confederate officer to the ground, and held him until the remaining Union troopers reached the scene of the struggle and disarmed Ashby.

The white horse had instantly stopped when Ashby was pulled from his back, and the captive was allowed to ride him back to the Union lines, slightly in advance of his captors, Sergeant Pierson at his side. The detachment had gone but a short distance when the mysterious white horse wheeled suddenly to one side, bounded over the high plantation fence which lined the roadside, and dashed away across the fields. Before the Union troops could recover from their surprise, Ashby was again free, and it was not long before he was once more reported by the Federal scouts as standing on a distant hill, engaged in caressing his faithful horse.

Only a few weeks later, this famous horse, which had become so familiar to the Union troops, was shot and killed by a sharpshooter belonging to the Fifth Michigan, who was attempting to bring down Ashby. Not long after, while leading his men in a cavalry skirmish, at Harrisonburg, during

[172]

MEN WHO TRIED TO CATCH MOSBY

GUARDING THE CAPITAL—CAMP OF THE THIRTEENTH NEW YORK CAVALRY

The Thirteenth New York horsemen were constantly held in the vicinity of Washington endeavoring to cross swords with the elusive Mosby, when he came too near, and scouting in the Virginia hills. This shows their camp at Prospect Hill at the close of the war. During most of their service they were attached to the Twenty-second Army Corps. The Administration policy of always keeping a large army between the Confederates and Washington resulted in the turning of the National Capital into a vast military camp. Prospect Hill became the chief center of cavalry camps during the latter part of the war.

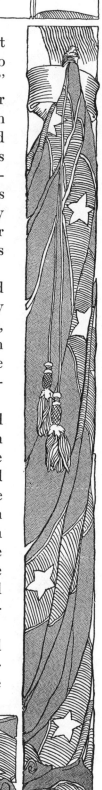

"Stonewall" Jackson's famous Valley campaign, Ashby met his own death, on June 6, 1862. As he fell, his last words to his troopers were: "Charge men! For God's sake, charge!"

Next to the gallant Ashby there was no partisan leader whose death created a greater loss to the South than John Hunt Morgan. He was a slightly older man than Ashby and had seen service in the Mexican War. When the call to arms sounded, he was one of the first to organize a company of cavalry and pledge his support to the Southern cause. He was fearless and tireless, a hard rider, and a man of no mean ability as a tactician and strategist. Morgan's men were picked for their daring and their horsemanship, and until the day of his death, he was a thorn in the flesh of the Union commanders.

Starting before daybreak, Morgan and his troopers would rush along through the day, scarcely halting to rest their weary and jaded horses. When, worn to the very limit of endurance, the exhausted animals refused to go farther, the cavalrymen would quickly tear off saddle and bridle, and leaving the horse to live or die, would hurry along to the nearest farm or plantation and secure a fresh mount.

At night, far from their starting-point, the dust-covered troopers threw themselves, yelling and cheering, on the Union outposts, riding them down and creating consternation in the camp or bivouac. Then, with prisoners or perhaps captured wagon trains, the rangers rode, ghostlike, back through the night, while calls for reenforcements were being passed through the Federal lines. By dawn, Morgan and his weary horsemen would have safely regained their own lines, while oftentimes the Union troops were still waiting an attack at the spot where the unexpected night raid had been made. Morgan's famous raid through the State of Ohio exerted a moral and political influence which was felt throughout the entire North.

On their raids, Morgan's men were usually accompanied by an expert telegraph operator. They would charge an isolated telegraph office on the railroad communications of the

GENERAL JOHN H. MORGAN, C.S.A.

Morgan was a partisan leader who differed in method from Mosby. His command remained on a permanent basis. In the summer of 1863 Bragg decided, on account of his exposed condition and the condition of his army, weakened by detachments sent to the defense of Vicksburg, to fall back from Tullahoma to Chattanooga. To cover the retreat he ordered Morgan to ride into Kentucky with a picked force, breaking up the railroad, attacking Rosecrans' detachments, and threatening Louisville. Morgan left Burkesville July 2d, with 2,640 men and four guns. Ten thousand soldiers were watching the Cumberland but Morgan, exceeding his instructions, effected a crossing and rode northward. After a disastrous encounter with the Twenty-fifth Michigan at a bridge over the Green River, he drew off and marched to Brandenburg, capturing Lebanon on the way. By this time Indiana and Ohio were alive with the aroused militia, and Morgan fled eastward, burned bridges and impressed horses, marched by night unmolested through the suburbs of Cincinnati, and was finally forced to surrender near New Lisbon, Ohio, on July 26th. He escaped from the State Penitentiary at Columbus, Ohio, by tunneling on November 27, 1863, and took the field again.

Union army, and, capturing the operator, would place their own man at the telegraph key. In this way they gained much valuable and entirely authentic information, which, as soon as known, was rushed away to the headquarters of the army.

At other times, Morgan's operator would "cut in" on the Federal telegraph lines at some distant point, and seated on the ground by his instrument, would read the Union messages for many hours at a time. This service to the Confederate leaders was of inestimable value, and created a feeling among the Union signal-men that even cipher messages were not entirely safe from Morgan's men.

As Morgan was promoted from grade to grade, and the size of his command increased accordingly, he became more and more of an annoyance and even a terror to the North. His troopers were no longer mere rangers, but developed into more or less trained cavalry. Yet even then, his command showed a partiality for sudden and highly successful attacks upon Union outposts and wagon trains. The death of Morgan occurred near Greeneville, Tennessee, on September 4, 1864, when, being surrounded, he was shot down in a dash for life.

Colonel John S. Mosby, with his raiding detachments of varying size, was probably the best known and the most anxiously sought by the Union forces of any of the partisan leaders. Mosby's absolute fearlessness, his ingenious methods of operating, as well as his innate love of danger and excitement, all combined to make his sudden descents upon the Federal lines of communication spectacular in the extreme.

His almost uniform success and the spirit of romance which surrounded his exploits, drew thousands of recruits to his leadership, and had he desired, he could have commanded a hundred men for every one who usually accompanied him on his forays. But he continued throughout the war using small detachments of from twenty to eighty men, and much of his success was probably due to this fact, which permitted sudden appearances and disappearances. From beginning to end

BRIGADIER–GENERAL TURNER ASHBY, C. S. A.

Such a will-o'-the-wisp was Turner Ashby, the audacious Confederate cavalryman, that he was looked upon by many officers and men in the Union armies as a purely mythological character. It was widely declared that no such man existed, and that the feats accredited to Ashby's rangers were in reality the work of many different partisan bands. His habit of striking at different and widely divergent points in rapid succession went far toward substantiating this rumor. He would fall upon an isolated wagon-train at dawn, and by twilight of the same day would strike a Federal camp thirty miles or more away. But Ashby was a real character, a daring soldier, a superb horseman, and the right-hand man of "Stonewall" Jackson. Careless of the additional danger, he customarily rode a beautiful white horse. After he was captured by the First Michigan cavalry, it was due to the courage and splendid jumping ability of this animal that he was able to make good his escape. Ashby met his death in a "Valley" cavalry skirmish at Harrisonburg on June 6, 1862, crying to his troopers in his last words: "Charge, men! For God's sake, charge!"

of the war, Mosby's raiders were a constant menace to the Union troops, and the most constant vigilance was necessary to meet successfully his skilfully planned stratagems.

On March 8, 1863, Mosby performed one of the most daring and effective feats of his career. In this case, as well as in others, it was the supreme boldness of the act which alone made it possible. Even with their knowledge of Mosby's methods, the Union officers could hardly conceive of such an apparently rash and unheard-of exploit being successful.

With a small band of carefully picked men, Mosby rode safely through the Union picket-lines, where the sentries believed the party to be Federal scouts returning from a raid. Upon reaching the vicinity of Fairfax Court House, Mosby entered the house used as headquarters by General Edwin H. Stoughton, woke the general, and demanded his surrender. Believing that the town had surrendered, the Union leader made no resistance. Meanwhile, each trooper in Mosby's little command had quietly secured several prisoners. Stoughton was forced to mount a horse, and with their prisoners Mosby and his cavalcade galloped safely back to their lines.

It was with similar strokes, original in conception and daring in execution, that Mosby kept thousands of Federal cavalry and infantry away from much-needed service at the front. After he became well established as a partisan ranger, his men were never organized as a tactical fighting body, and never had, as with other troops, an established camp. Through his trusty lieutenants, the call would be sent out for a designated number of men "for Mosby." This was the most definite information as to their mission that these volunteers ever received. In fact, they always moved out with sealed orders, but at the appointed time and place the rangers would assemble without fail. That Mosby wanted them was sufficient.

Many of these men were members of regular cavalry regiments home on furlough, others were farmers who had been duly enlisted in the rangers, and were always subject to call,

PROTECTION AGAINST THE "JAYHAWKERS" OF LOUISIANA

The lookout tower in the midst of this Federal cavalry camp in the northwest part of Baton Rouge, Louisiana, is a compliment to the "jayhawkers"—soldiers not affiliated with any command—and nondescript guerilla bands which infested this region along the banks of the Mississippi. Here the land is so level that lookout towers were built wherever a command stopped for more than a few hours. The soldiers found it safer also to clear away the brush and obstructing trees for several hundred yards on all sides of their camps, in order to prevent the roving Confederate sharpshooters from creeping up and picking off a sentry, or having a shot at an officer. The guerilla bands along the Mississippi even had some pieces of ordnance, and used to amuse themselves by dropping shells on the Union "tin-clad" gunboats from lofty and distant bluffs.

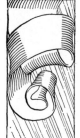

still others were troopers whose mounts were worn out, and whose principal object was to secure Northern horses. The Union cavalry always claimed that among Mosby's men were a number who performed acts for which they were given short shrift when caught. Of course, the nature of the service performed by these rangers was subversive of discipline, and it is quite possible that many deeds were committed which the leader himself had absolutely nothing to do with and would not have sanctioned. But this is true with all warfare.

Mosby's expeditions often led him far within the Union lines, and the command was often nearly surrounded. On such occasions Mosby would give the word and the detachment would suddenly disintegrate, each trooper making his way back to his own lines through forests and over mountains as best he could. Frequently his men were captured. But Mosby seemed to bear a charmed life, and in spite of rewards for his capture and all manner of plans to entrap him, he continued his operations as a valuable ally to the main Confederate army.

Of course much of his success was due to the fact that he was ever operating in a friendly country. He could always be assured of authentic information, and wherever he went was certain of food, fresh horses, and means of concealment.

In 1864, Mosby was shot during one of his forays, and was left, apparently dying, by the Union troops, who failed to recognize him, in the house where he had been surprised. Learning soon after that the wounded Confederate was the famous leader of Mosby's rangers, the troops hastily returned to capture him or secure his dead body. But in the meantime, Mosby's men had spirited him away, and within a short time he and his men were again raiding Federal trains and outposts.

Until the very end of the war he kept up his indefatigable border warfare, and it was not until after the surrender at Appomattox, that Mosby gathered his men about him for the last time, and telling them that the war was over, pronounced his command disbanded for all time.

CHAPTER
EIGHT

CAVALRY
PICKETS, SCOUTS
AND COURIERS

A VETERAN SCOUT
OF THE
THIRTEENTH NEW YORK CAVALRY

WHY FEDERAL

CAVALRY HISTORY

BEGAN LATE

These four Federal troopers holding their horses, side by side with an equal number of infantry, are typical of the small detachments that split up the cavalry into units of little value during the first two years of the war. The cavalry also furnished guides, orderlies, and grooms for staff officers. The authorities divided it up so minutely among corps, division, and brigade commanders as completely to subvert its true value. It was assigned to accompany the slow-moving wagon-trains, which could have been equally well guarded by an infantry detail, and was practically never used as a coherent whole. "Detachments

CAVALRY WITH INFANTRY

ON

PROVOST-GUARD DUTY

from its strength were constantly increased, and it was hampered by instructions which crippled it for all useful purposes." This photograph was taken in February, 1865, after the cavalry had proved itself. The companies attached at that time to the provost-guard were Company K of the First Indiana Cavalry, Companies C and D of the First Massachusetts Cavalry, and the Third Pennsylvania Cavalry. The officer is inspecting the arms of the Zouaves at the right, and the troopers with their white gauntlets are much more spick and span than if they were assigned to the long rides and open air life of active campaigning.

CAVALRY GUARDING THE ORANGE & ALEXANDRIA RAILROAD, 1864

Here it is apparent why the Northern generals found it necessary to detach large portions of their armies along their lines of communication, to guard against the impending raids of the Confederate cavalry.   The destruction of the bridge in this photograph, part of Grant's line of communication in the Wilderness campaign, would have delayed his movements for days and have compelled him to detach a strong body to recapture the railroad, and another to rebuild the bridge.   Hence this strong force detailed as a guard.   Cavalry boots

READY TO FORESTALL A CONFEDERATE RAID

and sabers are visible in the photograph, with the revolver, distinctive of that branch of the service.   The photographer evidently posed his men.   Note the hands thrust into the breasts of their jackets, or clasped in front of them, the folded arms, and the jaunty attitudes. The two boys at the left of the picture seem hardly old enough to be real soldiers.   The tangle of underbrush along the banks suggest the mazes of the Wilderness where Grant was baffled in his overland campaign.

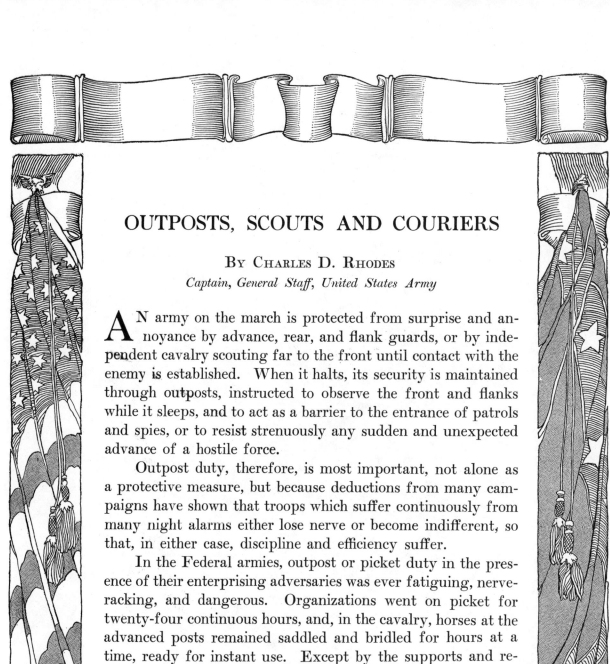

OUTPOSTS, SCOUTS AND COURIERS

By Charles D. Rhodes
Captain, General Staff, United States Army

AN army on the march is protected from surprise and annoyance by advance, rear, and flank guards, or by independent cavalry scouting far to the front until contact with the enemy is established. When it halts, its security is maintained through outposts, instructed to observe the front and flanks while it sleeps, and to act as a barrier to the entrance of patrols and spies, or to resist strenuously any sudden and unexpected advance of a hostile force.

Outpost duty, therefore, is most important, not alone as a protective measure, but because deductions from many campaigns have shown that troops which suffer continuously from many night alarms either lose nerve or become indifferent, so that, in either case, discipline and efficiency suffer.

In the Federal armies, outpost or picket duty in the presence of their enterprising adversaries was ever fatiguing, nerveracking, and dangerous. Organizations went on picket for twenty-four continuous hours, and, in the cavalry, horses at the advanced posts remained saddled and bridled for hours at a time, ready for instant use. Except by the supports and reserves, the lighting of fires and cooking of food, when in close contact with the Confederates, were forbidden, but many a strip of bacon and occasionally a stolen chicken were fried surreptitiously in a safe hiding-place. Although a farmhouse was oftentimes available, horses and troopers were usually without shelter, and this, in rainy or freezing weather, made outpost duty an uncomfortable, if not a thrilling, experience.

The nervous period for the vedette was between midnight

CAVALRY AT SUDLEY'S FORD
BULL RUN

Not until the time this photograph was taken—March, 1862—did the Union cavalrymen revisit this little ford after the disastrous rout of the inchoate Federal army the July previous. The following March, the Confederate commander Johnston left his works at Centerville for the Peninsula, having learned that McClellan's move on Richmond would take that direction. This group of cavalrymen is advancing across the stream near the ford where they had so gallantly protected the Federal flight only a few months before. At the time this was taken, the Federal Government had already changed its first absurd decision to limit its cavalry to six regiments of regulars, and from the various States were pouring in the regiments that finally enabled the Union cavalry to outnumber and outwear the exhausted Southern horse in 1864 and 1865.

and daybreak, when all was still and dark and mysterious. For the inexperienced soldier, with eyes and ears at extraordinary tension, the grunting of a predatory hog or the browsing of a calf was quite sufficient to create alarm.

Again, when the excitement had subsided, and eyes had grown drowsy from lack of sleep, steps among the trees would bring the sharp challenge and colloquy:

"Halt! Who comes there?"

"A friend."

"Advance, friend, with the countersign."

Sometimes the "friend" was an officer, making his rounds of inspection; sometimes a countryman who had never heard of the countersign. Occasionally the answer to the countersign was a rush of feet, a blow, and the driving-in of the outpost by a force of the foe, or by guerrillas.

The tendency of the raw recruit was to see a gray uniform behind every stump, tree, or bush, and in the early period of the Civil War, the rifle-firing by opposing pickets, especially at night, was constant and uninterrupted. Many a time, too, the lone sentinel or vedette was shot down in cold blood.

A member of one of the first organized companies of Union sharpshooters tells a story of creeping with his comrades, in the early morning hours, upon a Confederate outpost. The break of a lovely day was just showing red in the eastern sky. The range to the hostile picket was considerable, but the rifles of the sharpshooters were equipped with telescopic sights.

Through the glass, a tall, soldierly-looking cavalry officer in Confederate gray could be seen through the morning mist, sitting motionless on his black charger, admiring the dawn. The rifles were leveled; the telescopic sights were adjusted on the poor fellow's chest; the triggers were pulled in unison, and although too distant to hear a sound from the outpost, the cavalryman was seen to fall dead from his horse. To the narrator, an inexperienced New England lad, such deeds were wanton murder, and he made haste to transfer to a cavalry command,

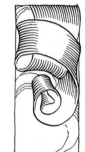

GUARDING A PONTOON-BRIDGE

These cavalrymen posted at the strategic point known as Varuna Landing, across the James River, in 1864, are engaged in no unimportant task. The Federals were by no means sure that Lee's veterans would not again make a daring move northward. However, by this time (1864) the true value of the Federal cavalry had been appreciated by the authorities; it was being used in mass on important raids, and had been given a chance to show its prowess in battle. But not until after Hooker reorganized the Army of the Potomac in 1863 was the policy definitely abandoned of splitting up the cavalry into small detachments for minor duties, and of regarding it merely as an adjunct of the infantry.

not equipped with telescopic sights and hair-trigger rifles. But as the war progressed, this constant firing by sentinels and vedettes disappeared, and opposing pickets began to comprehend that this was not war. To the guerrillas, who killed to rob and loot, it was, of course, a different matter.

The time came when the "Yankee" troopers exchanged newspapers, bacon, or hardtack with the "Johnny Rebs," for tobacco or its equivalent, or they banteringly invited each other to come out and meet half-way between the lines of outposts.

It was two years before the true rôle of cavalry was understood by the Federal commanders. During that early period, the constant use of the mounted branch as outposts for infantry divisions and army corps, was largely responsible for cavalry inefficiency, and for the tremendous breaking-down of horse-flesh. Indeed, it was not until 1864 that Sheridan impressed upon Meade the wastefulness of thus rendering thousands of cavalry mounts unserviceable through unnecessary picket duty, which could be as well performed by infantry.

But many opportunities for brave and gallant deeds occurred on outpost duty, albeit many such were performed in obscurity, and were thus never lauded to the world as heroic.

One such deed, which fortunately did not escape recognition, was that of Sergeant Martin Hagan, of the Second United States Cavalry. When the city of Fredericksburg was evacuated by the Union army on December 13, 1862, Sergeant Hagan was left behind in charge of an outpost detachment of seven troopers, with orders to remain until relieved.

For some reason or other, Hagan was not relieved, and remained at his post with his pitiably small force until the Confederate Army of Northern Virginia began entering the town. Then Hagan and his troopers succeeded in delaying the advanced troops by skirmishing. Subsequently learning that the bridges over the Rappahannock behind him had been removed, and that his outpost was the only Union force in Fredericksburg, he retired, stubbornly disputing every foot of his

A FEDERAL CAVALRY "DETAIL" GUARDING A WAGON-TRAIN, 1862

These troopers bending over their saddles in the cold autumn wind, as the wagon-train jolts along the Rappahannock bank, are one of the many "details" which dissipated the strength and impaired the efficiency of the cavalry as a distinct arm of the service during the first two years of the war. They carried revolvers, as well as their sabers and carbines, for they had to be ready for sudden attack, an ambush, a night rush, or the dash of the swift Southern raiders who helped provision the Confederate armies from Northern wagon-trains.

way with a brigade of Confederate cavalry, until the banks of the Rappahannock were reached. Here, seeing his men and their horses well over the river, he plunged in himself under a shower of balls, and swam across without the loss of a man, horse, or article of equipment. For this gallant act of " valor and fidelity," this cavalry sergeant was awarded the Congressional Medal of Honor.

Scouting

At the beginning of the Civil War, what is now known as military information or intelligence was not appreciated as it was later. The organization of the scout service was not perfected; accurate military maps of the theater of operations were almost wholly lacking, and many commanders accepted the gage of battle with no very comprehensive idea of the foe's numbers, position, and *morale*, and with no accurate conception of the topography of the battlefield.

As the military organization of the Union armies was perfected, however, and the newly made officers learned their lesson in the stern school of experience, the importance of scouting became apparent, and this use of cavalry developed into a necessary preliminary to every serious encounter.

Perhaps no branch of the military operations of the Civil War gave such opportunities for individual intelligence, initiative, nerve, daring, resourcefulness, tact, and physical endurance, as the constant scouting by the cavalry of the opposing armies between the great battles of the war. It required bold riding combined with caution, keen eyesight and ready wit, undaunted courage—not recklessness—an appreciation of locality amounting to a sixth sense, and above all other things a mind able to differentiate between useful and useless information.

The increased importance given to scouting, as the cavalry of the Federal armies gained in experience and efficiency, by no means did away with the use of paid civilian spies. But the

WATCHING AT RAPPAHANNOCK STATION

A FEDERAL CAVALRY PICKET IN '62

IN DANGER AT THE TIME

THIS PHOTOGRAPH WAS TAKEN

This picture of August, 1862, shows one of the small cavalry details posted to guard the railroad at Rappahannock Station. The Confederate cavalry, operating in force, could overcome these details as easily as they could drive away an equal number of infantry, and unless it was on account of their superior facilities for flight, there was little use in using the mounted branch of the service instead of the infantry. On the other hand the Union cavalry was so constantly crippled by having its strength dissipated in such details that it was unable to pursue the Confederate raiders. Before this scene, the summer and fall of 1862, Pope and Lee had been maneuvering for position along each side of the Rappahannock River. Pope had established a *tête-de-pont* at this railroad station, and on August 22d Longstreet feinted strongly against it in order to divert Pope's attention from Jackson's efforts to turn his right flank. Longstreet and Stuart burned the railroad bridge, and drove the Federals from the *tête-de-pont*, after a contest of several hours' duration.

information furnished by soldier scouts served as a check upon untrustworthy civilians—sometimes employed as spies by both sides—and enabled the Union commanders to substantiate valuable information secured from prisoners, newspapers, and former slaves. As in a great many other things, the Confederate cavalry excelled in the use of trained officers as scouts— officers' patrols, as they are called nowadays—men whose opinion of what they observed was worth something to their commanders; while the Federal leaders were very slow to appreciate that false or faulty military information, in that it is misleading, is worse than no information at all.

In many cases loyal inhabitants of the border States were utilized as scouts, men who knew each trail and by-path, and who were more or less familiar with Confederate sentiment in their own and adjoining counties. These men were placed in a most uncomfortable position, suspected by their friends and neighbors at home, and looked upon with suspicion by their military employers. Their service to their country was oftentimes heroic, and they frequently laid down their lives in her cause.

General Sheridan was one of the first of the Union commanders who appreciated, at its true value, the importance of the information service—a part of headquarters which should be systematically organized and disciplined, and whose reports as to topography and the location of the foe could be absolutely relied upon. Indeed, this was one of the secrets of Sheridan's almost uniform success. He was always well informed as to his opponent's movements, strength, and probable intentions.

After Sheridan's engagements in the Shenandoah valley at Clifton and Berryville, he decided to dispense almost entirely with the use of civilians and alleged Confederate deserters, and to depend entirely on Union scouts. For this purpose he organized a scout battalion recruited entirely from soldiers who volunteered for this dangerous duty. These troopers were disguised in the Confederate uniform when necessary, and were paid from secret-service funds.

CAVALRY TO KEEP THE PEACE—THE "ONEIDA" COMPANY

Cavalrymen playing cards, washing, smoking pipes, whittling sticks, indolently leaning against a tree, do not fulfill the usual conception of that dashing arm of the service. These are the Oneida Cavalry, used as provost-guards and orderlies throughout the war. Not a man of them was killed in battle, and the company lost only ten by disease. This does not mean that they did not do their full share of the work, but merely that they exemplified the indifference or ignorance on the part of many military powers as to the proper rôle of the cavalry. The "Oneidas" were attached to Stoneman's cavalry command with the Army of the Potomac from the time of their organization in September, 1861, to April, 1862. They did patrol duty and took care of the prisoners during several months in the latter year. Thereafter they acted as headquarters escort until they were mustered out, June 13, 1865, and honorably discharged from the service.

This assumption of the Confederate uniform, giving these soldiers the character of spies, caused Sheridan's scouts to be more or less disliked by the Cavalry Corps, and it has been stated on good authority that they were frequently fired upon deliberately by their own side, under the pretense of being taken for the foe. These scouts literally took their lives in their hands, and it required all their ready wit to escape being killed or captured by either the one side or the other. But the independence of the service, its constant risk, as well as patriotic impulses in the case of many, fascinated and appealed to a certain class of men, and they kept Sheridan well informed at all times.

The specially selected scouts of the Federal armies usually were mounted on the best available horses, and were furnished fresh remounts whenever occasion required—or they helped themselves to what the country afforded. The best scouting was done by cavalry troopers working in pairs, on the principle that two pairs of eyes are better than one pair. So in case of surprise, at least one scout might escape.

Sheridan's scouts were usually excellent pistol shots, and were encouraged to carry several revolvers in their belts or saddle holsters. They carried no sabers lest the rattle of scabbards or the gleam of bright metal attract the attention of the Southern scouts and betray their presence. The most experienced scouts traveled light. Many times they were forced to ride for their lives, and an extra pound or two made a difference in the weight-carrying speed of their horses. They usually left their grain and clothing in the headquarters' wagons, and managed to live off the country.

Sheridan's disguised scouts became expert in picking up the stragglers of the opposing army and in questioning them, and even went to the extent of riding around the Confederate columns and wagon trains. If detected, their fleet horses usually put considerable distance between them and their pursuers, but they were ever ready to shoot, and instances have been recorded of one of their number holding off four men.

BUILDING A CAVALRY CAMP

Waving sabers in battle, as the cavalryman soon learned, consumed but a small part of his time as compared with handling pickaxes and felling trees. In this photograph the cavalry detail at the head-quarters of General Adelbert Ames is breaking ground to build a camp. The men have just arrived, and the horses are still saddled. A barrel is supplying draft for a temporary fireplace, and even the dog is alert and excited. The faces gazing out of the photograph below are of men who more than once have looked death in the face and have earned their comparative rest. A pleasant change from active service is this camp of Companies C and D of the First Massachusetts Cavalry. They had served at Antietam, at Kelly's Ford, at Brandy Station, at Gettysburg, in the Wilderness, at Spotsylvania, and in a host of minor operations before they were assigned to provost duty near the end of the war.

A REST IN THE WOODS

COURIERS

The risk taken by the despatch bearers of both armies, when occasion demanded, is well illustrated in the story of the fate of private William Spicer, of the Tenth Missouri Cavalry, who undertook to carry an order through the Confederate lines while Sherman was conducting his campaign in Mississippi. The cavalry of General Smith, numbering nearly seven thousand men, had been detached from the remainder of the army and sent away along the Mobile and Ohio Railroad, with orders to join the army near Meridian, on February 10, 1864.

Meanwhile, the main body had marched to Meridian, and there Sherman waited for Smith until the 18th, without receiving any tidings of the missing troopers. Then the remainder of the Federal cavalry, under Winslow, was ordered to scout twenty miles toward the direction from which Smith was expected, and to convey new orders to him. Winslow's forces reached their objective point at Lauderdale Springs, and still no news had been heard of Smith.

Scouts that traveled far into the surrounding country obtained no further news. As Winslow's orders allowed him to go no farther, he abandoned the search, but it was necessary that Smith receive Sherman's orders, and a volunteer was called for to carry the despatch through a country occupied by Forrest's cavalry, and other portions of Polk's army. The messenger would be forced to locate Smith in whatever manner he could, and then to reach him as quickly as possible.

From many volunteers, Private Spicer was finally chosen. He was an Arkansas man, and as many Confederate troops had been enlisted there, he was less likely to be suspected than a man from any of the Northern States. Spicer considered all the features of the case, and his final decision was to risk detection in the gray uniform of a Confederate. The Federals were supplied with uniforms taken from prisoners and captured wagons, which were kept for use in such an emergency

KEEPING FODDER DRY

Fodder and equipment were scarcer in the field than men. Whether the trooper slept in the open or not, he took advantage of any and every facility to keep the fodder dry and protect his horses. This photograph shows a half-ruined and deserted house utilized for these two purposes. The saddles were laid beneath the shelter; those covered with rawhide instead of leather soon split if wet, and when cracked were far from comfortable. This, like the scene below, was taken near City Point in 1864.

A HOME BECOMES A CAVALRY STABLE

QUICKLY IMPROVISED STALLS

QUARTERS FOR HORSES

The trooper's first regard was for the comfort of his horse, not only in the matter of feeding and watering, but also in respect to providing him with comfortable quarters. Along the crest of the hill stretches a row of stalls improvised with poles, to afford each horse room enough to lie down and not be walked on or kicked by his neighbor—room was essential for the hard-worked horses. The haze in the distance indicates the Virginia summer of 1864—a trying one for members of the mounted service.

as this, and Spicer was provided with one that fitted him well. It was the evening of February 23d, when he rode northward, on his search for the missing cavalry.

With the tact of a scout well drilled in his work, he followed each little clue on his northward ride, until he had learned where Smith could be found. On the morning following his exit from his camp, he met several bodies of Confederates, who passed him with little notice.

Then another band was met. Spicer saluted; the salute was returned, and the Confederates were passing him, as the others had. But suddenly one of the party stopped and looked closely at the lone rider. The Confederates halted and Spicer was ordered to dismount. The man who had called the commander's attention to the courier stepped before Spicer. The courier recognized him as a neighbor in Arkansas.

With all the ingenuity at his command the courier fought to allay the suspicions of the Confederates, but slowly and surely the case against him was built up. Then a drumhead court martial was held in the middle of the road. The verdict was soon reached, and Spicer was hanged to a near-by tree.

One of the swiftest and most daring courier trips of the war was made, immediately after the second battle of Bull Run, by Colonel Lafayette C. Baker, a special agent of the War Department, acting as courier for Secretary Stanton. He was sent from Washington with a message to General Banks, whose troops were at Bristoe Station, and, as was then believed, cut off from Pope's main army. Riding all night, making his way cautiously along, Baker passed through the entire Confederate army, and at daylight had reached Banks.

Waiting only for a response to the message, the despatch bearer remounted his horse and started the return trip to Washington in broad daylight. For a time he eluded the Confederates, but finally, as he attempted to pass between certain lines, he was seen, and a party of cavalrymen started in pursuit of him. In spite of the distance traveled, his horse

CAVALRY SCOUTS NEAR GETTYSBURG—1863

Nothing could illustrate better than this vivid photograph of scouts at White's house, near Gettysburg, a typical episode in the life of a cavalry scout. The young soldier and his companions are evidently stopping for directions, or for a drink of water or milk. The Pennsylvania farmers were hospitable. The man of the family has come to the front gate. His empty right sleeve seems to betoken an old soldier, greeting old friends, and asking for news from the front. The lady in her hoop-skirt remains on the porch with her little boy. His chubby legs are visible beneath his frock, and he seems to be hanging back in some awe of the troopers who are but boys themselves. The lady's hair is drawn down around her face after the fashion of the day, and the whole picture is redolent of the stirring times of '63.

raced away at a speed that soon left a number of the cavalry-men in the rear. Finally, the number of pursuers dwindled to three, and the courier, crossing the brow of a small hill, turned his horse into the woods bordering the turnpike.

The ruse was successful, and the three Confederate cav-alrymen dashed on down the hill. A short distance farther along one of the horsemen abandoned the chase and started to return. As he came abreast of Stanton's courier, a movement of Baker's horse attracted the Confederate's attention and he stopped. The cavalryman saw the courier and started to cover him with his rifle, but Baker was prepared. The Federal's revolver cracked, and the Southerner fell from his saddle.

The other Confederates had given up the chase and were returning when they heard the shot. They rushed back in time to see Baker's steed galloping across an open field to reach the road in front of them, and dashed to intercept him. The Federal was the first to reach the road, and again the pur-suit commenced. Baker turned into the fields, and with the pursuers close behind him started a last race for Bull Run.

The despatch bearer's horse was panting and exhausted, but, with the grit of a blooded racer it struggled on, holding the pursuers almost at the same distance. With a final dash Baker reached the bank, leaped into the stream and started for the opposite shore. The creek was little more than twelve yards wide at that point and the horse soon reached the other side, but there a steep bank several feet high confronted it, and it could not climb out. With revolver ready the courier waited, prepared to offer his last resistance, when a shot rang out. It was the pickets of the Federal army firing on the Confed-erates, who abandoned their pursuit at the first shot. The messenger made his way into Centreville, and mounting an-other horse dashed on toward Washington.

It was late afternoon when he delivered the messages from Banks to the Secretary. In twenty-four hours the cou-rier had ridden nearly one hundred miles.

A CHANGE OF BASE—THE CAVALRY SCREEN

This photograph of May 30, 1864, shows the Federal cavalry in actual operation of a most important func-
tion—the "screening" of the army's movements. The troopers are guarding the evacuation of Port Royal
on the Rappahannock, May 30, 1864. After the reverse to the Union arms at Spottsylvania, Grant ordered the change of base from the Rappahannock to McClellan's former starting-point, White House on
the Pamunkey. The control of the waterways, combined with Sheridan's efficient use of the cavalry, made
this an easy matter. Torbert's division encountered Gordon's brigade of Confederate cavalry at Hanover-
town and drove it in the direction of Hanover Court House. Gregg's division moved up to this line; Russell's division of infantry encamped near the river-crossing in support, and behind the mask thus formed
the Army of the Potomac crossed the Pamunkey on May 28th unimpeded. Gregg was then ordered to reconnoiter towards Mechanicsville, and after a severe fight at Hawes' shop he succeeded (with the assistance of
Custer's brigade) in driving Hampton's and Fitzhugh Lee's cavalry divisions and Butler's brigade from the
field. Although the battle took place immediately in front of the Federal infantry, General Meade declined
to put the latter into action, and the battle was won by the cavalry alone. It was not to be the last time.

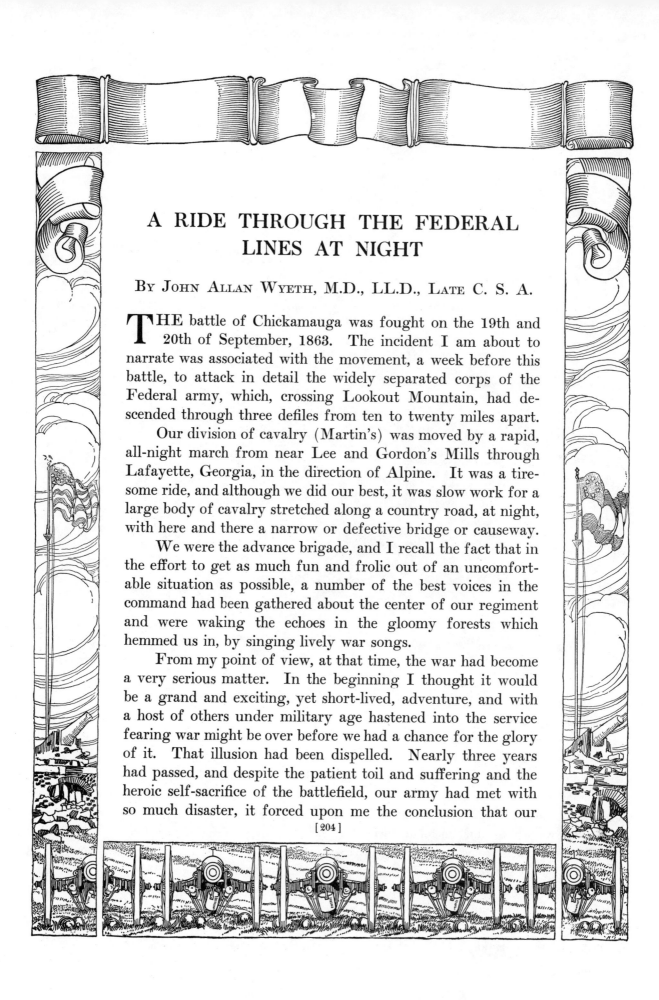

A RIDE THROUGH THE FEDERAL LINES AT NIGHT

By John Allan Wyeth, M.D., LL.D., Late C. S. A.

THE battle of Chickamauga was fought on the 19th and 20th of September, 1863. The incident I am about to narrate was associated with the movement, a week before this battle, to attack in detail the widely separated corps of the Federal army, which, crossing Lookout Mountain, had descended through three defiles from ten to twenty miles apart.

Our division of cavalry (Martin's) was moved by a rapid, all-night march from near Lee and Gordon's Mills through Lafayette, Georgia, in the direction of Alpine. It was a tiresome ride, and although we did our best, it was slow work for a large body of cavalry stretched along a country road, at night, with here and there a narrow or defective bridge or causeway.

We were the advance brigade, and I recall the fact that in the effort to get as much fun and frolic out of an uncomfortable situation as possible, a number of the best voices in the command had been gathered about the center of our regiment and were waking the echoes in the gloomy forests which hemmed us in, by singing lively war songs.

From my point of view, at that time, the war had become a very serious matter. In the beginning I thought it would be a grand and exciting, yet short-lived, adventure, and with a host of others under military age hastened into the service fearing war might be over before we had a chance for the glory of it. That illusion had been dispelled. Nearly three years had passed, and despite the patient toil and suffering and the heroic self-sacrifice of the battlefield, our army had met with so much disaster, it forced upon me the conclusion that our

THE EVACUATION OF PORT ROYAL NEARLY COMPLETED

This photograph, taken shortly after the one preceding, witnesses how quickly an army accomplishes its movements. The pontoon-bridge leading out to the boats has been practically cleared; all but a few of the group of cavalrymen have ridden away, and the transports are whistling "all aboard," as can plainly be seen from the sharp jets of steam. A few of the cavalry remain with the headquarters wagon which stands near the head of the pontoon. Sterner work awaits the troopers after this peaceful maneuver. Grant needs every man to screen his infantry in its attempt to outflank the brilliantly maneuvered army of Lee.

struggle was hopeless, and that if we fought on as we had determined to do, death was the inevitable end. That was my conviction, and I believe it accounts for the fact that I volunteered to go on the errand which I undertook that night.

About two o'clock word was passed down from the head of the column to stop the singing, and for the entire column to move in silence. When we heard the order, we knew we were coming close to the foe. About four o'clock we were again halted, and another message was started at the head of the column and came back down the line in a low tone, for it was the custom on night marches, on account of the darkness and the crowded condition of the roadway, to transmit orders in this fashion. An aide or courier could not get through the crowded highway or ride through the thick underbrush and woods on either side. The message was, in effect, a call for a volunteer to go on a special errand.

My messmate, Lieutenant Jack Weatherley, who was killed soon after at Big Shanty, rode with me to the head of the column where, in the darkness, I made out a number of men, presumably officers and aides, some mounted and some on the ground. The general in command—Wheeler or Martin—asked if I were willing to go inside the foe's lines. I replied I would go provided I could wear my uniform, but not as a spy. He said: " You can go as you are. I want you to find a detachment of cavalry which has been sent around the right of the enemy's lines, and which by this time should be in their rear, about opposite our present position. It is important that they be found and ordered not to attack, but to rejoin this column by the route which they have already traveled. In order to reach them," he added, "you will proceed upon a road which leads through the enemy's lines, and should bring you in contact with their pickets about one mile from this point."

The message was entirely verbal. I carried nothing but one army six-shooter. Lieutenant Weatherley, Colonel Hambrick, in command of our regiment at the time, and a guide

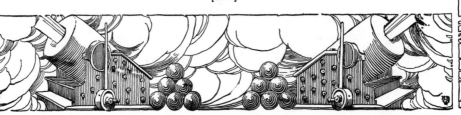

COURIERS AT BEVERLY HOUSE—WARREN'S HEADQUARTERS AT
SPOTSYLVANIA

The couriers doing duty before this farmhouse, headquarters of General G. K.
Warren, are kept riding day and night at breakneck speed. The Fifth Army
Corps, of which he was in command, occupied a position northwest of Spotsylvania Court House on the right of the Federal line, where it remained from May
9th to May 13th. On the evening of May 10th Warren made two assaults on the
position at his front, at a loss of six thousand men. Again, on the 12th, the dogged
Grant persisted in his hammering tactics and ordered heavy assaults at different
points. The Federal loss on that day was approximately seven thousand men
all told. For another week Grant made partial attacks all along the line,
but Lee's veterans withstood every onset. In two weeks Grant lost thirty-
six thousand men. The Fifth Corps bore the brunt of much of the heavy
work. One can imagine with what rapidity the couriers gathered around
Beverly's house wore out their horses in transmitting all-important commands.

accompanied me a few hundred yards down the road. As I started, our colonel said: "This is an important matter, and I hope you will succeed. If you do, I will see that you have a furlough for as long a period as you wish."

The officers soon left me, and the guide accompanied me half a mile further to where the road forked. He indicated the route I should travel which was to the right, as we were going, and then telling me that the Federal pickets were at a point half a mile beyond, he turned back. By this time, it must have been nearly five o'clock.

To the normal human being in times of peace and quiet, the love of life is so natural and so strong that it is difficult to appreciate, until one has passed into and through it, that strange and unusual mental condition in which the value of existence becomes a minor consideration. I look back upon this occasion as the one supreme moment when I came nearest to the elimination of every selfish consideration from the motive with which I was then actuated. I do not overstate the case in saying that death was preferable to life with failure in the accomplishment of my errand.

I had determined, if halted, to ride over every obstacle at full speed, and not to fire my pistol unless in dire extremity, although I had taken it from the holster and had it cocked and ready for quick use. I was riding a splendid horse, strong, swift, and mettlesome, and so alert that nothing escaped his quick observation.

I have no means of knowing how far I had gone, probably half a mile or more, when suddenly I felt my horse check himself as if he were about to change his gait. This movement told me that he had seen something more than the ordinary inanimate object. At the same instant he lifted his head, and in such a knowing way, that I was convinced the moment had come, and that the Federal outposts were here. Without waiting to be halted, I tightened the reins, and crouching down close to the saddle and the horse's neck, touched him with the spurs, and

A COURIER AT HEADQUARTERS

Located as they were near the Orange and Alexandria Railroad and at times between the hostile lines, the dwellings near Fairfax Court House passed time and again from the hands of one army to the other. The home in this photograph was used at different times by General Beauregard and General McClellan as headquarters. Even now a Union orderly is waiting to dash off on one of the powerful chargers. The assigning of troopers to such duties as these was part of the system which crippled the Federal cavalry till it passed under the control of efficient and aggressive Sheridan. The details of the picture indicate a hurried departure of the former occupants. The house itself is a fine example of the old Colonial Southern architecture—white columns in front of red brick. The white stucco has fallen away in places from the brick of the columns—a melancholy appearance for a home.

HORSES THAT CARRIED THE ORDERS OF THE GENERAL-IN-CHIEF

Crack horses were a first requisite for Grant's staff, escort, and couriers. This photograph shows several at Bethseda Church, the little Virginia meeting-house where the staff had halted the day before Cold Harbor. The staff consisted of fourteen officers only, and was not larger than that of some division commanders. Brigadier-General John A. Rawlins was the chief. Grant's instructions to his staff showed the value that he placed upon celerity and the overcoming of delays in communicating orders. He urged his

WAITING ON GRANT AT BETHESDA CHURCH, JUNE, 1864

officers to discuss his orders with him freely whenever it was possible in the course of an engagement or battle, to learn his views as fully as possible, and in great emergencies, where there was no time to communicate with headquarters, to act on their own initiative along the lines laid down by him without his specific orders. The result was an eager, confident, hard-riding staff that stopped at no danger, whether to horse or man. What was even more important, its members did not hesitate to assume responsibility.

AN ESCORT THAT MADE HISTORY

These men and boys formed part of the escort of General Grant during the Appomattox campaign. The same companies (B, F, and K of the Fifth United States Cavalry, under Captain Julius W. Mason) were with him at the fall of Petersburg. Perhaps they won this high distinction by their intrepid charge at Gaines' Mill, when they lost fifty-five of the two hundred and twenty men who participated. With such gallant troopers on guard, the North felt reassured as to the safety of its general-in-chief. The little boy

MEN OF THE FIFTH "REGULAR" CAVALRY

buglers, in the very forefront of the making of American history, stand with calm and professional bearing. Although but fifteen and sixteen years old, they rode with the troopers, and not less bravely. One boy of similar age was severely wounded in one of the numerous fights between Stuart and the Second United States Cavalry near Gettysburg. His captain, whom he was faithfully following, left him for dead upon the field. Many years after the young man sent the captain his photograph to prove that he was whole and sound.

he bounded forward like the wind. His clear vision was not at fault, for as I flew by, I saw two men leap up in front of me from the edge of the roadway and jump into the shadows of the woods and undergrowth at one side. They said something to me, and I replied, but my excitement was so intense, expecting every moment the crack of their rifles, that no part of the picture which flashed through my mind remains clearly registered except the forms of two men and the swift scurry of the horse.

Fortunately they did not fire. It may be that they felt something of the excitement and fright I was experiencing, but more than likely they were drowsy or asleep, and the soft, sandy road enabled me to approach them so closely without being heard (for in the darkness they could not have seen farther than a few feet), that they were taken by surprise, and moreover, they may have thought I was a Federal picket, since I was riding into their lines. In any event, in less time than it takes to tell it, I had scurried away beyond their vision and out of range of their guns. Although I believed a large body of Federals was on either side of the road, I was riding along at such a rapid gait, that in the darkness I saw no sign of troops. I cannot even now estimate how far I went at the speed I was making—probably two or three miles. I know I had slowed up, and was riding again at a canter when daylight came, and with it I noticed in the valley below a cloud of dust not more than half a mile away. This told me of the moving cavalry, and in a few minutes more I had the great good fortune of riding into the column I was sent to intercept.

A few days after the battle of Chickamauga, all of the good mounts in the cavalry were organized to cross the Tennessee River and break up General Rosecrans' communications, and I went with this flying column. We took the great wagon train in the Sequatchie valley on the 2d of October, and on the 4th I was captured and taken to the military prison at Camp Morton, Indiana, where I remained until the latter part of February, 1865.

CHAPTER

NINE

———

CAVALRY BATTLES
AND CHARGES

———

ON THE WAY TO THE BATTLE OF GETTYSBURG
COMPANY L, SECOND "REGULARS"

The "Second" fought in the reserve brigade under General Merritt, during the second day of the battle. The leading figures in the picture are First-Sergeant Painter and First-Lieutenant Dewees. Few photographs show cavalry thus, in column.

THE WAGONS WITH THE RIGHT OF WAY

The ammunition-train had the right of way over everything else in the army, short of actual guns and soldiers, when there was any possibility of a fight. The long, cumbrous lines of commissary wagons were forced to draw off into the fields to the right and left of the road, or scatter any way they could, to make way for the ammunition-train. Its wagons were always marked, and were supposed to be kept as near the troops as possible. Soldiers could go without food for a day or two if necessary; but it might spell defeat

AMMUNITION-TRAIN OF THE THIRD DIVISION, CAVALRY CORPS

and capture to lack ammunition for an hour. This is a photograph of the ammunition wagons of the Third Cavalry Division commanded by General James H. Wilson. They are going into bivouac for the night. The wagons on the right are being formed in a semi-circle, and one of the escort has already dismounted. A led mule is attached to the wagon on the right, for even mule power is fallible, and if one dies in the traces he must be promptly replaced. The men with these trains often held the fate of armies in their hands.

THE BATTLE–LINE—AN ENTIRE CAVALRY REGIMENT IN FORMATION

This stirring picture shows some of the splendid cavalry that was finally developed in the North arrayed in battle-line. Thus they looked before the bugle sounded the charge. One can almost imagine them breaking into a trot, increasing gradually to a gallop, and finally, within a score of yards of the Confederates' roaring guns, into a mad dash that carried them in clusters flashing with sabers through the struggling, writhing line. This regiment is the Thirteenth New York Cavalry, organized June 20, 1863. Two weeks after the regiment was organized these men were patroling the rear of the Army of the Potomac at Gettysburg. The following month they were quelling the draft riots in New York, and thereafter they were engaged

THE THIRTEENTH NEW YORK CAVALRY DRILLING NEAR WASHINGTON

in pursuing the redoubtable and evanescent Mosby, and keeping a watchful eye on Washington. They participated in many minor engagements in the vicinity of the Capital, and lost 128 enlisted men and officers. The photograph is proof enough that they were a well-drilled body of men. The ranks are straight and unbroken, and the company officers are keeping their proper distances. The colonel, to the extreme right in the foreground, has good reason to sit proudly erect. Note the white-horse troop in the rear, where the war chargers can be seen gracefully arching their necks. This is a triumph of wet-plate photography. Only by the highest skill could such restless animals as horses be caught with the camera of '65.

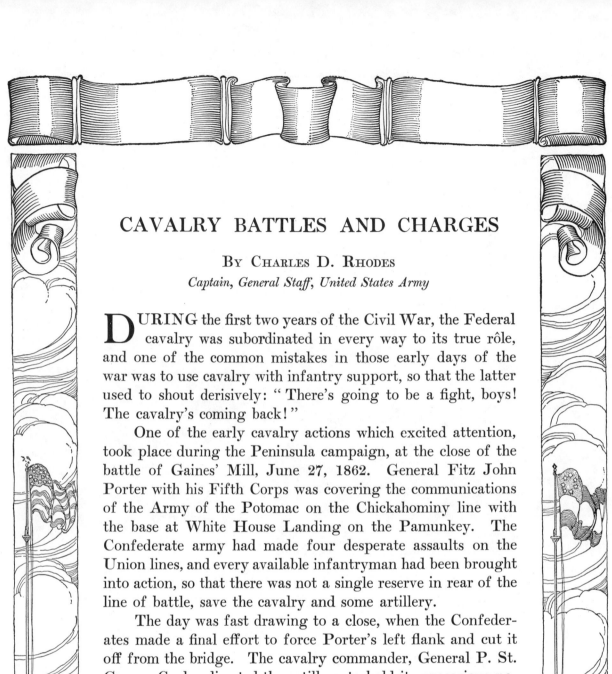

CAVALRY BATTLES AND CHARGES

By Charles D. Rhodes
Captain, General Staff, United States Army

DURING the first two years of the Civil War, the Federal cavalry was subordinated in every way to its true rôle, and one of the common mistakes in those early days of the war was to use cavalry with infantry support, so that the latter used to shout derisively: "There's going to be a fight, boys! The cavalry's coming back!"

One of the early cavalry actions which excited attention, took place during the Peninsula campaign, at the close of the battle of Gaines' Mill, June 27, 1862. General Fitz John Porter with his Fifth Corps was covering the communications of the Army of the Potomac on the Chickahominy line with the base at White House Landing on the Pamunkey. The Confederate army had made four desperate assaults on the Union lines, and every available infantryman had been brought into action, so that there was not a single reserve in rear of the line of battle, save the cavalry and some artillery.

The day was fast drawing to a close, when the Confederates made a final effort to force Porter's left flank and cut it off from the bridge. The cavalry commander, General P. St. George Cooke, directed the artillery to hold its precarious position, and ordered Captain Whiting, commanding the Fifth United States Cavalry, to charge the advancing infantry.

Numbering but two hundred and twenty sabers, the little force moved out under heavy fire, and striking the foe intact with a portion of its line, the charging troopers were only stopped by the woods at the bottom of the slope. The casualties of the charging force were fifty-five, with twenty-four

GENERAL

PHILIP ST. GEORGE

COOKE

COMMANDING

THE FIRST GREAT

FEDERAL

CAVALRY CHARGE OF THE

CIVIL WAR

Had it not been for General Philip St. George Cooke and his cavalry, Major-General Fitz-John Porter and his staff would not be enjoying the luxuries portrayed in the lower photograph, taken nineteen days after the battle of Gaines' Mill. The typical old-time Virginia cook, and the pleasant camping-ground on the banks of the river, suggest little of the deadly peril that faced the Federals June 27, 1862. The line of battle formed the arc of a circle, almost parallel to the Chickahominy. During the day the Confederate forces made four desperate assaults on the Union lines, and every available infantryman was brought into action. The only reserve on the left of the line was the cavalry and considerable artillery. As night was falling, the Confederates made a final effort to force the left flank and cut it off from the bridge across the Chickahominy. The artillery was directed to maintain its position, and General Cooke ordered Captain Whiting, commanding the Fifth United States Cavalry, to charge with his troopers. The little force of 220 sabers charged the advancing lines of Confederate infantry; a portion of the line struck the enemy intact and were stopped only by the woods at the bottom of the slope. Their casualties were fifty-five men—but under cover of the charge the artillery was safely withdrawn, and the sacrifice was well worth the results attained.

GENERAL FITZ–JOHN PORTER AND STAFF, JUNE, 1862

horses killed—a sacrifice well worth the results attained. Of this action, the Comte de Paris wrote fifteen years later: " The sacrifice of some of the bravest of the cavalry certainly saved a part of the artillery, as did, on a larger scale, the Austrian cavalry on the evening of Sadowa."

General Wesley Merritt, U. S. A., one of the ablest cavalry officers of his time, who was present at Gaines' Mill as an aide-de-camp to General Cooke, thus described this affair: *

During the early part of this battle the Union army held its ground and gained from time to time some material success. But it was only temporary. In the afternoon the writer of this, by General Cooke's direction, reported at the headquarters of the commanding general on the field, Fitz John Porter, and during his attendance there heard read a despatch from General McClellan congratulating Porter on his success. It closed with directions to drive the rebels off the field, and to take from them their artillery. At the time this despatch was being read, the enemy were forcing our troops to the rear. Hasty preparations were made for the retreat of the headquarters, and everything was in the most wretched confusion. No orders could be obtained, and I returned to my chief reporting the condition of affairs. It was apparent from movements in our front that the Confederates would make a supreme effort to force the left flank of Fitz John Porter's command, and cutting it off from the bridge over the Chickahominy, sever it from McClellan's army, and capture or disperse it.

It was growing late. Both armies were exhausted by the exertions of the day. But the prize at hand was well worth the effort, and the Confederates with renewed strength were fighting to make their victory complete. The Union cavalry commander seized the situation at a glance. The cavalry had been posted behind a plateau on the left bank of the Chickahominy, with ground to its front free of obstacles and suitable for cavalry action. To the right front of the cavalry the batteries of the reserve artillery were stationed. . . .

The events of that day at Gaines' Mill are pictured on the mind of the writer of this imperfect sketch as on a never fading photograph. The details of the battle are as vivid as if they had occurred yesterday. As

* Journal United States Cavalry Association, March, 1895.

MECHANICSVILLE, IN 1862, WHERE THE TROUBLE STARTED

At this sleepy Virginia hamlet the series of engagements that preceded the struggles along the Chickahominy in front of Richmond began. Early in June, 1862, as the Army of the Potomac extended its wings along both banks of the Chickahominy, Mechanicsville fell into its possession. There was a struggle at Beaver Dam Creek and on the neighboring fields, the defenders finally retreating in disorder down the pike and over the bridge toward Richmond, only three and a half miles away. The pickets of the opposing armies watched the bridge with jealous eyes till the Union lines were withdrawn on the 26th of June, and the Confederates retook the village.

OFFICERS OF THE FIFTH UNITED STATES CAVALRY, IN THE FAMOUS CHARGE

the Confederates came rushing across the open in front of the batteries, bent on their capture, one battery nearest our position was seen to limber up with a view to retreating. I rode hurriedly, by direction of General Cooke, to its captain, Robinson, and ordered him to unlimber and commence firing at short range, canister. He complied willingly, and said, as if in extenuation of his intended withdrawal, that he had no support. I told him the cavalry were there, and would support his and the other batteries. The rapid fire at short range of the artillery, and the daring charge of the cavalry in the face of an exhausted foe, prevented, without doubt, the enemy seizing the Chickahominy bridge and the capture or dispersion of Fitz John Porter's command. No farther advance was made by the Confederates, and the tired and beaten forces of Porter withdrew to the farther side of the Chickahominy and joined the Army of the Potomac in front of Richmond. The cavalry withdrew last as a rear guard, after having furnished torch and litter bearers to the surgeons of our army, who did what was possible to care for our wounded left on the field.

But it was not until a year later (March 17, 1863), at Kelly's Ford on the Rappahannock, that the Union cavalry first gained real confidence in itself and in its leaders.

In this engagement, following the forcing of the river crossing, two regiments of cavalry dismounted, with a section of artillery, and held the foe in front, while mounted regiments rolled up the Confederate flanks; their entire line was thrown into confusion and finally driven from the field.

The decisive cavalry battle at Brandy Station, or Beverly Ford, on June 9th, following, having for its object a reconnaissance in force of the Confederate troops on the Culpeper-Fredericksburg road, was the first great cavalry combat of the war. It virtually "made" the Union cavalry.

Buford's division of the Federal cavalry corps accompanied by Ames' infantry brigade, had been directed to cross the Rappahannock at Beverly Ford, and move by way of St. James' Church to Brandy Station. A second column composed of Gregg's and Duffié's divisions, with Russell's infantry

MAJOR CHARLES JARVIS WHITING

Major (then Captain) Whiting was the man who led the charge of the Fifth United States Cavalry upon the advancing Confederate infantry ordered by General Philip St. George Cooke at Gaines' Mill, June 27, 1862. He could entertain no hope of victory. The Confederates were already too near to allow of an effective charge. It was practically a command to die in order to check the Confederate column until infantry reenforcements could be rushed forward to save some imperiled batteries. Over twenty-five per cent. of the troopers who rode through the Confederate lines were killed, wounded, or missing.

GAINES' MILL

From this rural Virginia spot the battle of June 27th took its name. At the close of that fearful day the building fell into use as a hospital. It was later burned during a Federal raid, and nothing but the gaunt walls remain. The skull that lies in front of the mill evidently belonged to one of those brave cavalrymen who gave up their lives to save their comrades. He may have received a soldier's hasty burial, but it was by no means unusual for the heavy rains to wash away the shallow covering of soil, and to have exposed to view the remains of the men who had gone to their reward.

brigade, was to cross the river at Kelly's Ford—Gregg to push on by way of Mount Dumpling to Brandy Station, and Duffié to proceed to Stevensburg. By a strange coincidence, that brilliant cavalry leader, Stuart, planned on the same day to cross the Rappahannock at Beverly and the upper fords, for the purpose of diverting the attention of the Army of the Potomac from General Lee's northward dash into Maryland.

Under cover of a heavy fog, Buford's column crossed the river at four o'clock in the morning, surprising the Southern outposts and nearly capturing the Confederate artillery. Here, in spite of superior numbers, the Union commander, General Pleasonton, formed his cavalry in line of battle, covering the ford in less than an hour, but he could make no perceptible movement forward until Gregg's guns on the extreme left had made a general advance possible.

The Confederates fell rapidly back, and the headquarters of Stuart's chief of artillery, with all his papers and Lee's order for the intended movement, were captured. A junction was soon formed with Gregg, and with heavy losses on both sides, the foe was pushed back to Fleetwood Ridge. Of this part of the action General Stuart's biographer says:

A part of the First New Jersey Cavalry came thundering down the narrow ridge, striking McGregor's and Hart's unsupported batteries in the flank, and riding through and between guns and caissons from right to left, but were met by a determined hand-to-hand contest from the cannoneers with pistols, sponge-staffs, and whatever else came handy to fight with. The charge was repulsed by artillerists alone, not a single friendly trooper being within reach of us.

On Fleetwood Ridge the Confederate infantry rallied to the support of Stuart's cavalry, and the object of the reconnaissance having been gained, a general withdrawal of the Union cavalry was ordered, Gregg by way of the ford at Rappahannock Bridge, and Buford by Beverly Ford. But as the order was about to be executed, the Confederates fiercely

A BRIDGE OVER THE MUDDY CHICKAHOMINY—1862

This is a photograph of the insignificant stream that figured so largely in the calculations of the opposing generals before Richmond. Under the effect of the almost tropical rains, in a day luxuriant meadows would become transformed into lakes, and surging floods appear where before were stagnant pools. Thus it became doubtful in June whether the struggling Union army could depend upon the little bridges. It was said by some of the Union engineers that it was only the weight of the troops passing over them that held some in place. One was swept away immediately after a column had crossed. The muddy banks show more plainly than words what the little Chickahominy could do when it was thoroughly aroused.

attacked the Union right, and the most serious fighting of the day resulted. At four o'clock in the afternoon, a large Confederate infantry force being reported at Brandy Station, General Pleasonton began a general withdrawal of the Union cavalry, a movement which was executed in good order and completed by seven o'clock in the evening without molestation by the Confederates.

This great cavalry battle lasted for over ten hours, and was preeminently a mounted combat, the charges and counter-charges of the opposing horsemen being of the most desperate character. During the day, the First New Jersey Cavalry, alone, made six regimental charges, besides a number of smaller ones; the fighting and charging of the regular and Sixth Pennsylvania Cavalry was kept up for over twelve hours; and the other regiments were almost equally engaged through the eventful day.

Commenting on this defeat of the Confederate cavalry at Brandy Station, the *Richmond Examiner* of that period said:

The surprise of this occasion was the most complete that has occurred. The Confederate cavalry was carelessly strewn over the country, with the Rappahannock only between it and an enemy who has already proven his enterprise to our cost. It is said that their camp was supposed to be secure because the Rappahannock was not supposed to be fordable at the point where it actually was forded. What! Do the Yankees then know more about this river than our own soldiers, who have done nothing but ride up and down its banks for the past six months?

Brandy Station was really the turning-point in the evolution of the Federal cavalry, which had heretofore been dominated by a sense of its own inferiority to Stuart's bold horsemen. Even the Confederate writer, McClellan, has this to say of Brandy Station and its effect on the *morale* of the Union cavalry:

Up to this time, confessedly inferior to the Southern horsemen, they gained on this day that confidence in themselves and their commanders

REUNION OF OFFICERS

OF THE THIRD AND FOURTH PENNSYLVANIA

CAVALRY

The soldiers in a great war-game make merry while they can. This photograph shows the officers of the Third and Fourth Pennsylvania Cavalry picknicking on the banks of the river at Westover Landing in August, 1862. The Fourth Pennsylvania had taken part in the actions on the upper Chickahominy hardly a month before, when the Fifth United States Cavalry made their daring charge at Gaines' Mill. Both regiments had been active in the Peninsula campaign, although the Third Pennsylvania had been split up into detachments and on headquarters duty, and they were to be together on the bloody days at Antietam the middle of the following month. They have snatched a brief moment together now, and are hopefully pledging each other long lives. Neither the Union nor the Confederacy realized that the war was to stretch out over four terrible years.

which enabled them to contest so fiercely the subsequent battlefields of June, July, and October.

Passing by without comment the splendid stand of Buford's dismounted troops covering the approaches to the town of Gettysburg, in which less than three thousand cavalrymen and Calef's battery made possible the occupation by the delayed Union army of the dominating position along Cemetery Ridge and the Round Tops, the desperate battles of the cavalry on the right and left flanks at Gettysburg, are history.

On the Union left flank, Pleasonton had ordered Kilpatrick to move from Emmittsburg with his entire force to prevent a Confederate turning movement on the Round Tops, and, if practicable, to attack the Confederate flank and rear. Late on July 3, 1863, the reserve cavalry brigade under Merritt moved up and took position to the left of Kilpatrick. Custer's brigade had been detached to report to Gregg on the Union right. The fight which ensued on this third and last day of the great battle, was severe in the extreme.

Merritt's position on the left caused the Confederate general, Law, to detach a large force from his main line to protect his flank and rear. This so weakened the Confederate line in front of General Farnsworth, that Kilpatrick ordered the latter to charge the center of Law's line of infantry. The ground was most unfavorable for a mounted charge, being broken, covered with stone, and intersected by fences and stone walls.

Writing of this charge in "Battles and Leaders of the Civil War," Captain H. C. Parsons of the First Vermont Cavalry, says:

I was near Kilpatrick when he impetuously gave the order to Farnsworth to make the last charge. Farnsworth spoke with emotion: "General, do you mean it? Shall I throw my handful of men over rough ground, through timber, against a brigade of infantry? The First Vermont has already been fought half to pieces; these are too good men to kill." Kilpatrick said: "Do you refuse to obey my orders? If you are afraid to lead this charge, I will lead it."

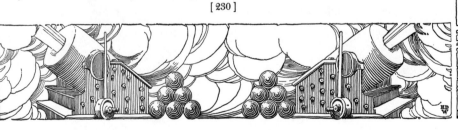

HELD BY THE CAVALRY AT ANTIETAM

The Federal cavalry bore its share of the work on the bloodiest single day of the war, September 17, 1862, at Antietam. At this bridge on the Keedysville road the gallant cavalry leader General Pleasonton had a most important part to play in the plan of attack on the Confederate positions west of Antietam Creek. In spite of galling cross-fire from the Confederate batteries, Pleasonton threw forward his mounted skirmishers, who held their ground until Tidball's batteries of the regular artillery were advanced piece by piece across the bridge. Opening with canister, the guns routed the sharpshooters, and soon four batteries were in position on the ridge beyond the creek. Here they held their ground till nightfall, at times running short of ammunition, but giving needed aid to Sumner's advance to their right and in Burnside's desperate struggle to cross the bridge below to their left. To the left of the bridge where Pleasonton's successful crossing on the morning of the 17th was accomplished stands Newcomers' Mill. On the ridge above, the cavalry and artillery held their positions, keeping open a way for reenforcements. These were much needed when the ammunition of the batteries ran low. More regular troops were sent forward, together with two more batteries from Sykes' division, under command of Captain Dryer. These reenforcements threw themselves splendidly into the fight. The cavalry had scored again.

NEWCOMERS' MILL ON ANTIETAM CREEK

Farnsworth rose in his stirrups—he looked magnificent in his passion—and cried, "Take that back!" Kilpatrick returned his defiance, but, soon repenting, said, "I did not mean it; forget it."

For a moment there was silence, when Farnsworth spoke calmly, "General, if you order the charge, I will lead it, but you must take the responsibility."

I did not hear the low conversation that followed, but as Farnsworth turned away, he said, "I will obey your order." Kilpatrick said earnestly, "I take the responsibility."

The charge was a daring and spectacular one. The First West Virginia, and Eighteenth Pennsylvania moved through the woods first, closely followed by the First Vermont and Fifth New York Cavalry, all mounted, and drove the foe before them until heavy stone walls and fences were reached. Two regiments cleared the obstacles, charged a second line of infantry, and were stopped by another stone wall, covering a third line of infantry. The First West Virginia was for a time entirely surrounded, but succeeded in cutting its way back with a loss of but five killed and four wounded, bringing with it a number of prisoners. When the body of Farnsworth was afterwards recovered, it was found to have received five mortal wounds.

General W. M. Graham, U. S. A. (Retired), says: *

The following is the account of Farnsworth's death as seen by a Confederate officer and by him related to me in the winter of 1876–77 at Columbia, South Carolina: I was introduced to Captain Bachman, who commanded the "Hampton Legion Battery," with which I was engaged (Battery K, First United States Artillery), at Gettysburg on July 3d. Naturally our conversation drifted to the war, and he remarked: "One of the most gallant incidents of the war witnessed by me was a cavalry charge at the battle of Gettysburg, on July 3d, made by a General Farnsworth of the Yankee army. He led his brigade, riding well ahead of his men, in a charge against my battery and the infantry supports; we were so filled with admiration of his bravery that we were reluctant

*Journal Military Service Institution for March, 1910, p. 343.

DUFFIÉ, WHO LED THE CHARGE AT KELLY'S FORD

Led by Colonel Alfred Duffié, the dashing cavalryman whose portrait is above, Federal cavalry had its first opportunity to measure itself in a real trial of strength with the hardy horsemen of the South at Kelly's Ford on March 17, 1863. Brigadier-General William W. Averell, in command of the Second Division, Cavalry Corps, Army of the Potomac, received orders to cross the river with 3,000 cavalry and six pieces of artillery, and attack and destroy the forces of General Fitzhugh Lee, supposed to be near Culpeper Court House. Starting from Morrisville with about 2,100 men, General Averell found the crossing at Kelly's Ford obstructed by abatis and defended by sharpshooters. The First Rhode Island Cavalry effected a crossing, and the battle-line was formed on the farther side of the river. Colonel Duffié on the Federal left flank, and Colonel McIntosh on the right led almost simultaneous charges. The entire body of Confederate cavalry was driven back in confusion. The Confederates made another stand three-quarters of a mile farther back in the woods, but when the Federal cavalry finally withdrew, their killed and wounded were 78, and those of the Confederates 133.

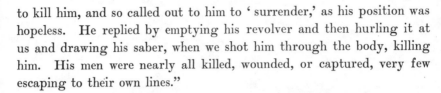

to kill him, and so called out to him to ' surrender,' as his position was hopeless. He replied by emptying his revolver and then hurling it at us and drawing his saber, when we shot him through the body, killing him. His men were nearly all killed, wounded, or captured, very few escaping to their own lines."

General Graham adds, " Bachman was a fine fellow who, like *all* those who *fought* on each side, had buried all bitterness of feeling."

All things considered, it seems wonderful that these four regiments did not suffer more severely (sixty-five casualties out of three hundred men in the charge). This fact can best be accounted for by the moral effect of the charge, the fearless troopers leaping the obstacles and sabering many of the Confederate infantry in their positions. The Confederate general, Law, said of this:

It was impossible to use our artillery to any advantage, owing to the close quarters of the attacking cavalry with our own men, the leading squadrons forcing their horses up to the very muzzles of the rifles of our infantry.

But while this was taking place on the Federal left flank, a great cavalry battle, fraught with tremendous responsibilities, was being waged on the right flank.

On July 3d, the Second Cavalry Division, under Gregg, had been ordered to the right of the line with orders to make a demonstration against the Confederates. About noon, a despatch reached Gregg that a large body of the Southern cavalry was observed from Cemetery Hill, moving against the right of the Union line. In consequence of this important information, Custer's brigade, which had been ordered back to Kilpatrick's command, was held by Gregg.

This Confederate column moving to the attack was Stuart's cavalry, which, belated by many obstacles, was advancing toward the lines of Ewell's corps. Stuart took position on a ridge, which commanded a wide area of open ground, and

THE HOLLOW SQUARE IN THE CIVIL WAR—A FORMATION USED AT GETTYSBURG

Many authorities doubted that the formation portrayed in this picture was used at the battle of Gettysburg. Not until the meeting of the survivors of the First Corps at Gettysburg in May, 1885, were these doubts finally dispelled. Late in the afternoon of July 1st General Buford had received orders from General Howard to go to General Doubleday's support. Buford's cavalry lay at that time a little west of the cemetery. Though vastly outnumbered by the advancing Confederate infantry, Buford formed his men for the charge. The Confederates immediately set to forming squares in echelon. This consumed time, however, and the respite materially aided in the escape of the First Corps, if it did not save the remnant from capture. Cavalry in the Civil War was not wont to charge unbroken infantry, the latter being better able to withstand a cavalry charge than cavalry itself. In such a charge the cavalry ranks become somewhat blended, and arrive in clusters on the opposing lines. The horses avoid trampling on the fallen and wounded, and jump over them if possible. Buford's threatened charge was a successful ruse.

TWO LEADERS OF THE FEDERAL CAVALRY AT GETTYSBURG

This martial photograph portrays two of the men who prevented the success of the Confederate General Stuart's charge on the third day at Gettysburg, when the tide of battle between the long lines of infantry had been wavering to and fro, and Pickett was advancing on Cemetery Ridge. Had the brilliant Stuart with his veteran cavalry gained the rear of the Federal line, the natural panic following might have been more than sufficient to win the day for the Confederate cause. About noon on July 3d, General Gregg was informed that a large body of Confederate cavalry was moving against the right of the line. General

PLEASONTON AND CUSTER, THREE MONTHS BEFORE THE BATTLE

Gregg held Custer's brigade, which had been ordered back to the left of the line, in order to help meet the attack. The Seventh Michigan Cavalry met the charge of a regiment of W. H. F. Lee's brigade, and this was followed by a charge of the First Michigan, driving back the Confederate line. Then followed counter-charges by the Confederates until a large part of both commands were fighting desperately. In this ter-rible cavalry combat every possible weapon was utilized. This photograph of Pleasonton on the right, who commanded all the cavalry at Gettysburg, and of the dashing Custer, was taken three months before.

SOME OF PLEASONTON'S MEN

AT GETTYSBURG

These men and mere boys stood seriously before the camera. Without a trace of swagger they leaned upon their flashing sabers; yet they had seen all the important cavalry fighting in the East before their final supreme test at Gettysburg. They had fought at Fair Oaks and the Seven Days around Richmond. They had played their part at Kelly's Ford and in the great cavalry battle at Brandy Station. They came to Gettysburg seasoned troopers, with poise and confidence in themselves. On the first day Gregg's Second Cavalry Division, of which they formed part, fought the Second Virginia on foot with carbines. On the second day they were deployed as dismounted skirmishers to meet Stuart's men. The Confederate cavalry leader hoped to charge at the opportune moment when Pickett was advancing, but Pleasonton's men frus-

COMPANY D

THIRD PENNSYLVANIA CAVALRY

trated this attempt. The desperate charges and counter-charges on the Union right on that third decisive day were the fiercest of the entire war. This photograph was taken seven months later at Brandy Station, a few weeks before the Third Pennsylvania went into the Wilderness. Their time intervening since the battle of Gettysburg has been spent scouting and picketing along the Rappahannock, including many a skirmish with their active adversaries. They have had time to spruce up a bit during one of their short rests, but their quiet veteran bearing reflects the scenes they have passed through. Their swords that gleam so brilliantly are the regulation light curved cavalry sabers. With these and all other needed articles of equipment they and most of the Federal cavalry are now thoroughly equipped.

his plan of attack was to engage the Federal troops in his front with sharpshooters, while he moved the Confederate brigades of Jenkins and W. F. H. Lee secretly through the woods in an effort to reach the Union rear. Stuart hoped to strike at the psychological moment when Pickett's famous infantry charge, on the center of the Union line of battle, would engage the entire attention of the Army of the Potomac.

The cavalry combat which followed was probably as desperate and as stubbornly contested as any in which the cavalry took part during the entire period of the war. A mounted charge by a regiment of W. F. H. Lee's brigade, was met by a countercharge of the Seventh Michigan Cavalry, the two regiments meeting face to face on opposite sides of a stone wall, and discharging their carbines point blank. The First Michigan Cavalry, aided by Chester's battery made a charge which, followed by a hand-to-hand fight, drove the Confederate lines back in confusion. Then followed charges and countercharges by each opponent, until a large part of both commands was involved in a general mêlée.

In this terrible cavalry combat every possible weapon was utilized, and after it was over, men were found interlocked in each other's arms, with fingers so firmly imbedded in the flesh as to require force to remove them. The casualties were heavy for both Stuart and Gregg, but the latter was able to stop the Confederate cavalry leader's critical turning movement. Had Stuart with his veteran cavalry been able to strike the rear of the Federal army simultaneously with Pickett's infantry charge in front, the result of this decisive battle of the war might have been different.

On April 4, 1864, General Sheridan assumed command of the cavalry of the Army of the Potomac, and thereafter a new order of things was inaugurated for the Union cavalry in the Eastern theater of operations.

Sheridan insisted that his cavalry should not be separated into fragments, but should be concentrated "to fight the

CAVALRY FROM INDIANA—A FIGHTING REGIMENT AT GETTYSBURG AND ELSEWHERE

Looking at the resolute faces and confident mien of these boys from what was then the far-western State of Indiana, the reader, even of a later generation, understands instantly how it was that the Western cavalry of the Federal army earned such an enviable reputation from '61 to '65. Not only did it protect the fast-spreading Federal frontier in the West; not only did it bear the brunt of the raids conducted by the dashing leaders Grierson, Smith, Wilson, and others, whereby the more southern portions of the Confederacy were cut off from their supplies and deprived of their stores; but States like Indiana also provided several of the most conspicuously gallant regiments that served with the Eastern armies. This Third Indiana, for instance, was busy East and West. At Nashville, at Stone's River, at Chattanooga, at Atlanta, and on Sherman's march to the sea, it did its duty in the West, while six companies of the regiment participated in Buford's stand at Gettysburg.

enemy's cavalry," and in deference to Sheridan's wishes, General Meade promptly relieved the cavalry from much of the arduous picket duty which it was performing at the time. But he gave little encouragement as yet to Sheridan's plans for an *independent* cavalry corps—a corps in fact as well as in name. By the end of July, the Cavalry Corps had succeeded in almost annihilating the Confederate cavalry and had accomplished the destruction of millions of dollars' worth of property useful to the Confederate Government. In all the important movements of the Army of the Potomac, the cavalry had acted as a screen, and by its hostile demonstrations against the Southern flanks and rear, had more than once forced General Lee to detach much-needed troops from his hard-pressed front.

On May 11th, at Yellow Tavern, Sheridan had fought an engagement which gave him complete control of the road to Richmond and resulted in the loss to the Confederates of Generals Stuart and James B. Gordon. Merritt's brigade first entered Yellow Tavern and secured possession of the turnpike. The other Union divisions being brought up, Custer with his own brigade, supported by Chapman's brigade of Wilson's division, made a mounted charge which was brilliantly executed, followed by a dash at the Southern line which received the charge in a stationary position. This charge resulted in the capture of two guns. Then, while Gibbs and Devin forced the Confederate right and center, Gregg charged in the rear and the battle was won.

At Deep Bottom, too, July 28th, occurred a brilliant fight which is worthy of more than passing notice.

The Second United States Cavalry led the advance on the 27th and took the New Market road in the direction of Richmond. When close to the Confederate pickets a dashing charge was made, forcing the foe back rapidly. On the afternoon of the following day the Union cavalry pickets were furiously attacked, and before the leading troops could dismount and conduct the led horses to the rear, an entire brigade of

WHERE THE CAVALRY RESTED—CASTLE MURRAY, NEAR AUBURN, VIRGINIA

In the fall of 1863 the headquarters of the Army of the Potomac were pitched for some days on the Warrentown Railroad near Auburn, Virginia. Near-by lay Dr. Murray's house, called the Castle, a picturesque gray stone edifice, beautifully contrasting with the dark green ivy which had partly overgrown it, and situated in a grove on an eminence known as Rockhill. Here General Pleasonton, commanding the cavalry, had his camp, his tents forming an effective picture when silhouetted by the setting sun against the gray walls of the Castle. At night the green lamps that showed the position of the general's camp would shine mysteriously over the trees, and the band of the Sixth United States Cavalry would make the stone walls echo to its martial music. The cavalry was resting after its desperate encounters at Gettysburg and its fights along the Rappahannock. But there remained much yet for the troopers to do.

Confederate infantry broke from the woods, and with colors flying advanced in splendid alignment across an open field. So closely were the advanced Union troops pressed, that despite the destruction wrought in the Southern ranks by the breech-loading carbines, there was danger of losing the led horses.

The following is quoted from the graphic description of this fight by Lieutenant (afterwards Colonel U. S. V.) William H. Harrison, Second United States Cavalry:

> With a cheer which makes our hearts bound, the First New York Dragoons, the First United States, and the Sixth Pennsylvania on the run, dismount, and form themselves on the shattered lines of the Second and Fifth. A few volleys from our carbines make the line of the enemy's infantry waver, and in an instant the cry is heard along our entire line, "Charge! Charge!" We rush forward, firing as we advance; the Confederate colors fall, and so furious is our charge that the North Carolina brigade breaks in complete rout, leaving three stands of colors, all their killed and wounded, and many prisoners in our hands. The enemy did not renew the fight, and we remained in possession of the field until relieved by our infantry.

It was, however, in the fall of the year (1864) that under Sheridan's brilliant leadership the Union cavalry won its greatest laurels. On September 19th, at Opequon Creek, Sheridan's infantry and cavalry achieved a victory which sent the Confederates under Early "whirling through Winchester," as Sheridan tersely stated in a telegram which electrified the people of the North.

While essentially a battle participated in by all arms, the brilliant part taken by Wilson's division in a mounted charge which gained possession of the Winchester-Berryville turnpike, and the subsequent demoralizing attack of Averell's and Merritt's cavalry divisions on the Confederate rear, had much to do with the Union victory.

The most severe fighting on the part of the cavalry took place in the afternoon. Breckinridge's Confederate corps had

BURNETT'S HOUSE, NEAR COLD HARBOR

A CLOSER VIEW

Three days before these photographs were taken Brigadier-General Alfred T. A. Torbert, with an isolated command of cavalry, was holding the breastworks at Cold Harbor in face of a magnificent attack by a brigade of Confederate infantry. The troopers busy beneath the trees are some of the very men who stood off the long gray lines blazing with fire. In the lower photograph they have moved forward, so that we can study them more closely. They seem quite nonchalant, considering their recent experience, but that is a veteran's way. Burnett's house, here pictured, stood not far from the road leading from Old Church Hotel to Old Cold Harbor. It was along this road that Torbert pursued the Confederates in the afternoon of May 30th, and it was near this house that his division of Sheridan's Cavalry Corps bivouacked that night. The following morning he continued his pursuit, first driving the Confederates into their breastworks at Cold Harbor, and then executing a flank movement to the left, which forced the Southern infantry to fall back three-quarters of a mile farther. Sheridan ordered him to withdraw from this isolated position, and he returned to the scene of his bivouac near Burnett's house.

OLD CHURCH HOTEL NEAR COLD HARBOR

The very attitude of the rough and ready cavalryman with his curved saber shows the new confidence in itself of the Federal cavalry as reorganized by Sheridan in April, 1864. Here the photographer has caught a cavalry detail at one of the typical cross-roads taverns that played so important a part in the Virginia campaigns of that year. So successful is the picture that even the rude lettering "Old Church Hotel" on the quaint, old fashioned swinging sign can be made out. The scene is typical of the times. The reorganized Federal cavalry was proving of the greatest help to Grant in locating the enemy, particularly ahead of the main column as in the case of the fight at Old Church. In Grant's advance toward Richmond from North Anna, Sheridan's cavalry corps served as an advance

FOUR DAYS AFTER THE CAVALRY CLASH OF MAY 30, 1864

guard. Torbert and Gregg with the First and Second Divisions formed the guard for the left flank. On May 27th Torbert crossed the Pamunkey at Hanover Ferry, captured Hanover Town, took part the following day in the sanguinary struggle at Hawes' Shop, and on the 29th picketed the country about Old Church Hotel seen in the picture, and toward Cold Harbor. At 4 P.M. on May 30th, the clash at Old Church took place, and it was necessary to put in General Merritt with the Reserve Brigade. The photograph was taken on June 4th, the day after the battle of Cold Harbor where the Federal loss was so severe. The horses look sleek and well-conditioned in spite of the constant marching and fighting.

fallen back on Winchester, leaving General Early's flank protected by his cavalry, which was successfully attacked by General Devin's Second Brigade and driven in confusion toward Winchester. Then within easy supporting distance of each other, the First Brigade, the Second Brigade, and the Reserve Brigade moved forward without opposition until the open fields near Winchester were reached.

What followed is well described in Lieutenant Harrison's recollections: *

While awaiting in suspense our next movement the enemy's infantry was distinctly seen attempting to change front to meet our anticipated charge. Instantly, and while in the confusion incident to their maneuver, the Second Brigade burst upon them, the enemy's infantry breaking into complete rout and falling back a confused and broken mass.

Immediately after, the Union reserve brigade under the gallant Lowell, formed to the left of the position from which the Second Brigade, under Devin, had just charged. They rode out fearlessly within five hundred yards of the Confederate line of battle, on the left of which, resting on an old earthwork was a two-gun battery. The order was given to charge the line and get the guns. Lieutenant Harrison continues:

At the sound of the bugle we took the trot, the gallop, and then the charge. As we neared their line we were welcomed by a fearful musketry fire, which temporarily confused the leading squadron, and caused the entire brigade to oblique slightly to the right. Instantly, officers cried out, "Forward! Forward!" The men raised their sabers, and responded to the command with deafening cheers. Within a hundred yards of the enemy's line we struck a blind ditch, but crossed it without breaking our front. In a moment we were face to face with the enemy. They stood as if awed by the heroism of the brigade, and in an instant broke in complete rout, our men sabering them as they vainly sought safety in flight.

* Everglade to Cañon, N. Y., 1873.

A CUSTER FAMILY GROUP

Two Union cavalrymen distinguished in the final "Valley" campaigns appear here—George A. Custer and his brother, Thomas W. The lady whose presence adds such charm to the striking group had become Mrs. George A. Custer just before Grant's campaign opened—in February, 1864. The September following, her husband took command of the Third Cavalry Division in Sheridan's army. In April, 1865, he recalled to his men an astonishing record for the division while serving under him. It had captured every piece of artillery that had opened upon it! A worthy brother to such a leader was "Colonel Tom." Having enlisted at sixteen, fought in the West, and served as aide-de-camp on his brother's staff, he became second lieutenant of Co. B., Sixth Michigan Cavalry, in November, 1864, when only nineteen. At Namozine Church, April 2, 1865, he captured a stand of colors, and four days later, at Sailor's Creek, performed the remarkable feat of leaping his horse over the Confederate works, and seizing another stand of colors. His horse was shot under him. He was severely wounded, but refused to go to the rear for treatment until his brother placed him under arrest. This record of two flag-captures is believed to have been held by no other officer in the Federal army. After the war, the daring *sabreur* entered the regular cavalry and rose to the rank of lieutenant-colonel. He served under his brother, and fell at his side on that fatal day in Montana, June 25, 1876—the "Custer Massacre."

The charging force emerged from the fight with two guns, three stands of colors, and over three hundred Confederate prisoners. Altogether there had been six distinct charges by parts of the First Cavalry Division—two by the Second Brigade and one by the First Brigade; one by the Second Brigade and one by the Reserve Brigade against Early's infantry; and one, the final charge, in which all three of the brigades joined. General Custer describes the scene in graphic language:

At this time five brigades of cavalry were moving on parallel lines; most, if not all, of the brigades moved by brigade front, regiments being in parallel columns of squadrons. One continuous and heavy line of skirmishers covered the advance, using only the carbine, while the line of brigades, as they advanced across the country, the bands playing the national airs, presented in the sunlight one moving mass of glittering sabers. This, combined with the various and bright-colored banners and battle-flags, intermingled here and there with the plain blue uniforms of the troops, furnished one of the most inspiring as well as imposing scenes of martial grandeur ever witnessed upon a battlefield.

The Union victory at Opequon came at a time when its moral effect was most needed in the North, and restored the fertile Shenandoah valley to the Union armies, after a long series of humiliating reverses in that granary of the Confederacy.

A month later Custer encountered three brigades of Confederate cavalry under Rosser near Tom's Brook Crossing. Merrit at about the same time struck the cavalry of Lomax and Johnson on the Valley pike, the Federal line of battle extending across the Valley. The fighting was desperate on both sides, being essentially a saber contest. For two hours charges were given and received in solid masses, boot-to-boot, the honors being almost equally divided—the Confederates successfully holding the center while the Federal cavalry pushed back the flanks.

This finally weakened the Confederates, and as both their

GENERAL TORBERT IN THE SHENANDOAH

This photograph, made in the Shenandoah Valley in the fall of 1864, shows General Alfred T. A. Torbert, immaculately clad in a natty uniform, on the steps of a beautiful vine-clad cottage. Virginia homes such as this fared but badly in that terrible October. The black shame of war spread over the valley and rose in the smoke from burning barns. Grant had resolved that Shenandoah should no longer be allowed to act as a granary for the armies of the Confederacy. Sheridan and his men had orders ruthlessly to destroy all supplies that could not be carried away. The Confederate cavalry clung desperately to his rear, and gave so much annoyance that on October 8th Sheridan directed Torbert "to give Rosser a drubbing next morning or get whipped himself." The saber contest that ensued at Tom's Brook was the last attempt of the Confederate cavalry to reestablish their former supremacy. The sight of the devastated valley spurred the Southern troopers to the most valiant attacks, in spite of their inferior equipment. Again and again were charges made and returned on both sides. For two hours the honors were almost even, the Confederates holding the center, while the Federal cavalry pushed back the flanks. Finally Merritt and Custer ordered a charge along the whole line, and at last the Confederates broke.

flanks gave way, Merritt and Custer ordered a charge along their entire line. The retreat of Rosser's force became a panic-stricken rout, which continued for twenty-six miles up the Shenandoah valley. Eleven pieces of artillery, three hundred and thirty prisoners, ambulances, caissons, and even the headquarters' wagons of the Confederate commanders were captured by the Federal troops.

Early ascribed his defeat to Sheridan's superiority in numbers and equipment, and to the fact that Lomax's cavalry was armed entirely with rifles and had no sabers; that as a consequence they could not fight on horseback, and in open country could not successfully fight on foot with large bodies of well-trained cavalry.

In the brilliant part taken by Sheridan's cavalry in retrieving the misfortunes of the morning of October 19, 1864, when the Union camp at Cedar Creek was surprised and routed—with "Sheridan only twenty miles away"—resulting in the final defeat and pursuit of the Confederate army, the Federal cavalry alone captured 45 pieces of artillery, 32 caissons, 46 army wagons, 672 prisoners, and an enormous quantity of other property.

This battle, which Sheridan's magnetic presence turned into a great victory, was followed by a number of small but highly successful cavalry movements, culminating on March 27, 1865, in Sheridan's veteran cavalry corps joining the Army of the Potomac in front of Petersburg for the final campaign against Lee.

In the Valley campaign Sheridan's cavalry captured 2556 prisoners, 71 guns, 29 battle-flags, 52 caissons, 105 army wagons, 2557 horses, 1000 horse equipments, and 7152 beef cattle. It destroyed, among other things, 420,742 bushels of wheat, 780 barns, and over 700,000 rounds of ammunition.

Meanwhile, during the years of vicissitudes which marked the evolution of the cavalry of the East, from a multitude of weak detachments lacking organization, equipment,

CAVALRY THAT CLOSED IN ON RICHMOND

While Sheridan's troopers were distinguishing themselves in the Shenandoah, the cavalry of the Army of the James, which was closing around Richmond, were doing their part. This photograph shows the Fifth Pennsylvania Cavalry, or "Cameron Dragoons," part of the second brigade, in winter-quarters. It was taken in the fall of 1864, on the scene of the engagement at Fair Oaks and Darbytown Road, October 29th of that year. Brigadier-General August V. Kautz had led them on a raid on the Petersburg and Weldon Railroad May 5th to 11th, and on the Richmond and Danville Railroad May 12th to 17th. On June 9th they went to Petersburg and remained there during the siege operations until the Southern Capital fell. During all this time they reversed the situation of the early part of the war, and incessantly harassed the Army of Northern Virginia by constant raids, cutting its communications, and attacking its supply trains.

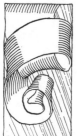

and training to a veteran army, filled with confidence in itself and in its commanders, the cavalry of the West had been equally unfortunate in its slow and discouraging development of fighting efficiency.

Under General Rosecrans, as early as 1862, the cavalry of the Army of the Cumberland was organized into three brigades under General David S. Stanley, but the mounted force actually at the disposal of its commander was but four thousand effective men. Although actively engaged, particularly in curbing the depredations of the Confederate cavalry under Forrest, its operations were not especially important. Nevertheless, at Stone's River, at Knoxville, at Chickamauga, and at other important battles, the cavalry of the West did desperate fighting and, considering its numbers, was not lacking in efficiency.

The cavalry which General Sherman assembled for his Atlanta campaign numbered about fifteen thousand sabers, organized into four divisions, and it participated with credit in all the celebrated movements and engagements of Sherman's army between May and August, 1864. Protecting the rear and preventing the destruction of the Nashville and Chattanooga Railroad by Wheeler's enterprising cavalry, some Union cavalry under Rousseau remained at Decatur until by a rapid and circuitous march around Johnston's Confederate army, in which he destroyed immense quantities of stores and damaged several railroads, Rousseau joined Sherman near Atlanta. After the fall of the latter city, a cavalry division of over five thousand men under Kilpatrick, accompanied Sherman on his famous march to the sea.

Up to this time the activities of the Union cavalry in the Southwest, while noted for boldness and celerity of movement, for endurance, and for accomplishment of results, though hampered by many drawbacks, were not yet distinguished by any of those great cavalry combats which marked the development of the cavalry of the Army of the Potomac.

RICHMOND AT LAST—APRIL, 1865

There is no need now for the troopers' carbines which can be seen projecting beside their saddles just as the cavalry rode into Richmond. The smoke still rising from the city's ruins seems to be the last great shuddering sigh of the Confederacy. The sight of the stark, blackened walls rising around them in the noonday sun brings but little joy to the hearts of the troopers. These ruined piles of brick and mortar are the homes of their brothers who fought a good fight. A few days from now, in the fullness of their hearts, the Union soldiers will be cheering their erstwhile foes at Appomattox. One more cavalry exploit, the capture of Lee's provision trains by Sheridan, which Grant in his delicacy did not reveal to the stricken commander, and the cavalry operations are over. Horses and men go back to the pursuits of peace.

Towards the close of October, 1864, however, General James H. Wilson, who had commanded a cavalry division in Sheridan's Army of the Shenandoah, and who had been instrumental in raising the efficiency of the cavalry service through the Cavalry Bureau, reported to Sherman, in Alabama, and began a thorough reorganization, a remounting and re-equipping of the cavalry corps of Sherman's army.

Wilson's cavalry corps speedily made itself felt as an integral part of the army, taking a prominent part in the battle of Franklin, scoring a decisive victory over Forrest's cavalry under Chalmers, and pressing the foe so closely that the Confederate troopers were actually driven into the Harpeth River. This decisive action of the Union cavalry prevented Forrest from turning Schofield's left flank and cutting his line of retreat.

In the battle of Nashville, which followed (December 15–16, 1864), Wilson's dismounted cavalry gallantly stormed the strong Confederate earthworks side by side with their comrades of the infantry. General Thomas mentions the part taken by this cavalry as follows:

Whilst slightly swinging to the left, [the cavalry] came upon a redoubt containing four guns, which was splendidly carried by assault, at 1 P.M., by a portion of Hatch's division, dismounted, and the captured guns turned upon the enemy. A second redoubt, stronger than the first, was next assailed and carried by the same troops that carried the first position, taking four more guns and about three hundred prisoners. The infantry, McArthur's division, on the left of the cavalry, . . . participated in both of the assaults; and, indeed, the dismounted cavalry seemed to vie with the infantry who should first gain the works; as they reached the position nearly simultaneously, both lay claim to the artillery and prisoners captured.

But the gallant part taken by Wilson's cavalry in these operations is best exemplified by the spoils of war. During and after the battle of Nashville, and including prisoners taken in the hospitals at Franklin, the Union cavalry captured 2 strong redoubts, 32 field guns, 11 caissons, 12 colors, 3232

THE FEDERAL CAVALRY AND THEIR REWARD—MAY, 1865

Shoulders squared, accouterments shining, all of the troops in perfect alignment, a unified, splendidly equipped and disciplined body, the Federal cavalry marched up Pennsylvania Avenue on that glorious sunshiny day in May when the Union armies held their grand review in Washington. What a change from the long night rides and the terrible moments of the crashing charge was this holiday parade, when not a trooper thought of sleeping in the saddle which had often proved his only bed. The battles are over now. Never again will their ears be riven by the agonized shriek of a wounded horse, said by many a cavalryman to be the most horrible sound in the field of battle. Never again will they bend over the silent body of a wounded friend. Men die more quietly than their mounts. This is an arm of the service that proved itself. From early disappointments and disasters, and dissipation of energy in useless details, it emerged a wonderfully effective fighting force that did much to hasten the surrender of the exhausted Confederacy.

prisoners (including 1 general officer), 1 bridge train of 80 pontoons, and 125 wagons. Its own losses were 122 officers and men killed, 1 field-gun, 521 wounded, and 259 missing.

The following spring, while Wilson and his horsemen were sapping the very life blood of the Confederacy, Sheridan and his cavalry of the Army of the Potomac had been playing a most important part in the grand operations of that remarkable army, now under the direction of the inexorable Grant.

After joining Grant in front of Petersburg on March 27, 1865, Sheridan received instruction from his chief to move with his three cavalry divisions of nine thousand men near or through Dinwiddie, reaching the right and rear of the Confederate army, without attempting to attack the Confederates in position. Should the latter remain entrenched, Sheridan was to destroy the Danville and South Side railroads, Lee's only avenues of supply; and then either return to the Army of the Potomac, or to join Sherman in North Carolina. History shows that two of the Confederate infantry divisions and all of Lee's cavalry failed to push back five brigades of Sheridan's cavalry, fighting dismounted, in an effort to cut off the Confederate retreat.

In the desperate fighting which took place in the days following, it was the same splendid cavalry at Five Forks, which dashed dismounted over the Southern entrenchments, carrying all before them.

And finally, on April 6th, at Sailor's Creek, after desperate and exhausting fighting by Custer's and Devin's divisions, it was Crook with his cavalry which intercepted the Confederate line of retreat, cut off three of Lee's hard-pressed infantry divisions, and made possible the surrender at Appomattox of the gallant but exhausted Army of Northern Virginia.

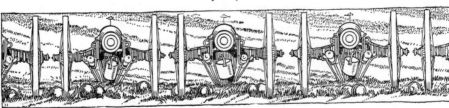

CHAPTER
TEN

CAVALRY LEADERS
NORTH AND SOUTH

CUSTER AND HIS DOG

SHERIDAN AND HIS RIGHT-HAND MEN

This photograph shows Sheridan and his leaders, who drove Early and the Confederate cavalry from the Shenandoah Valley, and brought the Federal cavalry to the zenith of its power. Sheridan stands at the extreme left of the picture. Next to him is General Forsyth, and General Merritt is seated at the table. General Devin stands with his hand on his hip, and Custer leans easily back in his chair. This is a ceremonious photograph; each leader wears the uniform of his rank. Even Custer has abandoned his favorite velvet suit. Together with the facing photograph, this offers an interesting study in the temperament of the Union cavalry leaders.

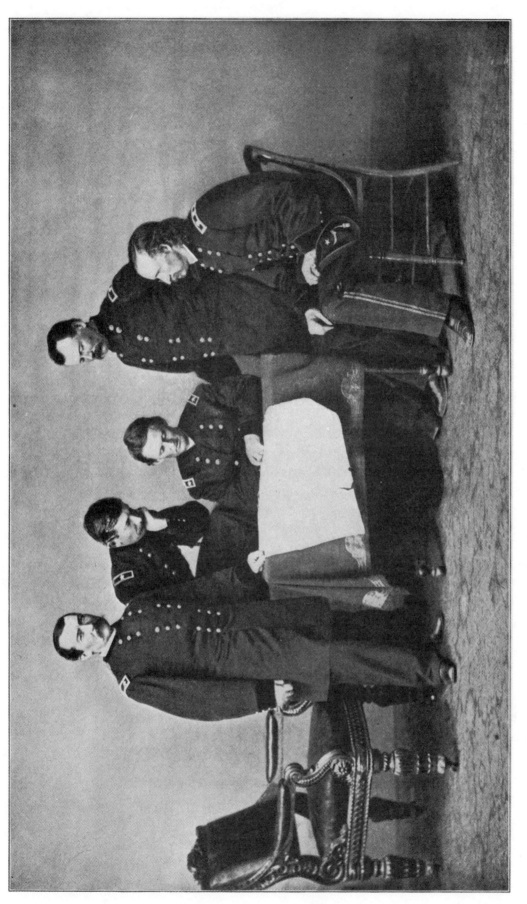

A STUDY IN TEMPERAMENT OF THE MEN WHO LED THE FEDERAL CAVALRY

The photographer has evidently requested the distinguished sitters to inspect a map, as if they were planning some actual movement such as that which "sent Early whirling through Winchester." All but Sheridan have been obliging. General Forsyth is leaning over, hand on chin, one foot on a rung of Merritt's chair. Merritt has cast down his eyes and bowed his head above the map. General Devin is leaning slightly forward in an attentive position. Custer alertly surveys his chief. But Sheridan, his hand clenched beside him, still gazes resolutely at the camera. These were the leaders who stood between the Confederate army and Washington, the capture of which might have meant foreign intervention.

SOME CAVALRY LEADERS

By Theo. F. Rodenbough
Brigadier-General, United States Army (Retired)

NO war of modern times has produced so many able cavalry leaders as the so-called "War of Secession." Sheridan, Stuart, Buford, Gregg, Wilson, Merritt, "Fitz" Lee, Pleasonton, Hampton, Lomax, Butler, Wheeler, Custer, Forrest, Grierson, Morgan, Kilpatrick, and others, have written their names on the roll of fame in letters of fire alongside those of Seydlitz and Ziethen of the Old World. Of the group mentioned who have "crossed the river" a few pen portraits by friendly hands, and true to the life, are here presented.*

GENERAL SHERIDAN †

The general is short in stature—below the medium—with nothing superfluous about him, square shouldered, muscular, wiry to the last degree, and as nearly insensible to hardship and fatigue as is consistent with humanity.

His face is very much tanned by exposure, but is lighted up by uncommonly keen eyes, which would stamp him anywhere as a man of quickness and force, while its whole character would betray him to be a soldier, with its firm chin, high cheek bones, and crisp mustache.

He is exacting on duty and hard on delinquents, and his ideas of duty are peculiar, as evinced by the fact that he has

* More or less personal sketches of famous Cavalry leaders will be found in other chapters of this volume and in the volume to be devoted to biography.

† With General Sheridan in Lee's Last Campaign. By a staff officer. (Philadelphia) J. B. Lippincott & Co., 1866.

MAJOR–GENERAL PHILIP HENRY SHERIDAN

General Sheridan was the leader who relieved the Union cavalry from waste of energy and restored it an arm of the service as effective and terrible to the Confederacy as the Southern cavalry had been to the North at the outset of the war. He was born at Albany, N. Y., 1831, and graduated at West Point in 1853. In May, 1862, he was appointed colonel of the Second Michigan Cavalry, and served in northern Mississippi. In July he was appointed brigadier-general of volunteers and distinguished himself on October 8th at the battle of Perryville. He commanded a division of the Army of the Cumberland at Stone's River, and was appointed major-general of volunteers early in 1863. He took part in the pursuit of General Van Dorn, afterwards aided in the capture of Manchester, Tennessee, on June 27th, and was in the battle of Chickamauga. In the battles around Chattanooga he attracted the attention of General Grant. In April, 1864, he was placed in command of the cavalry corps of the Army of the Potomac, and its brilliant exploits under his leadership culminated in the death of General J. E. B. Stuart at Yellow Tavern, where the Confederates were defeated. In August, 1864, he was placed in command of the Army of the Shenandoah. He defeated General Early at Opequon Creek, Fisher's Hill, and Cedar Creek, and captured 5,000 of his men and several guns. He drove the Confederates from the valley and laid it waste. On September 10th he was made brigadier-general, and in November major-general. In July, 1865, he received the thanks of Congress for his distinguished services. He died at Nonquitt, Mass., on August 5, 1888.

THE LEADER'S EYES

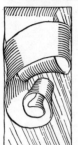

never issued orders of encouragement or congratulations to his troops before or after campaigns or battles. He has apparently taken it for granted that all under his command would do as well as they could, and they did so quite as a matter of course. And to this soldierly view the troops always responded. Understanding so well what they were fighting for and the issues at stake, they would not fight harder to accomplish results simply for the satisfaction of having them recounted. . . .

Though always easy of approach, the general has little to say in busy times. Set teeth and a quick way tell when things do not go as they ought, and he has a manner on such occasions that stirs to activity all within sight, for a row seems brewing that nobody wants to be under when it bursts. Notwithstanding his handsome reputation for cursing, he is rather remarkably low-voiced, particularly on the field, where, as sometimes happens, almost everybody else is screaming. "Damn you, sir, don't yell at me," he once said to an officer who came galloping up with some bad news, and was roaring it out above the din of battle. In such moments the general leans forward on his horse's neck, and hunching his shoulders up to his ears, gives most softly spoken orders in a slow, deliberate way, as though there were niches for all the words in his hearer's memory, and they must be measured very carefully to fit exactly, that none of them be lost in the carrying. . . .

The general has a remarkable eye for topography, not only in using to the best advantage the peculiarities of the country through which he is campaigning, either for purposes of marching, assaults, or defense, but he can foresee with accuracy, by studying a map, how far the country will be available for these purposes.

He has been called ruthless and cruel because, in obedience to the orders of the officers appointed over him, he was compelled, by the stern necessities of war, to destroy property in the Shenandoah valley, and to take from the war-ridden people

MAJOR–GENERAL JAMES EWELL BROWN STUART, C. S. A.

In the hat on General Stuart's knee appears the plume which grew to symbolize the dash and gallantry of the man himself. Plume and hat were captured, and Stuart himself narrowly escaped, at Verdiersville, August 17, 1862. "I intend," he wrote, "to make the Yankees pay for that hat." Less than a week later he captured Pope's personal baggage and horses, and for many days thereafter the Federal general's uniform was on exhibition in a Richmond store window—a picturesque and characteristic reprisal. Born in Virginia in 1833, Stuart graduated at the United States Military Academy in 1854. He saw service on the Texas frontier, in Kansas, and against the Cheyenne Indians before the outbreak of the war. On April, 1861, he resigned from the United States Army and joined the Confederacy in his native State. He won distinction at Bull Run, and also the rank of brigadier-general. Stuart rode twice around the Army of the Potomac when McClellan was in command, and played a conspicuous part in the Seven Days before Richmond. At the second Bull Run, at Antietam, by a destructive raid into Pennsylvania, at Fredericksburg, and at Chancellorsville Stuart added to his laurels. He was too late for anything except the last day of Gettysburg, where the strengthened Union cavalry proved his match. He was mortally wounded at Yellow Tavern May 11, 1864, in a pitched battle with Sheridan's cavalry.

there what their friends had left them of supplies for man and beast. As he rode down the Martinsburg pike in his four-horse wagon, heels on the front seat, and smoking a cigar, while behind him his cavalry was destroying the provender that could not be carried away, the inhabitants of the Valley doubtless regarded him as history regards the emperor who fiddled while Rome was burning, and would not now believe, what is the simple truth, that this destruction was distasteful to him, and that he was moved by the distress he was obliged to multiply upon these unfortunate people, whose evil fate had left them in the ruinous track of war so long. But the Shenandoah valley was the well-worn pathway of invasion, and it became necessary that this long avenue leading to our homes should be stripped of the sustenance that rendered it possible to subsist an army there.

GENERAL STUART

Stuart was undoubtedly the most brilliant and widely known *sabreur* of his time. The term is used advisedly to describe the accomplished horseman who, while often fighting dismounted, yet by training and the influence of his environment was at his best as a leader of mounted men.

Stuart as a cadet at the Military Academy is thus described by General Fitzhugh Lee:

"I recall his distinguishing characteristics, which were a strict attention to his military duties, an erect, soldierly bearing, an immediate and almost thankful acceptance of a challenge to fight from any cadet who might in any way feel himself aggrieved, and a clear, metallic ringing voice."

In the Indian country as a subaltern in the cavalry, his commanding officer, Major Simonson, thus wrote of him:

"Lieutenant Stuart was brave and gallant, always prompt in the execution of orders, and reckless of danger or exposure. I considered him at that time one of the most promising young officers in the United States army."

MAJOR–GENERAL JOHN BUFORD

General Buford was one of the foremost cavalry leaders of the North. He is credited by many with having chosen the field on which the battle of Gettysburg was fought. He was born in 1826 in Woodford County, Kentucky, graduated at West Point in 1848, and saw service against the Indians. In November, 1861, he attained to the rank of major, and in July, 1862, he was made brigadier-general of volunteers. While in command of a cavalry brigade in 1862, Buford was wounded in the second battle of Bull Run. In McClellan's Maryland campaign, at Fredericksburg, and in the spirited cavalry engagements at Brandy Station, he played his part nobly. In Pennsylvania he displayed remarkable ability and opened the battle of Gettysburg before the arrival of Reynolds' infantry on July 1st. The Comte de Paris says in his "History of the Civil War in America": "It was Buford who selected the battlefield where the two armies were about to measure their strength." After taking part in the pursuit of Lee and subsequent operations in central Virginia, he withdrew on sick leave in November, 1863, and died in Washington on December 16th, receiving a commission as major-general only on the day of his death.

As a Confederate colonel at the first Bull Run battle, General Early reported:

"Stuart did as much toward saving the battle of First Manassas as any subordinate who participated in it; and yet he has never received any credit for it, in the official reports or otherwise. His own report is very brief and indefinite."

In a letter to President Davis, General J. E. Johnston recommended Stuart's promotion, which was made September 24, 1861:

"He is a rare man, wonderfully endowed by nature with the qualities necessary for an officer of light cavalry. Calm, firm, acute, active, and enterprising, I know of no one more competent than he to estimate the occurrences before him at their true value. If you add a real brigade of cavalry to this army, you can find no better brigadier-general to command it."

In an account of the raid into Pennsylvania (October, 1862) Colonel Alexander K. McClure speaks of the behavior of Stuart's command in passing through Chambersburg:

"General Stuart sat on his horse in the center of the town, surrounded by his staff, and his command was coming in from the country in large squads, leading their old horses and riding the new ones they had found in the stables hereabouts. General Stuart is of medium size, has a keen eye, and wears immense sandy whiskers and mustache. His demeanor to our people was that of a humane soldier. In several instances his men commenced to take private property from stores, but they were arrested by General Stuart's provost-guard. In a single instance only, that I heard of, did they enter a store by intimidating the proprietor. All of our stores and shops were closed, and with very few exceptions were not disturbed." *

General John B. Gordon, in his "Reminiscences" relates:

"An incident during the battle of Chancellorsville [illustrates] the bounding spirits of that great cavalry leader, General 'Jeb' Stuart. After Jackson's fall, Stuart was

* Campaigns of Stuart's Cavalry.

[268]

LIEUTENANT–GENERAL WADE HAMPTON, C.S.A.

General Hampton was the leader selected three months after Stuart's death to command all of Lee's cavalry. Although it had become sadly decimated, Hampton lived up to his reputation, and fought effectively to the very end of the war. His last command was the cavalry in Johnston's army, which opposed Sherman's advance from Savannah in 1865. Hampton was born in Columbia, S. C., in 1818. After graduating in law at the University of South Carolina, he gave up his time to the management of his extensive estates. At the outbreak of the war he raised and equipped from his private means the "Hampton's Legion," which did good service throughout the war. He fought at the head of his Legion at Bull Run and in the Peninsula campaign, was wounded at Fair Oaks, and soon afterward was commissioned brigadier-general. He served brilliantly at Gettysburg, where he was wounded three times, and was made major-general on August 3d following. He was engaged in opposing the advance of Sheridan toward Lynchburg in 1864, and showed such high qualities as a cavalry commander that he was commissioned lieutenant-general in August of that year, and placed in command of all of Lee's cavalry. He was Governor of South Carolina from 1876 to 1878; then United States Senator until 1891. He was United States Commissioner of Railroads, 1893 to 1897. His death occurred in 1902.

designated to lead Jackson's troops in the final charge. The soul of this brilliant cavalry commander was as full of sentiment as it was of the spirit of self-sacrifice. He was as musical as he was brave. He sang as he fought. Placing himself at the head of Jackson's advancing lines and shouting to them ' Forward,' he at once led off in that song, ' Won't you come out of the Wilderness?' He changed the words to suit the occasion. Through the dense woodland, blending in strange harmony with the rattle of rifles, could be distinctly heard that song and words, ' Now, Joe Hooker, won't you come out of the Wilderness?'"

GENERAL BUFORD *

But something more than West Point and frontier service was needed to produce a Buford. He was "no sapling chance-sown by the fountain." He had had years of training and experience in his profession, and although they were precious and indispensable, they could not have produced the same results which were realized in him, had it not been for the honorable deeds of his ancestors and the hereditary traits developed and transmitted by them. Such men as Buford are not the fruit of chance. Springing, as he did, from a sturdy Anglo-Norman family long settled in the " debatable land " on the borders of England and Scotland, he came by the virtues of the strong hand through inheritance. His kinsmen, as far back as they can be traced, were stout soldiers, rough fighters, and hard riders, accustomed to lives of vicissitude, and holding what they had under the good old rule, the simple plan, " Those to take who have the power, and those to keep who can." Men of his name were the counsellors and companions of kings, and gained renown in the War of the Roses, and in the struggle for

* Major-General John Buford. By Major-General James H. Wilson, U. S. V., Brevet Major-General, U. S. A. Oration delivered at Gettysburg on July 1, 1895.

MAJOR–GENERAL WESLEY MERRITT

General Merritt did his share toward achieving the momentous results of Gettysburg. With his reserve brigade of cavalry on the Federal left, he caused Law to detach a large force from the Confederate main line in order to protect his flank and rear. Merritt served with distinction throughout the Civil War and later in the Spanish-American War. He was born in New York City in 1836, graduated at West Point in 1860, and was assigned to the Second Dragoons. In April, 1862, he was promoted to be captain. He rode with Stoneman on his famous Richmond raid in April and May, 1863, and was in command of the cavalry reserve at Gettysburg. Merritt commanded a cavalry division in the Shenandoah Valley campaign under Sheridan from August, 1864, to March, 1865, and in the final Richmond campaign the cavalry corps. After rendering service in the Spanish-American War, and commanding the forces in the Philippines, he was retired from active service in June, 1900. He died December 3, 1910.

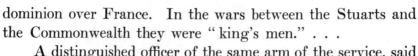
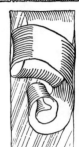

dominion over France. In the wars between the Stuarts and the Commonwealth they were "king's men." . . .

A distinguished officer of the same arm of the service, said of him that as a captain of dragoons "he was considered," in a regiment famed for its dashing and accomplished officers, "as the soldier *par excellence.*" He adds in loving admiration, that "no man could be more popular or sincerely beloved by his fellow officers, nor could any officer be more thoroughly respected by his men, than he was. His company had no superior in the service." The same distinguished officer, writing after his career had closed in death, says, "He was a splendid cavalry officer, and one of the most successful in the service; was modest, yet brave; unostentatious, but prompt and persevering; ever ready to go where duty called him, and never shrinking from action however fraught with peril." . . .

Speaking many years after of the part taken in this great day's work * by Buford's cavalry, General F. A. Walker, in the "History of the Second Army Corps," uses the following language: "When last it was my privilege to see General Hancock in November, 1885, he pointed out to me from Cemetery Hill the position occupied by Buford at this critical juncture, and assured me that among the most inspiring sights of his military career was the splendid spectacle of that gallant cavalry as it stood there, unshaken and undaunted, in the face of the advancing Confederate infantry." No higher commendation for the cavalry can be found. Its services have been generally minimized, if not entirely ignored, by popular historians, but no competent critic can read the official reports or the Comte de Paris' "History of the Civil War in America" without giving the cavalry the highest praise for its work on this day, and throughout this campaign. "To Buford was assigned the post of danger and responsibility. He, and he alone, selected the ground," says that trustworthy historian, "upon which unforeseen circumstances were about to bring the two armies into

* The First Day, Gettysburg, July 1, 1863.

MAJOR–GENERAL NATHAN BEDFORD FORREST, C.S.A.

General Forrest was one of the born cavalry leaders. Daring and resourceful in every situation, he and his hard-riding raiders became a source of terror throughout the Mississippi Valley. He was born near the site of Chapel Hill, Tennessee, on July 31, 1821, attended school for about six months, became a horse and cattle trader, and slave trader at Memphis. He cast in his lot with the Confederacy and entered the army as a private in June, 1861. In July he organized a battalion of cavalry, of which he became lieutenant-colonel. He escaped from Fort Donelson when it surrendered to Grant, and as brigadier-general served in Kentucky under Bragg. Transferred to Northern Mississippi in November, 1863, Forrest was made major-general on December 4th of that year, and at the close of the following year was placed in command of all the cavalry with the Army of the Tennessee. On January 24, 1865, he was put in command of the cavalry in Alabama, Mississippi, and east Louisiana, and was appointed lieutenant-general on February 28th. He met defeat at the hands of General James H. Wilson at Selma, Ala., in March, 1865, and surrendered to General Canby at Gainesville the following May. He remained in business in Tennessee until he died in 1877—one of the most striking characters developed by the war.

hostile contact. Neither Meade nor Lee had any knowledge of it. . . . Buford, who, when he arrived on the evening of [June] 30th, had guessed at one glance the advantages to be derived from these positions, did not have time to give a description of them to Meade and receive his instructions. The unfailing in-dications to an officer of so much experience, revealed to Buford the approach of the enemy. Knowing that Reynolds was within supporting distance of him, he boldly resolved to risk everything in order to allow the latter time to reach Gettys-burg in advance of the Confederate army. This first inspira-tion of a cavalry officer and a true soldier decided, in every respect, the fate of the campaign. It was Buford who selected the battlefield where the two armies were about to measure their strength."

GENERAL WADE HAMPTON

Wade Hampton entered the military service of the Con-federate States as colonel of the Hampton Legion, South Carolina Volunteers, June 12, 1861, said legion consisting of eight companies of infantry, four companies of cavalry, and two companies of artillery. With the infantry of his com-mand, Colonel Hampton participated in the first battle of Bull Run, July 21, 1861, where he was wounded. He bore a part as a brigade commander in the subsequent battles on the Peninsula of Virginia, from the beginning of operations at Yorktown until the battle of Seven Pines, where he was again wounded. . . .

I have been often asked if General Hampton was a good tactician. If in a minor, technical sense, I answer to the best of my judgment, " No." I doubt if he ever read a technical book on tactics. He knew how to maneuver the units of his command so as to occupy for offensive or defensive action the strongest points of the battlefield, and that is about all there

* Butler and His Cavalry, 1861–1865. By U. R. Brooks (Columbia S. C.). The State Company, 1909.

MAJOR–GENERAL GEORGE ARMSTRONG CUSTER WITH GENERAL PLEASONTON

The *beau sabreur* of the Federal service is pictured here in his favorite velvet suit, with General Alfred Pleasonton, who commanded the cavalry at Gettysburg. This photograph was taken at Warrenton, Va., three months after that battle. At the time this picture was taken, Custer was a brigadier-general in command of the second brigade of the third division of General Pleasonton's cavalry. General Custer's impetuosity finally cost him his own life and the lives of his entire command at the hands of the Sioux Indians June 25, 1876. Custer was born in 1839 and graduated at West Point in 1861. As captain of volunteers he served with McClellan on the Peninsula. In June, 1863, he was made brigadier-general of volunteers and as the head of a brigade of cavalry distinguished himself at Gettysburg. Later he served with Sheridan in the Shenandoah, won honor at Cedar Creek, and was brevetted major-general of volunteers on October 19, 1864. Under Sheridan he participated in the battles of Five Forks, Dinwiddie Court House, and other important cavalry engagements of Grant's last campaign.

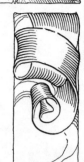

is in tactics. A successful strategist has a broader field for the employment of his military qualities. General Hampton appeared possessed of almost an instinctive topographical talent. He could take in the strong strategic points in the field of his operations with an accuracy of judgment that was surprising to his comrades. It was not necessary for him to study Jomini, Napoleon's "Campaigns," and other high authorities in the art of war. He was a law unto himself on such matters. According to the rules laid down in the books, he would do the most unmilitary things. He would hunt his antagonist as he would hunt big game in the forest. The celerity and audacity of his movements against the front, sometimes on the flank, then again in the rear, kept his enemies in a constant state of uncertainty and anxiety as to where and when they might expect him. With his wonderful powers of physical endurance, his alert, vigilant mind, his matchless horsemanship, no obstacles seemed to baffle his audacity or thwart his purpose.

GENERAL MERRITT *

Merritt was graduated in the class of 1860 at the Military Academy. He was twenty-four years of age. In scholarship he was rated at the middle of his class, and in the other soldierly qualities he was near the head. . . .

At the battle of the Opequon (Winchester), on September 19th, his division gave the most effective instance in a hundred years of war, of the use of a cavalry division in a pitched battle. He rode over Breckinridge's infantry and Fitzhugh Lee's cavalry and effectually broke the Confederate left. At this time Sheridan wrote to a friend, " I claim nothing for myself; my boys Merritt and Custer did it all.". . .

On the disastrous morning of October 19th, at Cedar

* General Wesley Merritt. By Lieutenant-Colonel Eben Swift, Eighth Cavalry. From the (March, 1911) Journal of the United States Cavalry Association.

MAJOR–GENERAL FITZHUGH LEE, C.S.A.

A nephew of the South's greatest commander, General Fitzhugh Lee did honor to his famous family. Along the Rappahannock and in the Shenandoah he measured swords with the Federal cavalry, and over thirty years later he was leading American forces in Cuba. He was born at Clermont, Va., in 1835, graduated at West Point in 1856, and from May, 1860, until the outbreak of the Civil War was instructor of cavalry at West Point. He resigned from the United States Army, and entered the Confederate service in 1861. He fought with Stuart's cavalry in almost all of the important engagements of the Army of Northern Virginia, first as colonel, from July, 1862, as brigadier-general, and from September, 1863, as major-general. He was severely wounded at Winchester, on September 19, 1864, and from March, 1865, until his surrender to General Meade at Farmville, was in command of all the cavalry of the Army of Northern Virginia. In 1896 he was sent to Cuba by President Cleveland as consul-general at Havana, and in May, 1898, when war with Spain seemed inevitable, was appointed major-general of volunteers, and placed in command of the Seventh Army Corps. He returned to Havana as Military Governor in January, 1899. He died in 1905.

Creek, Merritt's division blocked the way of Gordon's victorious Confederates, held its position north of Middletown all day, without assistance, then charged and, crossing the stream below the bridge, joined Custer in the pursuit to Fisher's Hill. In that campaign Merritt's division captured fourteen battle-flags, twenty-nine pieces of artillery, and more than three thousand prisoners. . . .

Merritt at his high prime was the embodiment of force. He was one of those rare men whose faculties are sharpened and whose view is cleared on the battlefield. His decisions were delivered with the rapidity of thought and were as clear as if they had been studied for weeks. He always said that he never found that his first judgment gained by time and reflection. In him a fiery soul was held in thrall to will. Never disturbed by doubt, or moved by fear, neither circumspect nor rash, he never missed an opportunity or made a mistake.

These were the qualities that recommended him to the confidence of that commander whose ideals were higher and more exacting than any other in our history. To his troops he was always a leader who commanded their confidence by his brave appearance, and his calmness in action, while his constant thoughtfulness and care inspired a devotion that was felt for few leaders of his rank.

GENERAL FORREST *

When the war broke out, Forrest was in the prime of his mental and physical powers. Over six feet in stature, of powerful frame, and of great activity and daring, with a personal prowess proved in many fierce encounters, he was a king among the bravest men of his time and country. He was among the first to volunteer when war broke out, and it was a matter of

* Recollections of a Virginian in the Mexican, Indian, and Civil Wars. By General Dabney Herndon Maury. (New York) Charles Scribner's Sons, 1894.

LIEUTENANT–GENERAL JOSEPH WHEELER, C.S.A.

Commander of Confederate forces in more than a hundred cavalry battles, General Wheeler well deserved the tribute of his erstwhile opponent, General Sherman, who once said: "In the event of war with a foreign country, Joe Wheeler is the man to command the cavalry of our army." He was born in 1836, and graduated at West Point in 1859. He served in the regular army until April, 1861, then entered the Confederate service. He commanded a brigade of infantry at Shiloh in April, 1862, and later in the year was transferred to the cavalry. He fought under Bragg in Kentucky at Perryville and in other engagements, and covered the retreat of Bragg's army to the southward. In January, 1863, he was commissioned major-general. In the Chattanooga campaigns Wheeler showed himself a brave and skilful officer. He harassed Sherman's flank during the march to Atlanta, and in August, 1864, led a successful raid in Sherman's rear as far north as the Kentucky line. In February, 1865, he was commissioned lieutenant-general, and continued in command of the cavalry in Johnston's army until its surrender. He served as a major-general in the Spanish-American War. He died in Brooklyn, January 25, 1906.

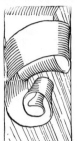

course that he should be the commander of the troops who flocked to his standard. From the very outset he evinced his extraordinary capacity for war, and in his long career of great achievement no defeat or failure was ever charged to him. . . .

When Forrest, with about twelve hundred men, set out in pursuit of Streight, he was more than a day behind him. Streight had several hundred more men in the saddle than Forrest, and being far in advance could replace a broken-down horse by a fresh one from the farms through which his route lay, while Forrest, when he lost a horse, lost a soldier, too; for no good horses were left for him. After a hot pursuit of five days and nights, during which he had lost two-thirds of his forces from broken-down horses, he overhauled his enemy and brought him to a parley. This conference took place in sight of a cut-off in the mountain road, Captain Morton and his horse artillery, which had been so long with Forrest, passing in sight along the road till they came to the cut-off, into which they would turn, reentering the road out of view, so that it seemed that a continuous stream of artillery was passing by. Forrest had so arranged that he stood with his back to the guns while Streight was facing them.

Forrest, in his characteristic way, described the scene to me. He said, " I seen him all the time he was talking, looking over my shoulder and counting the guns. Presently he said: ' Name of God! How many guns have you got? There's fifteen I've counted already!' Turning my head that way, I said, ' I reckon that's all that has kept up.' Then he said, ' I won't surrender till you tell me how many men you've got.' I said, ' I've got enough to whip you out of your boots.' To which he said, ' I won't surrender.' I turned to my bugler and said, ' Sound to mount!' Then he cried out ' I'll surrender!' I told him, ' Stack your arms right along there, Colonel, and march your men away down that hollow.'

" When this was done," continued Forrest, " I ordered my men to come forward and take possession of the arms.

MAJOR–GENERAL JAMES HARRISON WILSON AND STAFF

This brilliant cavalryman's demonstration of 1865 against Selma and Tuscaloosa, Alabama, in aid of General Canby s operations against Mobile and the center of the State, was one of the greatest cavalry raids in the West.   General Wilson was born in 1837, near Shawneetown, Illinois, and graduated at West Point in 1860. He was aide-de-camp to General McClellan on the Peninsula, and served in the engineering corps in the West until after Vicksburg and Chattanooga, when he was made brigadier-general of volunteers in October, 1863. In February, 1864, he was put in charge of the cavalry bureau at Washington, and later commanded the Third Division of Sheridan's reorganized cavalry.   October 5, 1864, he was brevetted major-general of volunteers for "gallant and meritorious services" during the war, and on the 24th of that month he was put in command of the cavalry corps of the Military Division of the Mississippi.   He took part in the battles of Franklin and Nashville, and in March, 1865, made his famous Selma raid.   In twenty-eight days Wilson had captured 288 guns and 6280 prisoners, including Jefferson Davis.   Five large iron works, three factories, numerous mills and immense quantities of supplies had been destroyed.   As a reward for these services, he was made major-general of volunteers on April 20, 1865.   General Wilson later served with distinction in the Spanish American War, and was also in command of the British and American troops in the siege at Pekin, China.

When Streight saw they were barely four hundred, he did rear! demanded to have his arms back and that we should fight it out. I just laughed at him and patted him on the shoulder, and said, ' Ah, Colonel, all is fair in love and war, you know.' ". . .

Forrest knew nothing about tactics—could not drill a company. When first ordered to have his brigade ready for review, he was quite ignorant, but Armstrong told him what commands to give, and what to do with himself. . . .

Forrest will always stand as the great exponent of the power of the mounted riflemen to fight with the revolver when mounted and with the rifle on foot. His troops were not dragoons " who fought indifferently on foot or horseback," nor were they cavalry who fought only mounted and with sabers. Few of his command ever bore sabers, save some of his officers, who wore them as a badge of rank. None of Forrest's men could use the saber. He himself had no knowledge of its use, but he would encounter half a dozen expert *sabreurs* with his revolver.

GENERAL CUSTER *

It was here (Hanover, Pennsylvania, June, 1863) that the brigade first saw Custer. As the men of the Sixth, armed with their Spencer rifles, were deploying forward across the railroad into a wheat-field beyond, I heard a voice new to me, directly in rear of the portion of the line where I was, giving directions for the movement, in clear, resonant tones, and in a calm, confident manner, at once resolute and reassuring. Looking back to see whence it came, my eyes were instantly riveted upon a figure only a few feet distant, whose appearance amazed, if it did not for the moment amuse me. It was he who was giving the orders. At first, I thought he might be a staff-officer, conveying the commands of his chief. But it was at once apparent

* Personal Recollections of a Cavalryman. By J. H. Kidd, formerly Colonel, Sixth Michigan Cavalry. (Ionia, Mich.) Sentinel Printing Co.

BRIGADIER–GENERAL JOHN R. CHAMBLISS, C.S.A.

General John R. Chambliss was a Confederate cavalry leader who distinguished himself at Gettysburg. At Brandy Station, June 9, 1863, W. H. F. Lee had been wounded, and Colonel Chambliss had taken command of his brigade. On the night of June 24th Stuart left Robertson's and Jones' brigades to guard the passes of the Blue Ridge and started to move round the Army of the Potomac with the forces of Hampton, Fitzhugh Lee, and Chambliss, intending to pass between it and Centerville into Maryland and so rejoin Lee. The movements of the army forced him out of his way, so on the morning of the 30th he moved across country to Hanover, Chambliss in front and Hampton in the rear with Fitzhugh Lee well out on the flank. Chambliss attacked Kilpatrick at Hanover about 10 A.M., but was driven out before Hampton or Lee could come to his support.

MAJOR HENRY GILMOR, C.S.A.

Major Gilmor was born in Baltimore County, Maryland, in 1838. He entered the Confederate army at the outbreak of the Civil War, and was commissioned captain in 1862. In 1862–63 he was imprisoned for five months in Fort McHenry, at Baltimore, and in the latter year he raised a cavalry battalion, of which he was made major. Subsequently he commanded the First Confederate Regiment of Maryland, and in 1864 headed the advance of the forces of General Jubal A. Early into that State, and, being familiar with the country, made a successful raid north of Baltimore. He captured Frederick, Md., and created great alarm by his daring exploit so far north of the customary battlefields. In 1874 he became police commissioner of his native city. He died in 1883.

that he was *giving* orders, not transmitting them, and that he was in command of the line.

Looking at him closely, this is what I saw: An officer, superbly mounted, who sat his charger as if to the manner born. Tall, lithe, active, muscular, straight as an Indian and as quick in his movements, he had the fair complexion of a school-girl. He was clad in a suit of black velvet, elaborately trimmed with gold lace, which ran down the outer seams of his trousers, and almost covered the sleeves of his cavalry jacket. The wide collar of a navy-blue shirt was turned down over the collar of his velvet jacket, and a necktie of brilliant crimson was tied in a graceful knot at the throat, the long ends falling carelessly in front. The double rows of buttons on his breast were arranged in groups of twos, indicating the rank of brigadier-general. A soft black hat with wide brim adorned with a gilt cord, and rosette encircling a silver star, was worn turned down on one side, giving him a rakish air. His golden hair fell in graceful luxuriance nearly or quite to his shoulder, and his upper lip was garnished with a blonde mustache. A sword and belt, gilt spurs and top-boots completed his unique outfit.

A keen eye would have been slow to detect in that rider with the flowing locks and gaudy tie, in his dress of velvet and of gold, the master-spirit that he proved to be. That garb, fantastic as at first sight it appeared to be, was to be the distinguishing mark which, during all the remaining years of the war, like the white plume of Henry of Navarre, was to show us where, in the thickest of the fight, we were to seek our leader —for, where danger was, where swords were to cross, where Greek met Greek, there he was, always. Brave, but not reckless; self-confident, yet modest; ambitious, but regulating his conduct at all times by a high sense of honor and duty; eager for laurels, but scorning to wear them unworthily; ready and willing to act, but regardful of human life; quick in emergencies, cool and self-possessed, his courage was of the highest moral type, his perceptions were intuitions.

[284]

MAJOR–GENERAL HUGH JUDSON KILPATRICK

This daring cavalry leader was born in 1836 near Deckertown, New Jersey, and graduated at West Point in 1861. He entered the Federal service as captain in the Fifth New York Volunteers, generally known as Duryea's Zouaves. He was wounded at Big Bethel, June 10, 1861, and on September 25th he became lieutenant-colonel of the Second New York Cavalry. In the second battle of Bull Run, and on the left at Gettysburg, he served with conspicuous gallantry. In December, 1862, he was promoted to be colonel, and in June, 1863, to be brigadier-general of volunteers while he received the brevet of major and lieutenant-colonel in the Regular Army for repeated gallantry. In March, 1864, he made his celebrated Richmond raid and in April accompanied Sherman in his invasion of Georgia. He was wounded at Resasca, and at the close of the war he was brevetted brigadier-general in the Regular Army for "gallant and meritorious services in the capture of Fayetteville, North Carolina," and major-general for his services during the campaign under Sherman in the Carolinas. In June, 1865, he obtained the regular rank of major-general of volunteers. He died at Santiago in December, 1881.

GENERAL FITZHUGH LEE *

Major-General Fitzhugh Lee, or " Our Fitz " as he was affectionately called by his old comrades, won high distinction as a cavalryman in the Army of Northern Virginia, and since the war won higher distinction as a citizen.

After serving for a year at Carlisle Barracks as cavalry instructor of raw recruits, he reported to his regiment on the frontier of Texas, and was greatly distinguished in several fights for gallantry. In a fight with the Comanches, May 13, 1859, he was so severely wounded, being pierced through the lungs by an arrow, that the surgeons despaired of his life (especially as he had to be borne two hundred miles across the prairie in a horse litter), but he recovered and rejoined his command, and led a part of his company in January, 1860, in a very notable and successful fight with the Indians, in which he greatly distinguished himself in a single combat with a powerful Indian chief. . . .

In the campaign against Pope, and the Maryland Campaign (1862) his cavalry rendered most important service, of which General R. E. Lee said in his official report: " Its vigilance, activity, and courage were conspicuous; and to its assistance is due in a great measure some of the most important and delicate operations of the campaign." . . .

When Hampton was sent south, Lee was put in command of the entire cavalry corps of the Army of Northern Virginia, and only the break-up at Richmond prevented him from receiving his merited commission as lieutenant-general, which had been decided on by the Confederate President. . . .

When the war with Spain broke out he was made major-general of volunteers, and put in command of troops destined to capture Havana. After the close of the war he was kept

* Thirty-sixth Annual Reunion of the Association of the Graduates of the United States Military Academy, at West Point, New York, June 13, 1905.

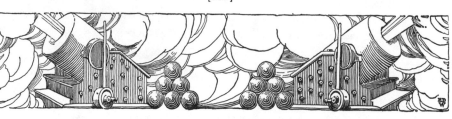

MAJOR–GENERAL LOVELL HARRISON ROUSSEAU

General Rousseau was born in Stanford, Lincoln County, Ky., in 1818. He fought in the Mexican War, distinguished himself at Buena Vista, and later settled in Louisville. In 1860 he raised the Fifth Kentucky regiment, of which he was made colonel, and in 1861 he was made brigadier-general. He served with great credit at Shiloh, and was made major-general of volunteers for gallant conduct at Perryville. He commanded the Fifth Division of the Army of the Cumberland at Stone River and at Chickamauga, and in 1864 made a cavalry raid into Alabama. In the Nashville campaign he had command of Fort Rosecrans under General Thomas, and did his share in achieving the notable results of that battle. At the time of his death in 1869 he was commander of the Department of the Gulf.

MAJOR–GENERAL GEORGE STONEMAN

General Stoneman was born at Busti, Chautauqua County, N. Y., in 1822, and graduated at West Point in 1846. Following some service in West Virginia in the early part of the war, he was appointed chief of cavalry in the Army of the Potomac. After the evacuation of Yorktown, he overtook the Confederate troops and brought on the battle of Williamsburgh in May, 1862. On November 15, 1862, he was made commander of the Third Army Corps, which he led at Fredericksburg on December 13, 1862. During Hooker's Chancellorsville campaign he led a cavalry raid toward Richmond. In April, 1864, he was made commander of a cavalry corps in the Army of the Ohio, and in the Atlanta campaign undertook a raid against Macon and Andersonville. For three months he was a prisoner.

for a time in Cuba as Commander of the District of Havana, and was made brigadier-general in the regular army, where he served with distinction until he was retired.

GENERAL WHEELER

One of the most versatile soldiers of the Civil War was Joseph Wheeler, Lieutenant-General, C. S. A., Brigadier-General, U. S. A., and in the opinion of General R. E. Lee one of " the two ablest cavalry officers which the war developed."

President Davis said that General Wheeler displayed " a dash and activity, vigilance and consummate skill, which justly entitled him to a prominent place on the roll of great cavalry leaders. By his indomitable energy he was able to keep the Government and commanders of our troops advised of the enemy's movements and by preventing foraging parties from leaving the main body, he saved from spoliation all but a narrow tract of country, and from the torch millions worth of property which would otherwise have certainly been consumed."

One of his biographers (Rev. E. S. Buford) states that: " General Wheeler has commanded in more than a hundred battles, many of which, considering the numbers engaged, were the most severe recorded in the history of cavalry. Always in the front of battle, he was wounded three times, sixteen horses were shot under him, eight of his staff-officers were killed and thirty-two wounded."

At the outbreak of the war with Spain, Wheeler was appointed a major-general, U. S. V., and during the short but sharp campaign in Cuba, displayed the same energy and ability which had distinguished him in a greater conflict. In 1899 he was ordered to the Philippines, serving there until June, 1900, when he was commissioned brigadier-general, U. S. A., and in September of the same year was retired from active service. His old opponent, General Sherman, paid this tribute to his worth: " In the event of war with a foreign country, 'Joe' Wheeler is the man to command the cavalry of our army."

CHAPTER
ELEVEN

———

FAMOUS CHARGERS

———

GRANT'S FAVORITE WAR-HORSE "CINCINNATI"

THREE CHARGERS THAT BORE A NATION'S DESTINY

These three horses can fairly be said to have borne a nation's destiny upon their backs. They are the mounts used by General Grant in his final gigantic campaign that resulted in the outwearing of the Confederacy. When photographed in June, 1864, they were "in the field" with the General-in-Chief, after the ghastly battle of Cold Harbor, and before the crossing of the James River that sealed the fate of Lee's army. On the left is "Egypt," presented to Grant by admirers in Illinois, and named for the district in

IN THE FIELD WITH GENERAL GRANT

which he was bred. The horse in the center, fully caparisoned, is "Cincinnati," also a present from a gentleman in St. Louis, who on his death-bed sent for Grant and presented him with "the finest horse in the world." The little black pony to the right is "Jeff Davis," captured in a cavalry raid on the plantation of Joe Davis, brother of the Confederate President, near Vicksburg. "Jeff Davis" looks indifferent, but "Cincinnati" and "Egypt" have pricked up their ears. Perhaps they were looking at General Grant.

WAR–HORSES

By Theo. F. Rodenbough
Brigadier-General, United States Army (Retired)

THE battle chargers of the general officers of the Confederate and Federal armies during the American Civil War, wrote their names upon the scrolls of history by their high grade of sagacity and faithfulness. They carried their masters upon the tedious march and over the bullet-swept battlefields, and seemed to realize their importance in the conflict. The horse of the commanding officer was as well known to the rank and file as the general himself, and the soldiers were as affectionately attached to the animal as was the master.

GENERAL GRANT'S HORSES

When the Civil War broke out, my father,* General Grant, was appointed colonel of the Twenty-first Illinois Volunteer Infantry and on joining the regiment purchased a horse in Galena, Illinois. This horse, though a strong animal, proved to be unfitted for the service and, when my father was taking his regiment from Springfield, Illinois, to Missouri, he encamped on the Illinois River for several days. During the time they were there a farmer brought in a horse called "Jack." This animal was a cream-colored horse, with black eyes, mane and tail of silver white, his hair gradually becoming darker toward his feet. He was a noble animal, high spirited, very intelligent and an excellent horse in every way. He was a stallion and of considerable value. My father used him until after the battle of Chattanooga (November, 1863), as an extra horse

* This account was furnished at the author's request by General Frederick Dent Grant, U. S. A.—T. F. R.

"STONEWALL" JACKSON'S WAR–HORSE SHORTLY AFTER HIS MASTER'S DEATH

The negative of this picture, made in 1863, not long after the terrible tragedy of General Jackson's death, was destroyed in the great Richmond fire of 1865. The print is believed to be unique, and here reproduced for the first time. All day long on May 2d of 1863, "Old Sorrel," as the soldiers called him, had borne his master on the most successful flanking march of the war, which ended in the Confederate victory at Chancellorsville. There have not been many movements in military history so brilliant and decisive in their effect. At nightfall Jackson mounted "Fancy" for the last time, and rode out to reconnoiter. Galloping back to avoid the Federal bullets, he and his staff were mistaken for foes and fired upon by their own men. Jackson reeled from the saddle into the arms of Captain Milburn, severely wounded. The horse bolted toward the Union lines, but was recovered and placed in the stable of Governor John Letcher at Richmond.

and for parades and ceremonial occasions. At the time of the Sanitary Fair in Chicago (1863 or '64), General Grant gave him to the fair, where he was raffled off, bringing $4,000 to the Sanitary Commission.

Soon after my father was made a brigadier-general, (August 8, 1861), he purchased a pony for me and also another horse for field service for himself. At the battle of Belmont (November 7, 1861), his horse was killed under him and he took my pony. The pony was quite small and my father, feeling that the commanding general on the field should have a larger mount, turned the pony over to one of his aides-decamp (Captain Hyllier) and mounted the captain's horse. The pony was lost in the battle.

The next horse that my father purchased for field service was a roan called "Fox," a very powerful and spirited animal and of great endurance. This horse he rode during the siege and battles around Fort Donelson and also at Shiloh.

At the battle of Shiloh the Confederates left on the field a rawboned horse, very ugly and apparently good for nothing. As a joke, the officer who found this animal on the field, sent it with his compliments, to Colonel Lagow, one of my father's aides-de-camp, who always kept a very excellent mount and was a man of means. The other officers of the staff "jollied" the colonel about this gift. When my father saw him, he told the colonel that the animal was a thoroughbred and a valuable mount and that if he, Lagow, did not wish to keep the horse he would be glad to have him. Because of his appearance he was named "Kangaroo," and after a short period of rest and feeding and care he turned out to be a magnificent animal and was used by my father during the Vicksburg campaign.

In this campaign, General Grant had two other horses, both of them very handsome, one of which he gave away and the other he used until late in the war. During the campaign and siege of Vicksburg, a cavalry raid or scouting party arrived at Joe Davis' plantation (the brother of Jefferson Davis,

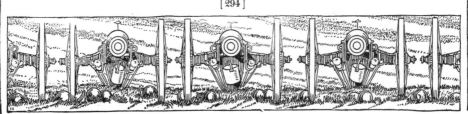

MEADE'S BATTLE–SCARRED MOUNT THREE MONTHS AFTER GETTYSBURG

"Baldy" was the horse that carried General George G. Meade from September, 1861, to the end of the war, except when "absent on sick leave." His war record is remarkable for the number of wounds from which he recovered, reporting for duty each time he was convalescent. He was wounded twice at the first battle of Bull Run, before he came into General Meade's possession. Left on the field for dead at Antietam, he was later discovered quietly grazing, with a deep wound in his neck. Again, at Gettysburg, a bullet lodged between his ribs and rendered him unable to carry his owner again until after Appomattox. "Baldy" was a bright bay horse, with white face and feet. This bullet-scarred veteran followed General Meade's hearse to his last resting-place in 1872, and survived him by a decade. The photograph was taken in October, 1863.

President of the Confederacy) and there captured a black pony which was brought to the rear of the city and presented to me. The animal was worn out when it reached headquarters but was a very easy riding horse and I used him once or twice. With care he began to pick up and soon carried himself in fine shape.

At that time my father was suffering with a carbuncle and his horse being restless caused him a great deal of pain. It was necessary for General Grant to visit the lines frequently and one day he took this pony for that purpose. The gait of the pony was so delightful that he directed that he be turned over to the quartermaster as a captured horse and a board of officers be convened to appraise the animal. This was done and my father purchased the animal and kept him until he died, which was long after the Civil War. This pony was known as " Jeff Davis."

After the battle of Chattanooga, General Grant went to St. Louis, where I was at the time, critically ill from dysentery contracted during the siege of Vicksburg. During the time of his visit to the city he received a letter from a gentleman who signed his name "S. S. Grant," the initials being the same as those of a brother of my father's, who had died in the summer of 1861. S. S. Grant wrote to the effect that he was very desirous of seeing General Grant but that he was ill and confined to his room at the Lindell Hotel and begged him to call, as he had something important to say which my father might be gratified to hear.

The name excited my father's curiosity and he called at the hotel to meet the gentleman who told him that he had, he thought, the finest horse in the world, and knowing General Grant's great liking for horses he had concluded, inasmuch as he would never be able to ride again, that he would like to give his horse to him; that he desired that the horse should have a good home and tender care and that the only condition that he would make in parting with him would be that the person receiving him would see that he was never ill-treated, and

GENERAL SHERIDAN'S "WINCHESTER"

"Winchester" wore no such gaudy trappings when he sprang "up from the South, at break of day" on that famous ride of October 19, 1864, which has been immortalized in Thomas Buchanan Read's poem. The silver-mounted saddle was presented later by admiring friends of his owner. The sleek neck then was dark with sweat, and the quivering nostrils were flecked with foam at the end of the twenty-mile dash that brought hope and courage to an army and turned defeat into the overwhelming victory of Cedar Creek. Sheridan himself was as careful of his appearance as Custer was irregular in his field dress. He was always careful of his horse, but in the field decked him in nothing more elaborate than a plain McClellan saddle and army blanket.

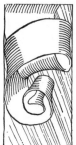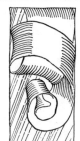

should never fall into the hands of a person that would ill-treat him. This promise was given and General Grant accepted the horse and called him "Cincinnati." This was his battle charger until the end of the war and was kept by him until the horse died at Admiral Ammen's farm in Maryland, in 1878.*

About this time (January, 1864) some people in Illinois found a horse in the southern part of that State, which they thought was remarkably beautiful. They purchased him and sent him as a present to my father. This horse was known as "Egypt" as he was raised, or at least came from southern Illinois, a district known in the State as Egypt, as the northern part was known as Canaan.

GENERAL LEE'S "TRAVELLER"

The most famous of the horses in the stables of General Lee, the Confederate commander, was "Traveller," an iron gray horse. He was raised in Greenbrier County, near Blue Sulphur Springs, and, as a colt, won first prize at a fair in Lewisburg, Virginia. When hostilities commenced between the North and the South, the horse, then known as "Jeff Davis," was owned by Major Thomas L. Broun, who had paid $175 (in gold) for him. Lee first saw the gray in the mountains of West Virginia. He instantly became attached to him, and always called him "my colt."

In the spring of 1862, this horse finally became the

* "Cincinnati" was the son of "Lexington," the fastest four-mile thoroughbred in the United States, time 7:19¾ minutes. "Cincinnati" nearly equaled the speed of his half-brother, "Kentucky," and Grant was offered $10,000 in gold or its equivalent for him, but refused. He was seventeen hands high, and in the estimation of Grant was the finest horse that he had ever seen. Grant rarely permitted anyone to mount the horse —two exceptions were Admiral Daniel Ammen and Lincoln. Ammen saved Grant's life from drowning while a school-boy. Grant says: "Lincoln spent the latter days of his life with me. He came to City Point in the last month of the war and was with me all the time. He was a fine horseman and rode my horse 'Cincinnati' every day."—T. F. R.

GENERAL ALFRED PLEASONTON AND HIS HORSE

This is the horse which General Pleasonton brought with him from Utah in 1861. This charger carried him through the Peninsular campaign when he was a major in the Second Cavalry, commanding the regiment and covering the march of the Federal army to Yorktown, August 18 and 19, 1862. It bore him at Antietam, Fredericksburg, and Chancellorsville, where Pleasonton distinguished himself by checking the flank attack of the Confederates on the Federal right, and perhaps it stepped forth a little more proudly when its owner was given command of the entire cavalry corps of the Army of the Potomac on June 7, 1863. This photograph was taken at Falmouth, Va., in the latter year. General Pleasonton is riding the same charger in the photograph of himself and Custer used to illustrate the battle of Gettysburg on page 237.

property of the general, who paid $200 in currency for him. He changed the name of his charger to "Traveller" and from the date of purchase it became almost a daily sight to see the commander astride the gray, riding about the camp.

There were a number of battle horses in Lee's stables during the war. There were "Grace Darling," "Brown Roan," "Lucy Long," "Ajax," and "Richmond," but of them all "Traveller" became the especial companion of the general. The fine proportions of this horse immediately attracted attention. He was gray in color, with black points, a long mane and long flowing tail. He stood sixteen hands high, and was five years old in the spring of 1862. His figure was muscular, with a deep chest and short back, strong haunches, flat legs, small head, quick eyes, broad forehead, and small feet. His rapid, springy step and bold carriage made him conspicuous in the camps of the Confederates. On a long and tedious march with the Army of Northern Virginia he easily carried Lee's weight at five or six miles an hour, without faltering, and at the end of the day's hard travel seemed to be as fresh as at the beginning.

The other horses broke under the strain and hardships; "Lucy Long," purchased by General "Jeb" Stuart from Stephen Dandridge and presented to Lee, served for two years in alternation with "Traveller," but in the fall of 1864 became unserviceable and was sent into the country to recuperate.* "Richmond," "Ajax," and "Brown Roan" each in turn proved unequal to the rigors of war.

* "Lucy Long," second to "Traveller" in Lee's affections, was recalled from the country just before the evacuation of Richmond; but during the confusion she was placed with the public horses and sent to Danville, and Lee lost all trace of his war-horse. A thorough search was made, and finally, in 1866, she was discovered and brought to Lexington to pass her days in leisure with General Lee and "Traveller." After a number of years the mare became feeble and seemed to lose interest in life, and when "Lucy Long" reached about thirty-three years of age a son of General Lee mercifully chloroformed the veteran war-horse of the Army of Northern Virginia.

[300]

GENERAL RUFUS INGALLS' CHARGER

Like General Grant's "Cincinnati," this horse was present at Lee's surrender at Appomattox. Major-General Rufus Ingalls was chief quartermaster of the Army of the Potomac. After the surrender he asked permission to visit the Confederate lines and renew his acquaintance with some old friends, class-mates and companions in arms. He returned with Cadmus M. Wilcox, who had been Grant's groomsman when he was married; James Longstreet, who had also been at his wedding; Heth, Gordon, Pickett, and a number of others. The American eagle is plainly visible on the major-general's saddle-cloth, which the charger is wearing. The whole outfit is spick and span, though the double bridle is not according to army regulations, and General Ingalls even enjoyed the luxury of a dog at the time this photograph was taken.

But "Traveller" sturdily accepted and withstood the hardships of the campaigns in Virginia, Maryland, and Pennsylvania. When in April, 1865, the last battle of the Army of Northern Virginia had been fought, the veteran war-horse was still on duty. When Lee rode to the McLean house at Appomattox Court House, he was astride of "Traveller," and it was this faithful four-footed companion who carried the Southern leader back to his waiting army, and then to Richmond.

When Lee became a private citizen and retired to Washington and Lee University, as its president, the veteran war-horse was still with him, and as the years passed and both master and servant neared life's ending they became more closely attached.* As the funeral cortège accompanied Lee to his last resting place, "Traveller" marched behind the hearse, his step slow and his head bowed, as if he understood the import of the occasion.

GENERAL McCLELLAN'S HORSES

While General McClellan was in command of the Army of the Potomac, in 1862, he had a number of war-horses. The favorite of them all was "Daniel Webster," soon called by the members of the general's staff "that devil Dan," because of his speed with which the staff officers had great difficulty in keeping pace. During the battle of the Antietam the great horse carried the commander safely through the day.

"Daniel Webster" was a dark bay about seventeen hands high, pure bred, with good action, never showing signs of fatigue, no matter how hard the test. He was extremely hand-

* During the life of "Traveller" after the war, he was the pet of the countryside about Lexington, Va. Many marks of affection were showered upon him. Admiring friends in England sent two sets of equipment for the veteran war-horse. Ladies in Baltimore, Md., bestowed another highly decorated set, and another came from friends at the Confederate capital, Richmond. But the set that seemed to most please "Traveller" was the one sent from St. Louis, in Missouri.

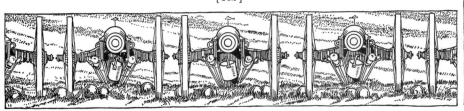

GENERAL RAWLINS' MOUNT

It is a proud little darkey boy who is exercising the horse of a general—John Aaron Rawlins, the Federal brigadier-general of volunteers, who was later promoted to the rank of major-general, U. S. A., for gallant and meritorious services during the campaign terminating with the surrender of the army under General Lee. The noble horse himself is looking around with a mildly inquiring air at the strange new instrument which the photographer is leveling at him.

some, with more than ordinary horse-sense. He was a fast walker, an important requisite in a commander's charger, but a disagreeable quality for the staff officers whose horses were kept at a slow trot. After McClellan retired to private life, "Dan" became the family horse at Orange, N. J., where he died at the age of twenty-three. McClellan said: "No soldier ever had a better horse than I had in 'Daniel Webster.'"

McClellan also had a charger named "Burns," a fiery black, named after an army friend who gave the horse to Mc-Clellan. His one failing was that at dinner time he would bolt for his oats regardless of how much depended on McClellan's presence on the battlefield at the critical moment, as in the battle of the Antietam. Running at dinner time became so much an obsession with "Burns" that McClellan was always careful not to be mounted on him at that hour of the day.*

GENERAL SHERMAN'S HORSES

General Sherman's best war-horse was killed early in the Civil War, at the battle of Shiloh, where he led the right wing of the Federal army against General A. S. Johnston's Confederate legions. Two of his other chargers were killed while being held by an orderly. Of the many horses that carried Sherman through the remaining years of the struggle, two had

* The Editor has vivid recollection of "Little Mac" in April, 1862 (then at the height of his popularity), during a ride from Fort Monroe to Big Bethel, being the first day's march of the Army of the Potomac toward Yorktown, Va. The writer commanded the escort (a squadron, Second U. S. Cavalry), and during the ten or twelve miles of the route covered at a gallop, between double lines of infantry, halted for the moment to permit the commanding general to pass, the air was literally "rent" with the cheers of the troops, filled with high hopes of an early entrance to the Confederate capital. As the brilliant staff, headed by the young chieftain of magnetic presence, with bared head, mounted on "Black Burns," swept along amid clatter of hoof, jingle of equipment, and loud hurrahs, the thought came to the writer that thus the "Little Corporal" was wont to inspire his devoted legions to loud acclaim of *Vive l'Empereur.* (T. F. R.)

GENERAL BUTTERFIELD, A WELL–MOUNTED INFANTRY GENERAL

This is a photograph of the well-mounted chief-of-staff and corps commander of the Army of the Potomac. It was the custom of generals who had been infantry officers to set their own pace, regardless of their cavalry escort. A cavalryman detailed to escort him tells the following story: "We started out with General Butterfield one day upon the Potomac to meet Confederate officers in relation to the exchange of prisoners. My regiment was ordered out to escort him. The infantry officers, accustomed to riding alone, made their way regardless of their escorts, and inside of half an hour my column was distributed over two miles of road; General Butter-field did not adapt his riding to the pace of the escort and made it very difficult for the cavalry to follow him."

a particular place in the general's affections—"Lexington" and "Sam." The former was a Kentucky thoroughbred, and his fine action attracted the admiration of all who saw him. When the Federal forces finally entered and occupied Atlanta, in 1864, Sherman was astride of "Lexington"; and after peace was declared, in 1865, the general rode the same horse in the final review of his army in Washington.

"Sam" was a large, half-thoroughbred bay, sixteen and a half hands high. He possessed great speed, strength, and endurance. The horse made one of the longest and most difficult marches ever recorded in history, from Vicksburg to Washington, through the cities of Atlanta, Savannah, Columbia, and Richmond. He had a rapid gait, and could march five miles an hour at a walk. While under fire "Sam" was as calm and steady as his brave master. He was wounded several times, while mounted, and the fault was usually due to Sherman's disregard of the horse's anxiety to seek cover. In 1865, Sherman retired "Sam" to a well-earned rest, on an Illinois farm, where he received every mark of affection. The gallant war-horse died of extreme old age, in 1884.

GENERAL JACKSON'S HORSES

General Thomas J. ("Stonewall") Jackson, the great Southern leader, had his favorite battle charger, which at the beginning of the war was thought to be about eleven years old. On May 9, 1861, while Jackson was in command of the garrison at Harper's Ferry, a train load of supplies and horses, on the way to the Federal camps, was captured. Among the horses was one that attracted Jackson's attention. He purchased the animal from his quartermaster's department for his own personal use. The horse, named "Old Sorrel," carried Jackson over many of the bullet-swept battlefields and was with Jackson when that officer fell before the volley of his own men at the battle of Chancellorsville. During the swift campaign through the Shenandoah, in 1862, when Jackson

AN "AIDE" OF GENERAL GRANT

A photograph of little "Jeff Davis," a pony that won General Grant's approval at the siege of Vicksburg by his easy gait. General Grant was suffering with a carbuncle and needed a horse with easy paces. A cavalry detachment had captured a suitable mount on the plantation of Joe Davis, brother of the President of the Confederacy, and that is how the little black pony came by his name. The great Union general was more apt to call him "Little Jeff." The general used him throughout the siege, but he felt that the commanding general on the battlefield should have a larger mount, and "Jeff Davis" in this photograph is apparently saddled for an orderly or aide. The little horse remained with General Grant until he died.

marched his "foot cavalry" towards the citadel at Washington, the horse was his constant companion.

In 1884, a state fair was held at Hagerstown, in Maryland, and one of the most interesting sights was that of the veteran war horse, "Old Sorrel," tethered in a corral and quietly munching choice bits of vegetables and hay. Before the fair was ended nearly all the mane and hair of his tail had disappeared, having been plucked by scores of relic hunters. For many years after the cessation of hostilities, Jackson's gallant old war-horse was held in tender esteem at the South.

When the veteran battle charger died, admirers of Jackson sent the carcass to a taxidermist and the gallant steed now rests in the Soldier's Home in Richmond, Virginia.*

GENERAL SHERIDAN'S "RIENZI"

General Sheridan's charger was foaled at or near Grand Rapids, Michigan, of the Black Hawk stock, and was brought into the Federal army by an officer of the Second Michigan Cavalry. He was presented to Sheridan, then colonel of the regiment, by the officers, in the spring of 1862, while the regiment was stationed at Rienzi, Mississippi; the horse was nearly three years old. He was over seventeen hands in height, powerfully built, with a deep chest, strong shoulders, a broad forehead, a clear eye and of great intelligence. In his prime he was one of the strongest horses Sheridan ever knew, very active, and one of the fastest walkers in the Federal army. "Rienzi" always held his head high, and by the quickness of his movements created the impression that he was exceedingly impetuous, but Sheridan was always able to control him by a firm hand and a few words. He was as cool and quiet under fire as any veteran trooper in the Cavalry Corps.

At the battle of Cedar Creek, October 19, 1864, the name of the horse was changed from "Rienzi" to "Winchester," a name derived from the town made famous by Sheridan's ride

* From the Confederate Veteran.

MOUNTS FOR ALL THE CAVALRYMEN

Behind this mixed command grouped in front of the camp stand a great number of horses. There is at least one for every cavalryman in the picture, a state of affairs that did not last long; the photograph was evidently taken before the Union armies were using up five hundred horses a day. The picture illustrates one of the few quiet hours that the Federal cavalrymen enjoyed. Infantry boys are evidently fraternizing with their comrades of the cavalry at an advanced post. The horn that shows on the cap of the second man at the left of the photograph is the insignia, adopted from European light infantry, of the infantry of the Army of the Potomac. The drummer boy also belongs to the infantry arm, and the leather scabbard of the officer kneeling near the center of the picture likewise indicates the infantry. Such photographs as these are rare. Both horses and men were resting for once.

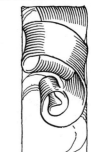

to save his army in the Shenandoah Valley. Poets, sculptors, and painters have made the charger the subject of their works. Thomas Buchanan Read was inspired to write his immortal poem, "Sheridan's Ride," which thrilled the North.

From an account of this affair in "Scribner's Magazine," by General G. W. Forsyth, who accompanied Sheridan as aide-de-camp, the following is quoted:

The distance from Winchester to Cedar Creek, on the north bank of which the Army of the Shenandoah lay encamped, is a little less than nineteen miles. As we debouched into the fields . . . the general would wave his hat to the men and point to the front, never lessening his speed as he pressed forward. It was enough. One glance at the eager face and familiar black horse and they knew him and, starting to their feet, they swung their caps around their heads and broke into cheers as he passed beyond them; and then gathering up their belongings started after him for the front, shouting to their comrades farther out in the fields, "Sheridan! Sheridan!" waving their hats and pointing after him as he dashed onward. . . . So rapid had been our gait that nearly all of the escort save the commanding officer and a few of his best mounted men had been distanced, for they were more heavily weighted and ordinary troop horses could not live at such a pace.

In one of the closing scenes of the war—Five Forks—Sheridan was personally directing a movement against the Confederates who were protected by temporary entrenchments about two feet high. The Federal forces, both cavalry and infantry, were suffering from a sharp fire, which caused them to hesitate. "Where is my battle-flag?" cried Sheridan. Seizing it by the staff, he dashed ahead, followed by his command. The gallant steed leaped the low works and landed the Federal general fairly amid the astonished Southerners. Close behind him came Merritt's cavalrymen in a resistless charge which swept the Confederates backward in confusion. The horse passed a comfortable old age in his master's stable and died in Chicago, in 1878; the lifelike remains are now in the Museum at Governor's Island, N. Y., as a gift from his owner.

TWO FINE HORSES—THE PROVOST-MARSHAL'S MOUNTS

A couple of examples of the care given to horses at Giesboro. These two serviceable chargers belonged to Colonel George Henry Sharpe, Provost-Marshal of the Army of the Potomac. The provost-marshal of a great army must be well mounted. It is the duty of the provost-guard to arrest all criminals, take charge of deserters, follow the army and restore strag-glers to their regiments. This was no easy matter with an army of 120,000 men. Prisoners of war were also turned over to its care to be sent back to the institutions in the North. It is no wonder that the chief provided himself with powerful mounts. This photograph was taken at Brandy Station just before the strenuous campaign of the Wilderness.

GENERAL STUART'S "HIGHFLY"

The battle horse, "Highfly," carried General "Jeb" Stuart through many campaigns and had become his favored companion. The intelligence and faithfulness of the steed had many times borne the dashing cavalier through desperate perils. In the summer of 1862, at Verdiersville on the plank road between Fredericksburg and Orange, in Virginia, Stuart was stretched out upon a bench on the porch of the tavern, awaiting the arrival of General Fitzhugh Lee with whom he desired to confer on the next movement of the cavalry. "Highfly" was unbridled and grazing in the yard near the road. The clatter of horses aroused the Confederate general, and he walked to the roadway, leaving behind on the bench his hat, in which was a black plume, the pride of Stuart's heart. Suddenly, horsemen dashed around the bend in the road and Stuart was within gunshot of Federal cavalry. He was nonplussed; he had expected to see Fitzhugh Lee. Mounting his faithful and speedy bay he soon left the chagrined cavalry far behind, but the foe carried away the hat with its black plume.

GENERAL MEADE'S "BALDY"

In the first great battle of the Civil War, at Bull Run, there was a bright bay horse, with white face and feet. His rider was seriously wounded. The horse was turned back to the quartermaster to recover from his wounds received that day. Later, in September, General Meade bought the horse and named him "Baldy." Though Meade became deeply attached to the horse, his staff officers soon began to complain of the peculiar pace of "Baldy," which was hard to follow. He had a racking gait that was faster than a walk and slow for a trot and compelled the staff, alternately, to trot and then to drop into a walk, causing great discomfort.

"Baldy's" war record was remarkable. He was wounded twice at the first battle of Bull Run; he was at the battle of Drainesville; he took part in two of the seven days' fighting

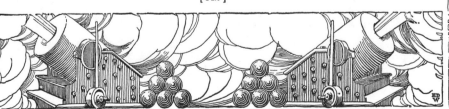

THE HALT

On this and the opposite page are shown types of the horses for which the Northern States were ransacked to furnish mounts for the staff and regimental officers of the Union armies. Small wonder that this magnificent, well-groomed animal has excited the admiration of his own master who is critically looking him over. The officer is Captain Harry Page, quartermaster of the Headquarters of the Army of the Potomac, subsequently colonel and chief quartermaster of the cavalry corps under Sheridan. This was one of the most arduous posts of duty in the entire service, and one whose necessities during the severe campaigns up the Shenandoah Valley, and around Richmond, kept the young colonel always upon his mettle. He has cultivated the ability to rest and relax when the opportunity arrives. He is evidently awaiting the arrival of his wagon-train, when he will again become active at the pitching of the tents and the parking of the wagons.

around Richmond in the summer of 1862; at Groveton, August 29th, at the second battle of Bull Run; at South Mountain and at Antietam. In the last battle the gallant horse was left on the field as dead, but in the next Federal advance "Baldy" was discovered quietly grazing on the battle-ground, with a deep wound in his neck. He was tenderly cared for and soon was again fit for duty. He bore the general at the battles of Fredericksburg and Chancellorsville. For two days "Baldy" was present at Gettysburg, where he received his most grievous wound from a bullet entering his body between the ribs, and lodging there. Meade would not part with the gallant horse, and kept him with the army until the following spring.

In the preparations of the Army of the Potomac for their last campaign, "Baldy" was sent to pasture at Downingtown, in Pennsylvania. After the surrender of Lee's army at Appomattox, Meade hurried to Philadelphia where he again met his faithful charger, fully recovered. For many years the horse and the general were inseparable companions, and when Meade died in 1872, the bullet-scarred war-horse followed the hearse. Ten years later "Baldy" died, and his head and two fore hoofs were mounted and are now cherished relics of the George G. Meade Post, Grand Army of the Republic, in Philadelphia.

GENERAL THOMAS' "BILLY"

The "Rock of Chickamauga," General George H. Thomas, possessed two intelligent war-horses, both powerful and large, and able to carry the general, who weighed nearly two hundred pounds. Both horses were bays; one named "Billy" (after Thomas' friend, General Sherman) was the darker of the two, about sixteen hands high, and stout in build. He was, like his owner, sedate in all his movements and was not easily disturbed from his habitual calm by bursting shells or the turmoil of battle. Even in retreat, the horse did not hurry his footsteps unduly, and provoked the staff by his deliberate pace.

"Billy" bore General Thomas through the campaigns in

AN OFFICER'S MOUNT

Captain Webster, whose horse this is, showed a just pride in his steed. Observe how the reins are hitched over the saddle to exhibit the arched neck to the best advantage. The equipment is regulation except for the unhooded stirrups. It has the preferable single line, curb bit, no breast strap and no martingale. The saddle is the McClellan, so-called because adopted through recommendations made by General George B. McClellan after his official European tour in 1860, although it was in reality a modification of the Mexican or Texas tree. It was an excellent saddle, and in an improved pattern remained after fifty years of trial still the standard saddle of the United States regular cavalry. In its original form it was covered with rawhide instead of leather, and when this covering split the seat became very uncomfortable to the rider. Captain Webster used a saddle cloth instead of the usual folded blanket. His horse's shiny coat shows recent thorough grooming.

middle Tennessee and northern Georgia. He was on the fields of Chickamauga and Chattanooga, and marched with the Federal host in the advance upon Atlanta. From Atlanta, he next moved to Nashville where his master engineered the crushing defeat to the Confederate arms in the winter of 1864, the last battle in which Thomas and "Billy" participated.

GENERAL HOOKER'S "LOOKOUT"

General Hooker first became acquainted with his famous charger, "Lookout," while the animal was stabled in New York, and when Louis Napoleon, the French emperor, and an English gentleman of wealth were bidding for its purchase. Napoleon repeatedly offered the owner a thousand dollars for the horse. Hooker finally obtained him and rode him in the campaigns in which he later participated.

"Lookout" was raised in Kentucky, and he was a three-quarters bred, out of a half bred mare by Mambrino. He was of a rich chestnut color, stood nearly seventeen hands high, and had long slender legs. Despite his great height, the horse was known to trot a mile in two minutes and forty-five seconds. When the battle of Chattanooga occurred, the horse was seven years old. It was here that the animal received its name of "Lookout." The grandeur of "Lookout's" stride and his height dwarfed many gallant war-horses and he has been termed the finest charger in the army.

GENERAL KEARNY'S HORSES

General Philip Kearny was a veteran of the Mexican War, with the rank of captain. It had been decided to equip Kearny's troop (First United States Dragoons) with horses all of the same color, and he went to Illinois to purchase them. He was assisted in the work by Abraham Lincoln and finally found himself in possession of one hundred gray horses. While engaged in battle before the City of Mexico, mounted upon one of the newly purchased grays, "Monmouth," Kearny was

WHEN SLEEK HORSES WERE PLENTIFUL—YORKTOWN, 1862

Confederate winter quarters near Yorktown, Virginia, which had passed into Federal hands. When McClellan moved to the Peninsula in the spring of 1862 he had but few cavalry, but every officer was provided with a handsome charger on which he pranced gaily up and down the lines. "Little Mac" himself rode preferably at full speed. His appearance was the signal for an outburst of cheering. It was to be a picnic parade of the well-equipped army to the Confederate capital. It is presumable that the portly officer in the center of the picture had lost some weight, and the chargers some sleekness before they were through with Lee and Jackson. To such an extent had overwork and disease reduced the number of cavalry horses during McClellan's retreat from the Peninsula that when General Stuart made his raid into Pennsylvania, October 11th of the same year, only eight hundred Federal cavalry could be mounted to follow him. Under date of October 21st, McClellan wrote to General Halleck: "Exclusive of the cavalry force now engaged in picketing the river, I have not at present over one thousand horses for service. Without more cavalry horses our communications from the moment we march would be at the mercy of the large cavalry force of the enemy."

wounded in an arm, which was finally amputated. During the Civil War, Kearny had many excellent animals at his command, but his most celebrated steed was "Moscow," a high-spirited white horse. On the battlefield, "Moscow" was conspicuous because of his white coat, but Kearny was heedless of the protests of his staff against his needless exposure.

Another war-horse belonging to General Kearny was "Decatur," a light bay, which was shot through the neck in the battle of Fair Oaks or Seven Pines. "Bayard," a brown horse, was ridden by Kearny at this battle, and his fame will ever stand in history through the poem by Stedman, "Kearny at Seven Pines." At the battle of Chantilly, Kearny and "Bayard" were advancing alone near the close of the struggle, when they met with a regiment of Confederate infantry. "Bayard" instantly wheeled and dashed from danger, with Kearny laying flat upon the horse's neck. A shower of bullets fell about the general and his charger. They seemed about to escape when a fatal bullet struck the general.

The leader of the Southern legions in the West, General Albert Sidney Johnston, rode a magnificent thoroughbred bay, named "Fire-eater," on the battlefield. The steed stood patiently like a veteran when the bullets and shells hurtled about him and his master, but when the command came to charge, he was all fire and vim, like that Sunday in April, 1862, the first day of the bloody battle of Shiloh.

Among the hundreds of generals' mounts which became famous by their conspicuous bravery and sagacity on the battlefields, were General Fitzhugh Lee's little mare, "Nellie Gray," which was killed at the battle of Opequon Creek; Major-General Patrick R. Cleburne's "Dixie," killed at the battle of Perryville; General Adam R. Johnson's "Joe Smith," which was noted for its speed and endurance; and General Benjamin F. Butler's war-horse, "Almond Eye," a name derived from the peculiar formation of the eyes of the horse.

CHAPTER
TWELVE

MOUNTING THE CAVALRY
OF THE UNION ARMY

AN ORDERLY WITH AN OFFICER'S MOUNT

A THOUSAND FEDERAL CAVALRY HORSES

Lovers of horses will appreciate, in this photograph of 1864, the characteristic friendly fashion in which the cavalry "mounts" are gathering in deep communion. The numerous groups of horses in the corrals of the great depot at Giesboro, D. C., are apparently holding a series of conferences on their prospects in the coming battles. Presently all those who are in condition will resolve themselves into a committee of the whole and go off to war, whence they will return here only for hospital treatment. The corrals at Giesboro could easily contain a thousand horses, and they were never overcrowded. It was not until the true value of

"TALKING IT OVER"

cavalry was discovered, from the experience of the first two years of warfare, that this great depot was established, but it was most efficiently handled. Giesboro was a great teacher in regard to the care of horses. Cavalrymen learned what to guard against. The knowledge was acquired partly from field service, but in a great measure from the opportunity for leisurely observation, an opportunity somewhat analogous to that of a physician in a great metropolitan hospital where every kind of a physical problem has to be solved.

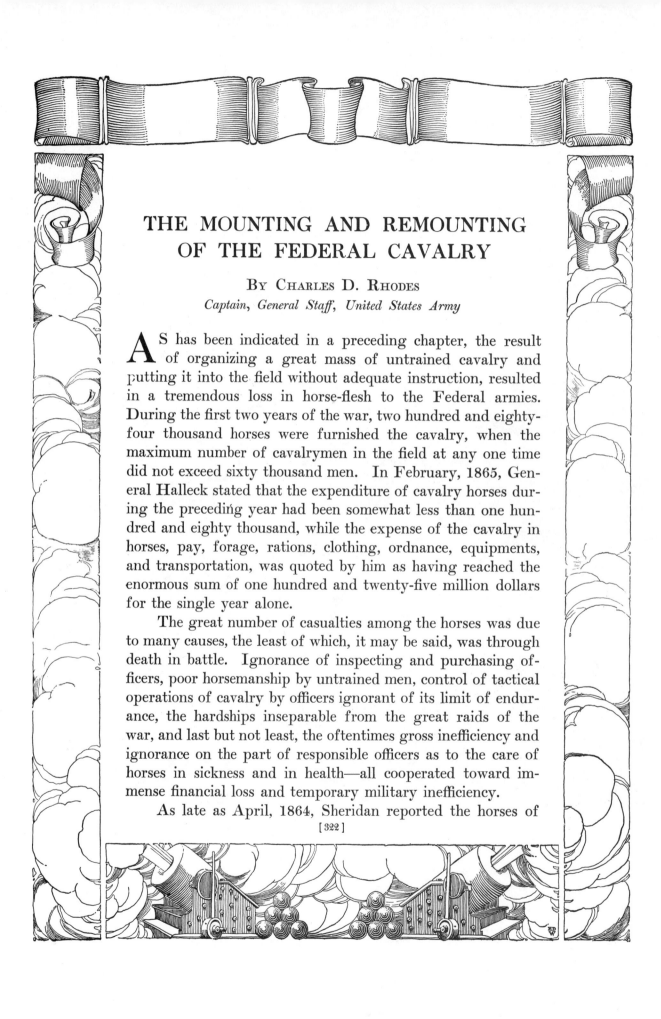

THE MOUNTING AND REMOUNTING
OF THE FEDERAL CAVALRY

By Charles D. Rhodes
Captain, General Staff, United States Army

AS has been indicated in a preceding chapter, the result of organizing a great mass of untrained cavalry and putting it into the field without adequate instruction, resulted in a tremendous loss in horse-flesh to the Federal armies. During the first two years of the war, two hundred and eighty-four thousand horses were furnished the cavalry, when the maximum number of cavalrymen in the field at any one time did not exceed sixty thousand men. In February, 1865, General Halleck stated that the expenditure of cavalry horses during the preceding year had been somewhat less than one hundred and eighty thousand, while the expense of the cavalry in horses, pay, forage, rations, clothing, ordnance, equipments, and transportation, was quoted by him as having reached the enormous sum of one hundred and twenty-five million dollars for the single year alone.

The great number of casualties among the horses was due to many causes, the least of which, it may be said, was through death in battle. Ignorance of inspecting and purchasing officers, poor horsemanship by untrained men, control of tactical operations of cavalry by officers ignorant of its limit of endurance, the hardships inseparable from the great raids of the war, and last but not least, the oftentimes gross inefficiency and ignorance on the part of responsible officers as to the care of horses in sickness and in health—all cooperated toward immense financial loss and temporary military inefficiency.

As late as April, 1864, Sheridan reported the horses of

CAVALRY STABLES AT ARLINGTON—THE GREAT CORRAL IN THE DISTANCE, 3½ MILES

INTERIOR VIEW OF CAVALRY STABLES AT ARLINGTON

The streets of Washington re-echoed throughout the war with the clatter of horses' hoofs. Mounted aides, couriers, the general staff, the officers of the various regiments stationed in and about the Capital all had their chargers, and Giesboro was too far away to stable them. In the left-hand corner of the upper picture, the Giesboro corral shown on the following pages can be seen in the distance. A glance at the photograph will show that the corral was too far away to be convenient for horses in use in Washington. It is three and a half miles as the crow flies from Arlington to the corral. The photographer has written on the face of the lower photograph the date, "June 29, 1864." At this moment Grant was swinging his cavalry toward Petersburg.

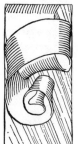

his command worn out by the mistaken use of mounted men to protect trains—a duty which could be as well and much more economically performed by infantry; and by the unnecessary picket-duty, encircling the great infantry and cavalry camps of the Army of the Potomac on an irregular curve of nearly sixty miles.

In October, 1862, when service in the Peninsula campaign and in that of the Army of Virginia, had brought the number of mounted cavalrymen down to less than a good-sized regiment, McClellan wrote Halleck:

It is absolutely necessary that some energetic measures be taken to supply the cavalry of this army with remount horses. The present rate of supply is 1,050 per week for the entire army here and in front of Washington. From this number the artillery draw for their batteries.

The demand for horses was so great that in many cases they were sent on active service before recovering sufficiently from the fatigue incident to a long railway journey. In one case reported, horses were left on railroad cars fifty hours without food or water, and were then taken out, issued, and used for immediate service in the field.

To such an extent had overwork and disease reduced the number of cavalry horses in the Army of the Potomac, that when the Confederate general, Stuart, made his daring raid into Pennsylvania, in October, 1862, only eight hundred Federal cavalrymen could be mounted to follow him.

Of course the original mounting of the cavalry, field-artillery, and field- and staff-officers caused a great demand for suitable chargers throughout the North. The draft animals required for transportation purposes increased the scarcity of suitable horses. Furthermore, with the unexpected losses during the first years of the war came such a dearth of animals suitable for the cavalry service, that in course of time almost any remount which conformed to the general specifications of a horse, was thankfully accepted by the Government.

SHELTER FOR SIX THOUSAND HORSES AT GIESBORO

Thirty-two immense stables, besides hospitals and other buildings, provided shelter for six thousand horses at the big cavalry depot, District of Columbia, but most of the stock was kept in open sheds or in corrals. The stockyards alone covered forty-five acres. The stables were large, well-lighted buildings with thousands of scrupulously clean stalls. The horses were divided into serviceable and unserviceable classes. About sixty per cent. of the horses received from the field for recuperation were returned to active service. Five thousand men were employed in August, 1863, to rush this cavalry depot to completion. Its maintenance was one of the costly items which aggregated an expenditure by the Union Government of $1,000,-000 a day during the entire period of the war—an expenditure running even as high as $4,000,000 a day.

THE BARRACKS AT GIESBORO

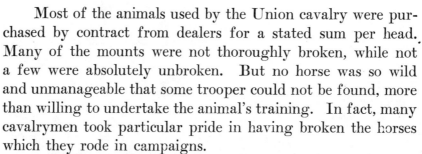

Most of the animals used by the Union cavalry were purchased by contract from dealers for a stated sum per head. Many of the mounts were not thoroughly broken, while not a few were absolutely unbroken. But no horse was so wild and unmanageable that some trooper could not be found, more than willing to undertake the animal's training. In fact, many cavalrymen took particular pride in having broken the horses which they rode in campaigns.

At the beginning of the war, when horses were being received from the West in car-load lots and shipped to the new regiments, some effort was made to organize troops of the same color—blacks, grays, bays, and sorrels—and to maintain this harmonious coloring from the remounts received from time to time. But after the regiments were fairly initiated into real campaigning and the losses in horseflesh became serious, all thought of coloring troops and regiments was abandoned, and the one idea was to secure serviceable mounts and remounts of any color, size, or description.

It is related of one cavalry colonel, whose regiment had been in several engagements and who had lost more than half his horses, that he appealed most eloquently to the quartermaster, for a supply of remounts. " Colonel," said the quartermaster in reply, " I'll tell you frankly that we haven't five pounds of horse for each man to be mounted." " That won't help much," retorted the colonel, testily; " we were thinking of riding the brutes, not of eating them."

The continual complaints as to the quality of the horses furnished, the tardiness with which remounts were supplied, and the inadequacy of conveniences for recuperating broken-down horses in the field, led to the establishment, in the year 1863, of the Cavalry Bureau, with General George Stoneman as its first chief, followed soon after by General Kenner Garrard. But it was under General James Harrison Wilson that the Cavalry Bureau reached its greatest efficiency.

This war bureau was charged with the organization and

IN BARRACKS

A COMFORTABLE SPOT

FOR THE CAVALRY TROOPER

These cavalrymen of '64 look comfortable enough in their barracks at Giesboro. When the cavalry depot was established there in '63, it was the custom to have the troopers return to the dismounted camp near Washington to be remounted and refitted. Some "coffee-coolers" purposely lost their equipments and neglected their horses in the field in order to be sent back for a time to the comfortable station. The order was finally given by General Meade to forward all horses, arms, and equipments to the soldiers in the field. While the men in this photograph are very much at ease and their lolling attitudes would seem to denote peace rather than war, they are probably none of them self-indulgent troopers who prefer this luxurious resting-place but are part of the garrison of the post charged with defending the valuable depot. There are many Civil War photographs of cattle on the hoof, but this picture contains the only representation of a sheep that has come to light.

equipment of the cavalry forces of the army, and with the providing of mounts and remounts. The inspection of horses for the latter purpose was ordered to be made by experienced cavalry officers, while the purchasing was under the direction of officers of the Quartermaster's Department of the army.

Under the general charge of the Cavalry Bureau, six principal depots were established at Giesboro, District of Columbia; St. Louis, Missouri; Greenville, Louisiana; Nashville, Tennessee; Harrisburg, Pennsylvania, and Wilmington, Delaware, for the reception, organization, and discipline of cavalry recruits, and for the collection, care, and training of horses.

The principal depot was at Giesboro, District of Columbia, on the north bank of the Potomac, below Washington, and consisted of a site of about six hundred and twenty-five acres for which the Government paid a rental of six thousand dollars per annum. Stables, stock-yards, forage-houses, storehouses, mess-houses, quarters, a grist-mill, a chapel, and wharves, were soon constructed, and within three months after taking possession (August 12, 1863) provision had been made for fifteen thousand animals; and within three months more, arrangement had been made for the care of thirty thousand animals, although twenty-one thousand was the largest number on hand at any one time. The wharves afforded facilities for three steamers of the largest class to load simultaneously; the hospitals had accommodation for two thousand six hundred and fifty horses; five thousand men were employed during the construction period, afterward reduced to fifteen hundred; while thirty-two stables, besides hospitals and other buildings, gave shelter to six thousand horses. Most of the stock was kept in open sheds or in corrals, these stock-yards alone covering forty-five acres, each yard being furnished with hay-racks and water-troughs, and having free access to the river. The estimated cost of the Giesboro Depot was $1,225,000.

The remount depot at St. Louis covered about four hundred acres, and had a force of nearly eleven hundred employees

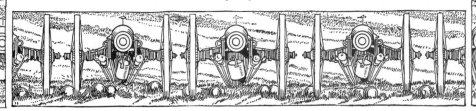

CAVALRY TO GUARD THE DISTRICT OF COLUMBIA.

Between June and December, 1863, just at the time that the Giesboro remount depot was established, four companies of the First District of Columbia Cavalry (A, B, C, and D) were organized. These commands were assigned to special service in the District of Columbia, subject only to the orders of the War Department. The thousands of mounts at Giesboro were not many miles from the track of the Confederate raiders, and presented a tempting prize to them. But early in 1864 the "District" cavalry were ordered away to southeastern Virginia, where they served with Kautz's cavalry division in the Army of the James, during the Petersburg and Appomattox campaigns. Colonel Lafayette C. Baker, in command of this cavalry, reported an encounter with Mosby, to whose depredations their organization was chiefly due, on October 22, 1863: "Sir: This morning about ten o'clock a detachment of my battalion, under command of Major E. J. Conger, and a detachment of the California battalion, under command of Captain Eigenbrodt, encountered a squad of Mosby's men some three miles this side of Fairfax Court House and near the Little River turnpike. One of Mosby's men (named Charles Mason) was shot and instantly killed. The celebrated guerrillas, Jack Barns, Ed. Stratton, and Bill Harover, were captured and forwarded to the Old Capitol Prison. These men state that they were looking for Government horses and sutlers' wagons. None of our force were injured." Colonel Baker was in the Federal Secret Service, and used these cavalrymen as his police. Eight additional companies were subsequently organized for the First District of Columbia Cavalry at Augusta, Maine, January to March, 1864, but after some service with Kautz's cavalry, these were consolidated into two companies and merged into the First Maine Cavalry.

—blacksmiths, carpenters, wagon-makers, wheelwrights, far-riers, teamsters, and laborers in many departments.

The stables were long, well-lighted buildings with thousands of scrupulously clean stalls. From five to ten thousand horses were usually present at the depot, nearly evenly divided between serviceable and unserviceable classes—the latter class being again divided into convalescents and condemned animals. The condemned horses were those declared unfit for further military service, and unless afflicted with some incurable disability, were sold at public auction.

About fifty per cent. of the horses received from the field for recuperation were returned to active service, "fit for duty." More than half of the remainder were recuperated sufficiently to be sold as condemned animals, while less than one-fourth of the unserviceable animals received, died at the depot or were killed to prevent further suffering.

The bane of the cavalry service of the Federal armies in the field was diseases of the feet. "Hoof-rot," "grease-heel," or the "scratches" followed in the wake of days and nights spent in mud, rain, snow, and exposure to cold, and caused thousands of otherwise serviceable horses to become useless for the time being.

Sore backs became common with the hardships of campaigning, and one of the first lessons taught the inexperienced trooper was to take better care of his horse than he did of himself. The remedy against recurrence of sore backs on horses was invariably to order the trooper to walk and lead the disabled animal. With a few such lessons, cavalry soldiers of but short service became most scrupulous in smoothing out wrinkles in saddle-blankets, in dismounting to walk steep hills, in giving frequent rests to their jaded animals, and when opportunity offered, in unsaddling and cooling the backs of their mounts after hours in the saddle. Poor forage, sudden changes of forage, and overfeeding produced almost as much sickness and physical disability as no forage at all.

A RIDING COB

IN WASHINGTON, 1865

NOT THE SORT

FOR CAVALRY

This skittish little cob with the civilian saddle, photographed at the headquarters of the defense of Washington south of the Potomac, in 1865, was doubtless an excellent mount upon which to ride back to the Capital and pay calls. But experience soon taught that high-strung hunters and nervous cobs were of little or no use for either fighting or campaigning. When the battle was on and the shells began to scream a small proportion of these pedigreed animals was sufficient to stampede an entire squadron. They took fright and bolted in all directions. On the other hand, they were far too sensitive for the arduous night marches, and lost in nerves what they gained in speed. A few of them were sufficient to keep a whole column of horses who would otherwise be patiently plodding, heads down, actually stumbling along in their sleep, wide awake and restive by their nervous starts and terrors. The short-barreled, wiry Virginia horses, almost as tireless as army mules, proved to be far their superiors for active service.

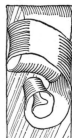

In its cantonment at Brandy Station, during the winter of 1864, the cavalry of the Army of the Potomac was nearly ruined by increasing the ration of grain to make up a deficiency in hay. During the famous Stoneman raid (March and April, 1863) an entire cavalry division was without hay for twenty-one days, in a country where but little grazing was possible. During Sheridan's last raid, in 1865, nearly three-fourths of the lameness of his horses was due to an involuntary change of forage from oats to corn.

But much of the breaking-down of cavalry horses was merely inseparable from the hardships and privations which every great war carries in its train, and which the most experienced leaders cannot foresee or prevent.

In General Sheridan's march from Winchester to Petersburg, February 27th to March 27, 1865, each trooper carried on his horse, in addition to his regular equipment, five days' rations in haversacks, seventy-five rounds of ammunition, and thirty pounds of forage. On General James H. Wilson's Selma expedition, each trooper carried, besides his ordinary kit, five days' rations, twenty-four pounds of grain, one hundred rounds of ammunition, and two extra horseshoes.

A remarkable case, illustrating the conditions surrounding the war service of cavalry regiments, was that of the Seventh Pennsylvania Cavalry. In April, 1864, this regiment started on a march from Nashville, Tennessee, to Blake's Mill, Georgia. It had nine hundred and nineteen horses fresh from the Nashville remount depot, and among its enlisted men were three hundred recruits, some of whom had never been on a horse before.

In a little over four months, the regiment marched nine hundred and two miles, not including fatiguing picket duty and troop scouting. During this period, the horses were without regular supplies of forage for twenty-six days, on scanty forage for twenty-seven days, and for seven consecutive days were without food of any kind. In one period of seventy-two

WHERE THE FEDERAL CAVALRY WAS TRAINED

Giesboro, D. C., where the cavalry of the Army of the Potomac was remounted after August, 1863, was also their drill and training camp.

A BIG RESPONSIBILITY—FORT CARROLL, GIESBORO, D. C.

Millions of dollars worth of Government property was entrusted to the men who occupied these barracks at Fort Carroll, Giesboro, D. C. The original cost of the cavalry depot was estimated at a million and a quarter dollars, and there were immense stores of fodder, medicine, cavalry equipment, and supplies at the depot, besides the value of the horses themselves. The Union Government's appropriations for the purchase of horses for the period of the war mounted to $123,864,915. The average contract price per head was $150, so that approximately 825,766 horses were used in the Union armies. Giesboro was the largest of the Government's cavalry depot, and it must have been an anxious time for those responsible for the preservation of all this wealth when Early threatened Washington.

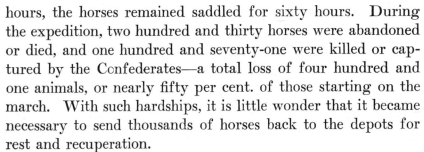

hours, the horses remained saddled for sixty hours. During the expedition, two hundred and thirty horses were abandoned or died, and one hundred and seventy-one were killed or captured by the Confederates—a total loss of four hundred and one animals, or nearly fifty per cent. of those starting on the march. With such hardships, it is little wonder that it became necessary to send thousands of horses back to the depots for rest and recuperation.

But, of course, one of the main purposes of the great horse-depots of the Civil War period, was not to recuperate horses already in the military service, but to receive, condition, and issue thousands of animals purchased throughout the country for army use.

During the fiscal year ending June 30, 1864, the Federal Government purchased 188,718 horses in addition to 20,308 captured from the Confederates and reported; while during the first eight months of the year 1864, the cavalry of the Army of the Potomac, alone, was supplied with two complete remounts or nearly forty thousand horses.

The price paid to contractors by Federal purchasing agents averaged about $150 per head, and occasionally really high-class horses found their way into the lots received at the depots. More often, however, the reverse was the case, and the inspectors of horses were usually at their wits' ends detecting the many frauds and tricks of the horse trade, which dealers attempted to perpetrate on the Government. Men otherwise known to be of the staunchest integrity seem to lose all sense of the equity of things when it comes to selling or swapping horses; and this is particularly the case when the other party to the transaction is the Government, a corporate body incapable of physical suffering and devoid of sentiment.

The Giesboro depot received between January 1, 1864, and June 30, 1866—a period of two and one-half years—an aggregate of 170,654 cavalry horses. Of this number, 96,006 were issued to troops in the field, 1574 were issued to officers,

AN ARTILLERY OFFICER'S MOUNT

A QUARTERMASTER'S MOUNT

Mounts were required by staff and regimental officers, as well as for the cavalry and mounted artillery. So great was the demand that during the second year of the war any quadruped that answered to the general specifications of a horse was seized upon. These fine animals look as if they had been obtained early in the war. The second and third show a "U. S." brand on the shoulder.

48,721 were sold, and 24,321 died. In addition to this number, over 12,000 artillery horses were handled at the depot.

While the capacity of the St. Louis depot was thirty thousand animals, it was never completely filled—the serviceable remounts being promptly forwarded to regiments in the field, and the recuperating animals being held only long enough to render them serviceable or to determine whether they would not respond to further rest or veterinary treatment. The hospitals for the accommodation and treatment of disabled animals were probably the most complete of their kind existing at that time; but after it had been demonstrated that an animal could not be nursed back to the military service, it was a matter of economy to dispose of him to some enterprising bidder for the average price of thirty dollars per head.

The depot system or caring for Government stock, receiving those newly purchased and recuperating those returning sick or disabled from the field, proved a measure of the greatest economy to the Federal Government, in addition to its marked effect on the military efficiency of the mounted service. The value of the animals returned to duty with regiments from the St. Louis depot alone, in excess of what the same animals would have been worth at public auction as condemned articles of sale, was in a single year nearly two hundred thousand dollars more than the entire operating expenses of the plant.

When it is remembered that there were six large depots, all engaged in handling the mounts and remounts of the great Federal armies, and that the depots at Giesboro and St. Louis comprised but a part of this complex system of administration and supply, the tremendous responsibilities imposed upon the Cavalry Bureau of the Federal War Department may be appreciated and understood.

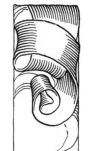

AN HONOR MAN OF THE REGULARS

First-Sergeant Conrad Schmidt of the Second United States Cavalry—a fine type of the "regular" trooper. He was decorated for galloping to the assistance of his captain, whose horse had been killed in a charge, mounting the officer behind him under fire and riding off to safety, although his own horse had been wounded in five places. This was at the Opequon, September 19, 1864.